'Written with heart, breathtaking courage, ambition and humility, *The Crossing* is as profound as it is moving— a tapestry of adventure, love and, of course, camels. Matterson inspires us to consider what lies in wait for us all, if only we have the courage to write the script of our own lives, while forever being open to the unknowns that destiny offers up.'
Tim Cope, author of *On the Trail of Genghis Khan*

'Sophie Matterson's gift for writing allows us to revel in the beauty of the Australian continent, the entire width of which she has trodden with her beloved camels, while also allowing us into her innermost world. She recounts the highs and lows of an epic journey that took courage, tenacity and love to complete. A compelling read.'
Chrissie Goldrick, Editor-in-Chief, *Australian Geographic*

the crossing

sophie matterson

A memoir of love,
adventure and finding
your own path

ALLEN&UNWIN
SYDNEY·MELBOURNE·AUCKLAND·LONDON

First published in 2023

Allen & Unwin
Cammeraygal Country
83 Alexander Street
Crows Nest NSW 2065
Australia
Phone: (61 2) 8425 0100
Email: info@allenandunwin.com
Web: www.allenandunwin.com

*Allen & Unwin acknowledges the Traditional Owners of the Country on which we
live and work. We pay our respects to all Aboriginal and Torres Strait Islander
Elders, past and present.*

A catalogue record for this
book is available from the
National Library of Australia

ISBN 978 1 76106 882 9

Maps by Mika Tabata
Set in 11.5/18 pt Sabon LT Pro by Midland Typesetters, Australia
Printed in Australia by Pegasus Media & Logistics

10 9 8 7 6

The paper in this book is FSC® certified.
FSC® promotes environmentally responsible,
socially beneficial and economically viable
management of the world's forests.

This book is dedicated to Jude—
a legend and my best bud.

'Above all, do not lose your desire to walk.
Every day, I walk myself into a state of
well-being and walk away from every illness.
I have walked myself into my best thoughts,
and I know of no thought so burdensome
that one cannot walk away from it . . . thus
if one just keeps on walking, everything will
be all right.'

Søren Kierkegaard

Contents

The middle of nowhere

A sharp tug from the lead rope woke me from my pleasant daydream. In a split second, all hell broke loose. Jude was dragging me forward at a rate that my legs could not keep up with. Four tonnes' worth of straining camels pulled me to the ground and I slid along the dirt, lead rope still in my outstretched hand, watching camping equipment tumble down around me. I couldn't hold the rope any longer. I let go and watched my five camels lurch forward. Jude's violent movement at the front had pulled the back camels over, as it had done me. Delilah and Charlie were scrambling, Clayton was skidding along on his knees and Mac had completely toppled onto his side. It seemed inevitable that one of them would break a leg. But as I struggled to my feet as quickly as possible, so did they. All six of us were up, limbs intact. And then . . . they bolted.

In the weeks and months leading up to my camel trip, I had considered the possibility of this scenario. In my head, the camels would run for a short time until they quickly became tired, or slowed to eat a delicious bush. I would then calmly walk up to them, take hold of the lead rope, regain control, and we would all go on our way. At no point did I imagine that my camels would keep on running, disappearing into the great expanse of Australian outback, leaving me alone, standing dumbfounded with nothing on me except the clothes I was wearing and a small pocketknife attached to my belt.

A panicked voice inside me yelled 'RUN!' and I took off after my fleeing camels.

The ground was undulating: a mix of red dirt and submerged red rock. My heart pounded in my chest, as though it was being squeezed by my diaphragm up and out through my ears. How was I so unfit? I had been walking now for two and a half months. Between gulps of air, I tried to steady my voice enough to call out to my camels.

'Steady Jude, stand Jude.' I hoped my voice might make it sound as if everything was okay. But it wasn't. My swag was hanging halfway down Jude's side, no doubt spooking him even more, as the camels ran faster and further away. I had to keep running. My mind was racing as fast as my feet. My lungs were on fire and the seriousness of the situation was becoming clearer with every pace I took. I felt for my phone in my pocket as I ran. It wasn't there; it had slipped from my hand as the camels yanked me to the ground. This was my worst nightmare. My phone was my GPS and map, and I never moved anywhere without it for fear of becoming lost. I'd been running after the camels in such a panicked state I had already become completely disorientated, and now had no idea where I was—but turning back to retrieve my phone was not an option. I had to get my camels back.

More sickening realities were dawning on me. I wasn't on a road or a track—I was in the middle of the bush, several hundred kilometres from the nearest town. No one knew where I was, and everything I needed to survive was strapped to my camels. Why did I put the sat phone, emergency beacon and navigational equipment into saddle bags? I wasn't even carrying any water—it was all on my camels. Here, water was the most vital element for survival. I was walking across the driest inhabited continent on Earth, where many explorers had perished due to lack of water.

Trying to keep my footing on the uneven ground, I kept losing sight of the camels as they disappeared up and over a rise or down a dry creek bed. I paused just long enough to locate their direction by the sound of the water jerry can racks smashing against Mac's saddle. I noticed small pools of water in the shallow indents of the rocks I was leaping over—short-lived traces of light rain the previous day. My mind a whirr, I tried to remember landmarks around these pools, in case I lost the camels and needed to drink from them to survive. I knew, however, that with the day heating up, the water would evaporate in a matter of hours. I crested a small hill and spotted the camels on an exposed section of sloping rock. They had slowed to a jog because of the hard and uneven ground. *This was my chance!*

I raced towards them, feeling for my pocketknife—the one survival item that remained in my possession. I flipped it open, clinging to the little tool like a lifeline. If I just caught up with the last two camels, I could cut the rope that joined them. Clayton's eyes were wide with terror, white foam seeping from his mouth. As I drew even and thrust the tip of the knife out for the rope, Clayton was jerked forward by the others, his front legs knocking me to the ground. With my face in the dirt, I saw a scramble of long camel legs running off again.

My camels, wild and terrified, would not stop. But without them I had nothing, was nothing—so there was nothing for it but to keep on running.

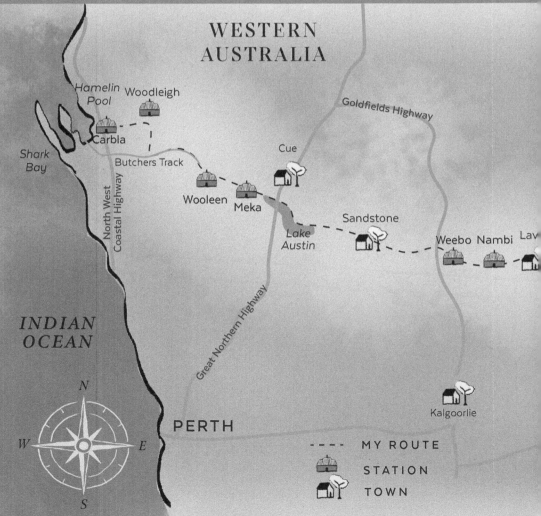

WESTERN
AUSTRALIA

Goldfields Highway

Hamelin
Pool   Woodleigh

Carbla

Shark
Bay

Butchers Track

Cue

Wooleen   Meka

Lake
Austin

Sandstone

Weebo Nambi   Lav

North West
Coastal Highway

INDIAN
OCEAN

Great Northern Highway

Kalgoorlie

N

W   E

S

PERTH

- - - -   MY ROUTE

STATION

TOWN

PART 1

casting off

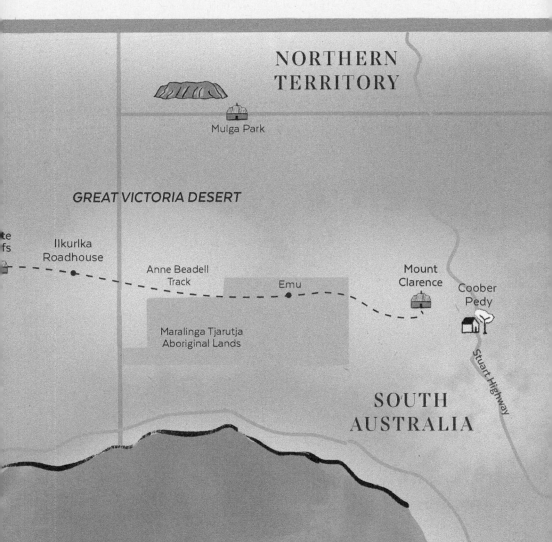

NORTHERN
TERRITORY

Mulga Park

GREAT VICTORIA DESERT

te
fs

Ilkurlka
Roadhouse

Anne Beadell
Track

Emu

Mount
Clarence

Coober
Pedy

Maralinga Tjarutja
Aboriginal Lands

SOUTH
AUSTRALIA

Stuart Highway

1

The Beginning of the End

SHARK BAY TO CARBLA HOMESTEAD—15 KM

The Indian Ocean. I stood with my ankles in the shallows, awestruck. The water was the turquoise blue you see in travel photos advertising tropical islands, so clear you can see right through to the white sand below. But instead of palm trees lining the shoreline of this paradise, here the rich red dirt of Australia's arid interior ran down to the sand. It was nothing like the east coast of Australia, where I grew up. It was new for the camels too; they had never seen the ocean before. But while I stood mesmerised, they looked out on the wide blue waters with complete indifference, the magic clearly lost on them. They had no idea what this moment meant: we had finally reached the starting line of our huge adventure. I had made it to Shark Bay, the westernmost point of the west coast of Australia, and was planning to walk with my five camel companions all the way to Byron Bay, the most easterly point of the country—a distance of 4000 kilometres as the crow flies, and probably about 5000 kilometres by the time I zigzagged a bit along the way.

This shoreline represented the start of my odyssey, but it also represented the end. The end of years of planning that had consumed my entire being. It had taken four years to learn how to work with the five large animals that stood behind me, to feel confident enough to attempt a journey of my own with them. I had been lucky to meet a diverse mix of talented camel handlers around Australia, and the world, who inspired and shared with me their knowledge. At Uluru, a year before I set off for my trip, I was able to obtain my own camels, train them, and learn the craft of making my own saddles.

Amid the heartbreak of a relationship break-up, the final year at Uluru had been a never-ending list of 'to-dos', with so much equipment to be bought. On ten-hour round trips to Alice Springs I would anguish over an inordinate amount of small decisions in the aisles of Bunnings, such as which length of tie-downs would be best for strapping food boxes to my camels.

A mountain of paperwork came with applying for a firearms licence, and then more paperwork when it came to buying the rifles—a powerful .308 and a .22. I shook when I held the .308, practising on a target in the dunes. It took me forever to find the target through the scope, and I pretended I understood what it meant to 'sight the rifle for 100 metres'.

There was also a long list of phone calls to be made. I hated these awkward cold calls, where I would stammer down the phone, 'Umm, sorry to call out of the blue, but um . . . I'm kind of doing a bit of a camel trek and I was wondering if um . . . if I might be able to walk across your property with my camels?'

I spent weeks salting meat, drying beef jerky and dehydrating vegetables before carefully packaging them. I sat on my living room floor surrounded by masses of long-life food, meticulously sorting it into piles to be packed into boxes that would be delivered at intervals on my way to the west coast, then picked up as resupply boxes as I walked back east. I hoped I would still tolerate muesli every day for breakfast and tinned tuna every day for lunch in nine months' time.

In the lead-up to my departure, my days began at 3 a.m. I'd spend a quiet hour or two poring over topographical maps on my Hema Maps app, searching for a thread that made a route across the country—all before taking tourists on a sunrise camel ride. Maps fed my imagination, and despite the early starts, I loved the silence of those witching hours.

When I was finally ready to head to the start line, it took six days and 2300 kilometres on mainly rough dirt roads to drive from Uluru to Shark Bay with my recently acquired truck licence and all of one day's truck-driving experience. I racked up some serious on-the-job training along the way. My friend Greg had agreed to do the trip with me to the west coast. Grinding through gears and gripping the steering wheel with white knuckles, we arrived in Western Australia with my precious camel cargo. However, the elation of completing this cross-country camel road trip was soon quelled by the outbreak of the global Covid-19 pandemic. When I left Uluru, no one had been taking the virus from China particularly seriously—but a week after I arrived in Western Australia, the borders shut. The world was scared. International backpackers were being told to return home, and Australians were being told to stay at home, with only 'essential travel' allowed. All the preparation for my trip came crashing down around me and uncertainty hung heavy in the air. Would I be allowed to travel? How long would the pandemic last? What did a lockdown mean for me? I was now homeless, my address 'on the road with five camels'. All I could do was to start walking and hope for the best.

So there I was, staring out at the Indian Ocean, at the beginning of the end of a huge preparation phase. I coaxed the camels down the sloping red dirt towards the beach. We crunched across a bed of millions of tiny white shells. They were reflecting the glare of the bright summer sun and I squinted. The shells became finer and finer until they formed smooth sand at the ocean's glassy edge. I couldn't believe I was here. In the past, my many crazy schemes for adventures had always fizzled out—but for some undefinable reason, the driving passion for this one had stuck. Even if I failed to make it across the country, I couldn't help feeling proud at simply having made it to the start.

I pulled my boots off and waded in, gently tugging at Jude's lead rope. He followed me without question into the water. Bringing his long neck down, he took a slurp, and then, surprised by its saltiness, withdrew his head quickly, flinging it around in circles and expelling water from his loose lips in great arcs all over me and the other camels. Delilah, who stood behind Jude, looked disgruntled.

Jude's attempt to drink from the ocean didn't surprise me; he had always been curious, like a bowerbird stopping to examine shiny objects. He particularly loved any kind of rubbish on the track—stopping mid-walk to investigate an old beer can left behind in the sand, forcing all the other camels behind him to grind to a sudden halt. When I first began training the camels at Uluru, they would stand in the corner of the stockyard, observing me warily. I started wheeling in wheelbarrows full of green vegetation, but even then they continued to stare at me suspiciously—except for Jude, who wandered over and ate gleefully. It didn't take long before I was feeding him from my hand, well before the others dared venture anywhere near me. He would pick up big clumps of prickly green weeds in his mouth and toss them about to separate them, before devouring them with gusto.

I knew early on Jude would be my lead camel—the camel at the front of the string. This is a very important role. You have to work one-on-one with your lead camel, and they have to trust you implicitly, because they are in turn leading the camels behind them, roped together from their halter to the shoulders of the camel in front. With his innate curiosity, Jude and I had a relationship from day one. He was a darkish male, roughly seven years old—a teenager in camel years, with about another year of growing before he reached full size. He was one of four boys in my group. There was Mac, a blond seven-year-old camel and the largest, and six-year-olds

7

Charlie and Clayton. Charlie was lanky and greyish, all long limbs like a young teenage boy who hasn't developed any muscle yet, while small and compact Clayton was dark brown, nearing black. Delilah was my only female, a mature-aged lady who, judging by her loose udder, had birthed several calves.

While Delilah looked put-out by the time-wasting experience of visiting the ocean, Jude appeared to be enjoying himself. The corners of his lips were turned upward, as if smiling. He lifted one of his big feet, a soft two-toed pad with prehistoric-looking nails, and let it fall back down into the water. *SPLASH*. He did it again, then dropped to his knees, the clear water lapping at his chest. I anticipated what would happen next. He wanted to roll.

'Not with your saddle on, Jude!' I said urgently, quickly wading back out of the water, removing the camels and my newly built saddles from harm's way. Further along the beach was a little shack, and beyond that, the sand led to some stunted coastal vegetation where I planned to unsaddle the camels and let them have a proper roll. The 'shack' was just four posts with a piece of green shadecloth loosely pinned down over the top. The 'Carbla Hilton', as I had heard it called, over-looked Hamelin Pool, the protected bay where, in 1977, Robyn Davidson had finished her journey with her camels across the western deserts from Alice Springs. This was where a *National Geographic* photographer, Rick Smolan, had taken pictures of Robyn in the water with her camels. Long before the outline of my own trip began to form, I had read her book, *Tracks*, and seen the subsequent movie. Her pioneering feat as a woman was undoubtedly inspirational, but it had never been my intention to replicate her trip. We were two different women conducting our adventures in different periods in history. Still, our stories ran parallel to one another's, and during many moments like this, I would often think of how they compared and what she must have felt.

As we approached the 'Carbla Hilton', part of the green shadecloth flapped about in the breeze. The rope went taut in my hand. The camels slammed on the brakes and stared wide-eyed at the innocent beach shack. It seemed inconceivable that they would be unaffected by their first sighting of the blue horizon of ocean, yet terrified by the sight of a man-made shack. A switch had been flicked: Jude was no longer 'smiling'. I looked at these five big wild animals and remembered that they were just that . . . wild animals.

Mustered from the wild at Mulga Park Station, having wandered there from the APY Lands and western deserts, my camels had been domesticated a mere year ago. Throughout the muster, adrenaline pumping, I had gripped the seat of an agile Mad Max–style vehicle that looked like it belonged in a redneck car show, as Shane, an imposing outback bloke wearing a sleeveless work shirt that revealed arms the size of tree trunks, wheeled the mustering buggy around. We were pelting through spinifex, weaving to avoid termite mounds as we chased the wild camels. Shane kept spotting small stray herds and brought them together to join the original group. Soon we were tailing fifty or so camels, who ran with their necks outstretched, heads bopping like toy dogs on the dashboard of a car. The wild camels ran freely through the yellow spinifex, with the red and rugged ranges behind them. I captured the moment in my mind; it was a beautiful image.

With the buggy, two motorbikes and a ute on the wings, we pushed the camels down a fenced laneway into a set of steel-railed cattle yards. I felt a tinge of sadness as I looked at these big, powerful animals, puffing and grinding their teeth, huddled together for security. But in the Outback, it is a necessity to be tough and practical. In Australia, feral camels are considered a 'pest', and it is a legal requirement for landowners to dispose of them. These camels were not mustered for my trip; they were being mustered for meat. The pragmatic side of me recognised that this muster was a better option than aerial culling; that was a waste of a potential resource.

My boss at Uluru Camel Tours, Chris, walked up behind me as I stood watching the large group of mustered camels in the yard that afternoon. Another tough outback character, he exuded authority. His persona oscillated between a man of few words, difficult to read, and a charismatic entertainer quick to make a lighthearted derogatory joke. But since I had told him about my plan to walk across Australia, he had taken me under his wing and become my mentor.

For months I had watched Chris like a hawk as he taught me how to train camels. The first afternoon, he showed me how to make a camel *hoosh*, which means 'sit down' in camel-speak, by looping a lasso around a front ankle and leveraging that leg in the air. This would drop the animal to its front knees, and the back legs would naturally fold to a sitting position. Accompanied by vocal commands, a camel could be taught to *hoosh* in a surprisingly short time. Once they have learnt it, they never forget it—just one of many things that, to me, proves their intelligence.

With ease Chris threw the lasso around a camel's front leg; he had close to thirty years' experience working with these animals. When I tried throwing the lasso I fumbled, feeling like the pathetic stereotype of a girl throwing a ball.

'For fuck's sake, darl! Stop fucking around changing your tampon and get on with it,' Chris hollered. Here in the Outback, I knew I had to get used to this crude approach. *Water off a duck's back*, I told myself, and picked up the lasso and tried again.

'Well done,' Chris grunted when I successfully looped the lasso around the camel's leg after several failed attempts. I basked in his approval—his few words of praise were like gold to me.

Standing beside me at the yards at Mulga Park Station, Chris looked thoughtfully at the freshly mustered camels.

'We could probably get you a couple of camels for your trip from this lot,' he said. I turned to him with wide eyes; I thought I had simply been invited along to experience a muster. Chris was here to select several camels for his tour company, but I didn't expect him to offer me camels of my own so soon. 'The deal is I get first choice, you can have what's left.' I thought that fair and felt a thrill of excitement. Chris had been incredibly generous in teaching me how to make saddles and giving me full rein of the saddlery shed.

He was also giving me a yard in which to train my camels, and had offered his own camels to help train mine.

The next day Chris drafted the best of the wild-caught camels, based on age, conformation and temperament. Once they had been trucked back to Uluru Camel Tours, it was time to get down to the gruesome business of nose-pegging and castrating. I wasn't afraid to get my hands dirty and volunteered to be Chris's assistant. I saw these experiences with Chris as a way of toughening up, adding calluses to my soft city hands, and readying me for the journey ahead.

After giving each of the bull camels both a local and general anaesthetic, I held their tails aloft as Chris donned chainmail gloves and wielded a scalpel like a knight from a medieval battle-field. I winced as the final tool—the 'emasculator'—was used, designed to sever, crush and cut at the same time. It was a neces-sary process; bull camels are notoriously difficult to work with. In winter the males will come into 'rut', a time when their testos-terone is pumping and their minds are singularly fixated on the two Fs—fighting and fucking.

'Here you go, darl, some outback mangos for your break-fast,' Chris joked, pointing at a wheelbarrow filled with camel balls.

When the castration was complete, and while the camels still swayed and drooled, their lips hanging low from the sedative, we inserted a peg into one nostril. Camels are cud-chewing animals, so you can't use a bit, as you would with a horse. The nose peg pierces sensitive skin, giving a stronger means of control than a halter and rope. Catching and domesticating wild camels may seem a brutal process, but the other alternative for my camels was to end up as steaks, burgers or sausages—or simply being shot and left to rot. I could justify my decisions when I remembered that.

Over the following weeks, Chris's hard shell cracked and his softer nature and generosity shone through. He had too many camels anyway, he said, and offered me most of those he had selected for himself. From a scared group of wild animals huddled in the corner of the yards, I chose my team.

I looked at Jude, Delilah, Clayton, Charlie and Mac now, happily rolling in the sand on the beach at Carbla. It always made me laugh how camels would roll onto one side and then the other, unable to roll the whole way across like a horse, because of their hump. In Australia we have only one-humped camels, the dromedaries. The other two-humped variety, bactrians, are cold-desert camels found in places like the Gobi Desert.

Jude stood up first to graze, followed by Clayton. Charlie, the most nervous, tailed Delilah, who was like a mother figure to him. Mac, never in a rush, was the last to get up, heaving himself up with a begrudging sigh to forage next to Delilah. It wasn't the first time I had watched this routine unfold, their personalities emerging as I trained them. It was one of the joys of the process, watching them go from fearful nameless animals to individuals, developing an understanding of who they all were and their relationships with each other. I had tried to use this understanding while training them, working with their personalities rather than against them.

Clayton, for example, had been inexplicably terrified of being touched. If he were a horse, you would say he was 'head shy'. I had always handled my camels softly, even after getting sprayed with hot, green, stinking cud. (Camels don't spit saliva; they have the rather disgusting habit of throwing up their entire stomach contents on you when they're upset.) I once spent hours sitting on a hay bale waiting for Clayton to make his own choice to approach me. Eventually I realised Clayton was very clever. He knew exactly what I wanted him to do, but he was independent and a bit of a loner. He disliked being touched and liked routine, as if he was on the autism spectrum, which I had heard was possible for animals. If I kept the stability of routine for him and gave him his space, he was happy.

I had never tried to push affection on any of them. Chris had always said, 'Don't you bloody kiss that camel, you'll ruin it.' He was right. The best reward you can give a wild camel is space. Once they trust you, they will eventually seek out affection, but until then, a human will only terrify or annoy them. I had seen many camels grow bitter from tourists insisting on patting them around the face, or from 'cameleers' (as the handlers are called) not understanding how to work with them. Because of their intelligence and power, a camel that has gone sour and dislikes people can be dangerous. They can kick 180 degrees with their back leg and strike out with their forelegs, and they can bite, too: the males have bear-like canine teeth on their upper jaw for fighting. At Uluru, I was once charged by a hulking camel named Hugo. I had been warned that he was capable of doing this, but didn't take the warning seriously. I knew from a little experience working with cattle that they could act with a lot of bravado, but if you turned and said 'boo' they would dash off in the other direction. Surely a camel was the same? I strode over to Hugo in the paddock with confidence. In a split second he was running at me, fierce intent in his eyes. No way was I going to stand my ground and say 'boo'. I sped like Usain Bolt across the paddock, Hugo hot on my heels, then dived through the gap between the feed trough and yard rail like a footballer scoring a touchdown. Had I hesitated, Hugo would have trampled me.

My camels were fresh from the wild, untainted by bad human handling. We were all new kids on the block, me and them. I had little idea how this inexperience would push us to our limits.

My first night on the beach didn't feel like a big deal. It wasn't the first time I had camped out with my camels. I had taken them on a few short three-day to six-day 'test' treks, camping around Uluru to get a sense of what it might be like.

I tied the camels to bushes for the night and stood eating a can of tuna with some crackers as the darkness descended. It didn't feel like the 'real' beginning; I hadn't even bothered to light a fire. The beach was only fifteen kilometres from the Carbla homestead where I had unloaded the camels from the truck, and I had left all the saddle bags and equipment there, only taking the bare minimum to the beach. I wouldn't feel like I had really left on my journey until all that equipment was with me. Then I would have to be entirely self-sufficient, relying only on myself and what I had packed.

The next morning, I saddled the camels and walked them back down to the beach. I could feel the heat of the day already, sweat beading on my top lip and brow. There was more humidity near the ocean, but at least the sea breeze was keeping the flies at bay. I walked the camels along the water's edge and paused at the end of the beach, looking at the track that led up the red dirt and back to Carbla homestead. I was restless to get going, knowing that the growing heat would make walking unpleasant, but I couldn't help having one last swim. It would be many months and several thousand kilometres before I would see the ocean again.

I stripped down naked, waded into the calm waters and dipped my head under, soaking up the quiet and picking up handfuls of fine sand from the ocean floor, letting it flow between my fingers. Sometimes I wondered why I had become so enamoured with desert-loving camels when I loved the ocean and craved the water so much. But I had given up many things in my single-minded pursuit of this goal. I loved surfing: the feel of salt on my skin, the surge of a wave as you paddled over its crest, and the quiet that fell about you under the ocean's surface.

It was the ocean that had brought Sam and I together. We were eighteen, fresh out of high school, in that delicious time between school finishing and 'real life' beginning, where there is no responsibility and the world is full of possibilities. I fell in love with him on a surf trip to Byron Bay, then we gathered a group of friends together and went to the Woodford Folk Festival, north of Brisbane. We thought we were hippies, wearing rainbow-coloured headbands and fire-twirling. We had my dad's farm at nearby Kilcoy to ourselves, retreating from the festival at intervals to fang about on motorbikes, swim in the dam and clamber onto the roof to listen to music and look at the stars. I felt alive and adventurous. I was hooked on him.

And then he joined the Army. He left for military school with a peace badge on his backpack. It was over, and we grew up and moved on with our lives. Eight years later, we bumped into each other, arranged to go surfing and ended up back together—in love with the waves and in love with each other. It was like the boy I knew had come back to me as the man I had wanted all along. It felt like serendipity.

I moved to Adelaide to be with Sam, until the Army called him to go to war in Iraq. We were used to this by now, frustratingly living our relationship with long-distance intervals, our lives never quite matching up—but the separation was bearable, because we had a big trip overseas planned when his Army days finished. When Sam returned from Iraq he left the Army, we bought a retro campervan in north-west America and spent six months driving down the west coast to Mexico, then flying to Chile, surfing and hiking our way back to the deep love we felt for one another. In the warm waters of Mexico, I pictured our future together, and imagined bringing our children there to surf one day.

The waters of Hamelin Pool were warm, too. They rippled on my naked body as I curled my way around the mushroom-shaped blobs on the sea floor. I knew not to touch them. They were not rocks, but rather microbial mats of living bacteria called stromatolites—the precursor of more complex life forms that had appeared on Earth 3.5 billion years ago, and had helped oxygenate the planet. David Attenborough had even been here to film their important yet humble presence. Nature filled me with awe, and I couldn't help feeling it was auspicious that I was starting my journey among some of the earliest life forms on Earth.

Finally, I emerged from the water. I untied my camels and turned to look at the sparkling ocean one last time.

It was time to get back to the homestead and pack my equipment so the journey could really begin.

2

Unexpected Certainty

**CARBLA HOMESTEAD TO THE END
OF THE DRIVEWAY—7 KM**

The camels were sitting, waiting to be saddled in the Carbla homestead yards. Goats and sheep milled about the outbuildings and woolshed. I could smell the pungent scent the billy goats exuded.

I never expected to start my trip with a huge farewell, with crowds of people wishing me luck and waving me goodbye—but I also never expected to begin it totally alone.

The only people present on the station were my friend Greg, who had helped me drive the camel truck from Uluru, and Sam, the station owner. But they had both left early that morning to muster goats. The one person I had relied upon to be there to see me leave was my dad, but the sudden border closures due to the pandemic had meant he was unable to fly from Queensland. We were both devastated. We had always been close. He'd become heavily invested in my trip, perhaps because it reminded him of his ultramarathon days, running 100-kilometre races around the island of Hong Kong, where I was born. He understood the desire to discover the limits of your own abilities; to push yourself.

I was alone now in the yards with my camels. Despite my disappointment, in a way I was thankful to be able to focus without distraction. Saddles, blankets and equipment lay about the camels, like pieces of a jigsaw puzzle not yet assembled. It reminded me of the way Sam used to lay out the contents of his Army backpack on our bed, ready to be packed meticulously. He would even cut his toothbrush in half to minimise the weight. The one time I tried to put on his enormous pack I fell over backwards, like a beetle flipped onto its back, helpless to right itself. We laughed hysterically, until he lifted me back up onto my feet.

I surveyed the equipment before me. On the ground were two hard plastic Pelican boxes, about a metre long. With a month's worth of food divided between the two, I was only just able to lift each box at a time. Twelve twenty-litre jerry cans for water sat in a line, four of them filled. Racks that Chris and Greg had built to hold the jerries and food boxes lay next to them. The swag that I would sleep in every night lay rolled up, with the rifles in the centre. Saddle bags were filled with every item that I would conceivably need to survive in the bush for the year—first-aid kit (filled with medications I couldn't pronounce the name of and hoped I never had to use), a tarp for wet weather, canvas tarps to cover saddlery and bags, cooking equipment, toiletries, clothes, emergency beacon, solar blanket and electronics, camera, chargers, drone, paper maps in a tube, a shovel, ammunition, camel medication, toilet paper. Then there were all the spares; I wouldn't be going through any towns with shops. There was spare saddlery—girths, halters, ropes, hobbles and leg straps—for the camels and spare boots for me, plus extra ammunition and extra gas to cook with if the weather turned bad. Then all the little things friends had given me as reminders that I wasn't really alone—beyond these quiet yards, a world out there was barracking for me and had helped me reach the beginning. The leather pocketknife pouch on my belt, made by my manager Bert at Uluru, the dried biltong meat from my friend Judi, a sarong from my housemate Huriana, the satellite phone my parents insisted I buy to keep me safe, crystals from my friend Keirin to hang in my swag, and a bunch of emu feathers, Greg's totem animal, bound by plaited red, black and gold wool, designed to protect me. The biggest surprise was from Chris, who had beautifully embossed in the leather of Jude's saddle the inscription: 'West. East. 2020.'—a thoughtful gesture that was predictably accompanied by a customary dig from Chris, 'Just in case you forget which way to go.'

Lots of friends, some of whom I had lost contact with over the years, had messaged me to wish me good luck. Sam had messaged too, as I was driving over in the truck—our first contact in a year. His message was light but heartfelt. It was nice that he had sent it, but it only brought him back into the forefront of my mind. Pain, regret and longing were dragged back into the light from the dark cave where I had tried to hide them. I shoved them away again; I had camels to load.

Five camels can carry a lot of equipment. But there was only one person loading that equipment on and off their backs: me. Two hours later, I still wasn't ready to go. The back of my shirt was drenched in sweat, and I blinked the flies away from the corners of my eyes as I pushed and squeezed, forcing bulging zips to shut. Each of the loads had to be weighted evenly on each side of the camels. I stood them up, walked around the back to access their loads from behind, then sat them back down again, unsatisfied and frustrated that they were not loaded right. I hoped this process would get quicker. I couldn't take this long every day. I was hot, tired and had necked litres of water—and I hadn't even left yet.

Finally, two and a half hours later, I was ready. It was the most understated departure that I could have imagined. For posterity more than anything, I simply took one fairly average photo of the camels standing there with a mountain of gear on their backs. Then I untied Jude's rope and led him and the other camels out of the yards.

We had taken less than ten steps when I almost trod on a huge goanna—a spectacular perentie, the largest of the goanna species, his scales dark grey with a yellow ringed pattern. He looked up at me and the camels, his tongue flicking in and out, tasting the air. I stood staring back at him and immediately thought of Uncle Steve, a Ngemba Aboriginal man Chris employed to help train camels for the tours at Uluru. He had helped me with Jude, giving me the confidence (and the subtle kick up the butt I needed) to start Jude off as lead camel. 'You just got to give him a go, darlin',' Steve had said as he walked beside me at Uluru, his round face grinning and his gentle, contagious chuckle filling me with confidence as I slowly relaxed my worried grip on Jude's lead rope. Steve's totem was the goanna—here he was, looking out for us.

'We've got this buddy,' I said to Jude, 'it's you and me.' I slowly moved forward, giving the goanna a respectfully wide berth. He turned and moved with a powerful snake-like motion back into the bush.

I looked on my phone at the orange circle that marked our location on the Hema Maps app. I had bought a fancy GPS for my trip, but so far had never used it. Even without reception, my phone could track my location on the map, and it was more visual than the GPS. I stared at the outline of the coast, the green patches marking nature reserves, the names of stations, the red line of the coastal highway running north–south, and the dirt tracks in dotted lines that I had only imagined walking all those months ago in my bedroom in Uluru. The map was sparse; Western Australia seemed to be sparse.

I didn't need the map today. We only had one dotted line to follow—the driveway of Carbla Station. I knew where I was going, and had already picked out a spot to camp on the side of the road, when we drove down the driveway in the truck. The map was simply a security blanket, giving me the sensation that I was tracking forward, even if the orange circle hovered barely a fraction off the coast. Today was only a short day's walk—an easy seven kilometres—but I knew the walks had to get longer soon. It was 1 April and I had given myself nine months to complete the trek. To walk through the hottest, most arid regions of central Australia in summer would be impossible, unless I planned to walk at night. So, like a fitness instructor devising a workout regime, I had planned that the camels and I would slowly increase the number of kilometres each month, as well as the amount of water weight Mac would carry, ready for the desert stretch in the middle. Like humans, camels can't just jump straight into running a marathon with a pack on their back. The first month we would do ten kilometres a day, followed by fifteen, eighteen, twenty-one and twenty-five by the time we reached the desert; I had it all organised . . .

After the physicality of saddling the camels, the relative stillness of ambling down the Carbla driveway settled upon me. Their soft pads were silent on the dirt road. All I could hear was the slight creaking of equipment on their backs, and the muffled bells around their necks, which I had plugged with leather stoppers. I slowed my pace to match theirs. Camels walk much more slowly than people, their steady, stately pace conserving energy in a hot climate. And it was hot today—well over thirty degrees, even though it was the start of April.

Despite the heat, I had decided to walk with the camels rather than ride. This had come as a surprise to most people I had spoken to about my trip. 'Why would you want to walk all that way?' many had responded. But I liked the idea that

I would also take every step that my camels took. Besides, your bum gets sore in the saddle after so many hours, and I had always liked walking. I craved it to clear my mind and make me feel good.

The slow pace of walking with camels can be quite meditative, but it's also like driving a road train. We were one long, moving, living vehicle, and that first day, I couldn't switch off. I had to keep checking the rear-view mirror, constantly looking back over my shoulder, making sure Mac was keeping up at the back, none of the camels were pushing or rushing, none of the equipment had slipped or was leaning, making sure they all followed behind one another and didn't hook themselves on the side of a tree, weaving through bushes so they could eat.

We reached camp and I tried to squeeze the road train into the shade of a low twisted snakewood tree to escape the heat of the afternoon sun. I fell into the process that was to be my routine for the next nine months: check the area for good camel feed, *hoosh* the camels down one by one in a line, placing a strap and buckle around their front bent leg (this prevents their leg extending and is a signal to stay sitting), unpack my canvas tarp and lay it out next to the camels, unload saddle bags, jerry cans and food boxes, lining them up along the back of the tarp nearest the camel who carries them—then unsaddle the camels, hobble their front ankles, unplug their bells and undo their leg straps so they are free to graze. Always the needs of my animals first, me second. Dad had taught me this when we rode horses together. He would tell me of his childhood fox hunts in the United Kingdom with his parents in winter. He would be wet and cold, but the horses were always fed and washed down first, then mud scraped from the saddlery, before he was eventually allowed a shower and dinner.

My camels stood up one by one and shuffled off together in their hobbles to graze, like a chain gang heading out to plough the fields. While they might seem cruel, hobbles are designed to restrict an animal's movement so they can graze beyond the bounds of a fence and be caught again with ease. My camels were wearing loose cuffs on each foreleg. connected by a short length of chain that slowed their walk to a shuffling pace. Feed would have been too cumbersome to pack for five of them, so they would have to rely on what the land had to offer. I watched Delilah reach her long neck up into the bows of a prickly acacia, manoeuvring her soft lips through the spikes and shredding the leaves off with ease. I admired the camel's ability to survive on this coarse vegetation that most other animals are unable to digest. If I had chosen to travel through this arid landscape with horses, I would have needed vehicle support for feed and water. With camels I was self-sufficient and independent; we could survive on our own.

I pulled off my boots and socks to air my sweaty feet and stood barefoot on my tarp, looking around at all the bags. This was now my home—this three-square-metre green canvas tarp my 'house' on the move. The idea of living out of a bag was not entirely foreign to me. For most of my life, constantly shifting living locations was more familiar than staying put. My parents had been expats and had lived all around the world. Dad had worked for the HSBC bank. From Hong Kong we moved to Paris when I was four, and then to Mum's home town of Brisbane when I was six. From the suburbs we moved to an acreage and Dad became a hobby farmer, among other things. Life was filled with animals—the property came with forty goats and an old German shepherd. Two cats had travelled with us from Hong Kong, and we added to the growing menagerie with more cats and dogs, cows, horses and a boisterous bull named Humphrey, who would come running to me when I swung a bucket of unnecessary high-energy grain to feed him (how I was not trampled or hurt, I do not know). Dad and I shared a passion for horses, but Mum and I also shared a love for animals. Once, when we hit a noisy miner bird with our car, injuring its wing, Mum had an entire full-size aviary constructed for its recovery, taking daily walks to pick nectar flowers for it. In Paris the school rabbit was encouraged to roam around the house on its visits, and in Australia cats were allowed on the kitchen table, and the dogs always slept on the bed. A family friend once commented that they wished to be reincarnated as one of Mum's animals.

When I was twelve, my parents split up. From a child's perspective, their split was amicable. Mum bought a small property across the road from Dad. I now had two patches of land to explore, creating cubbyhouses in the bush with my best friend, Ness. Later, Dad would buy a larger farm at Kilcoy in south-east Queensland, and Mum would buy a house in the city to be closer to Brisbane Girls Grammar, where I attended high school. I was forever packing bags and moving between houses. Dad's new partner at the time called me The Bag Lady.

I spent my late teens and early twenties travelling across Europe, Asia, the United States and Canada, visiting and living in as many places as I could before I turned thirty—an invisible threshold, a time when I should be 'settled', even though the word unnerved me.

At twenty-five, I returned home from working in Canada. Having already taken more 'gap years' than most of my peers, and having attended a prestigious high school, I was feeling self-inflicted pressure to have a successful career. People would constantly ask, 'So, are you back for good now?', but the implied permanency of such a statement scared me. What did they mean 'for good'? Did I now have to choose somewhere to live forever, doing the same thing? I was meant to be settling down—but where, and doing what? Almost a decade after leaving high school, I was still plagued with uncertainty about what I wanted to do, now that I was 'grown up'. Between stints of travelling, I had studied film and television in Byron Bay, but I could never quite find my place within the industry. When I returned to Brisbane from Canada, I tried being every type of assistant there was—photography assistant, camera assistant, production assistant. In an industry of strong egos and convictions, I felt unsure where and even if I belonged. I realised that the glamour of flying to remote locations to film nature documentaries was a far-flung dream, and the reality was often far more mundane—corporate head shots, cheesy TV commercials and reality TV, where money was thrown around on projects that felt shallow and superficial. I loved the talented young guys and girls I worked with, and the fact that every day as a freelancer was different, but there was a restlessness in me for something that meant more.

It was at this time that I reconnected with Sam. I moved

to Adelaide to be with him, and the process of establishing a career started all over again, with the same uncertainty.

When he was called away to war in Iraq, I returned to Brisbane again. It was while picking up the pieces of my barely formed career, and biding my time until Sam's return, that camels entered my life.

One night, visiting Dad for dinner, he showed me a copy of *Queensland Country Life* newspaper.

'They're milking camels on the Sunshine Coast now,' he announced with bemusement.

By chance, not long afterwards, I told a few girlfriends from high school about the article. 'That'll be my Aunty Lauren's farm,' laughed Georgie. 'She's the crazy camel lady.'

'What!?' Curiosity sparked within me. I'd known Georgie since we were fifteen and couldn't believe I hadn't heard about this. 'Do you think I could go and meet the camels?'

A few weeks later I stood in a paddock full of these unusual animals, their necks stretching down, their noses sniffing me deeply. It was such a personal face-to-face greeting, as if they were reading my deepest being, getting to know who I was, how I was feeling and whether I could be trusted. I was hooked. I wanted to learn everything I could about these fascinating creatures. The calm I felt among the camels was a reprieve from the anxiety that had been clouding my return to Brisbane to start my 'career'. In that moment, it didn't matter that I didn't know what I wanted to do with my life. It was enough that I was here, connecting with such big, powerful and intelligent animals.

Before long, I was milking full-time at QCamel dairy, getting to know the camels in the hundred-strong herd individually by name and appearance. It felt like the perfect short-term job until Sam returned from the war, gave up the Army, and our surf trip down the US west coast would begin. I had no idea how my new-found affinity with these animals would snowball. Which it did—so much so that when we finished our campervan trip in Mexico, I wasn't ready to go home. I wanted to learn more about camels around the world, so I said goodbye to Sam at yet another airport. He returned to Australia while I travelled onwards for several more months. Being apart again seemed trivial to me at the time. Since our travels, we were more in love than ever, so what was another brief long-distance stint when we'd already made it through so many months apart?

My fascination with camels took me on a series of interesting travel experiences, and again I revelled in being dropped into foreign countries, forced to swim in cultures that were not my own. I lived with a family of Mennonites in Michigan, United States, who milked their dairy camels in a big red barn. I attended an international camel conference in Texas, and went on to India, where I walked with the Raika, the traditional Indian caste of camel keepers, nomads moving their camels across Rajasthan.

Somewhere between my travels with camels and my return to the camel dairy in Brisbane, in those early morning hours milking, watching the purple hues grow bold over the mismatched spires of the Glasshouse Mountains, with the camels grazing in the foreground, an idea took seed. I wanted to do a journey with my own camels. I didn't know where, I didn't even know how to 'trek' with camels, but somewhere along the line that little seed took hold and grew roots.

When I first showed an interest in camels, Sam bought me *Tracks* from a roadside bookstand. He'd written on the first page: *I can't wait to travel across one of many countries on camels, with greyhounds, kelpies and chickens.* I took the first part of his inscription as gospel and daydreamed about a journey across Australia with him and two of our more adventurous friends.

It never occurred to me that I might end up walking a path not just without Sam, but without anyone at all.

Dusk was settling upon us as I retrieved the camels and brought them back to my camp on the side of the Carbla driveway. What a strange turn my life had taken to lead me here, alone in the bush with my five camels. As I bent down and undid Jude's hobbles, I felt small and vulnerable, squatting in front of such powerful big front legs. I linked the hobble cuffs around the bell buckle that hung around his neck. Jude brought his head down so his face connected with mine and gave me a long and steady sniff with his soft nostrils. I closed my eyes and took a breath, exhaling slowly. In that moment, nothing else mattered except the connection between the two of us. It was the same feeling of presence I had felt four years earlier when I was first surrounded by the camels at the dairy. I might not remember when I had decided this trip would be a good idea, but I remembered the feeling of calm certainty the camels gave me.

I undid the other camels' hobbles, linked them together and walked them back to my three-square-metre home, my tarp. I tied Jude, Delilah, Clayton and Mac to bushes for the night, making sure they had plenty to eat and their ropes were not so long that they would get tangled around their legs in the night. Charlie I left untethered with his hobble on. I had worked out he wouldn't stray from his friends.

As I ate my dinner of half-charred risotto, Charlie came and sat by the fire with me. He folded his legs underneath him, packing himself into a neat sphinx-like pose, and we stared into the flames together. A sense of peace settled over the campsite. When I rolled out my swag and crawled in, flicking off my head torch and staring up at the multitude of stars, I could hear the camels chewing their cud—a sign that all was good in a camel's world.

'Goodnight Jude, goodnight Delilah, goodnight Clayton, goodnight Mac, goodnight Charlie,' I called softly into the darkness.

3

Into the Outback

NORTH WEST COASTAL HIGHWAY TO
BUTCHERS TRACK—155 KM

At the end of the Carbla driveway, I crossed the North West Coastal Highway with the camels and entered the great inland portion of Western Australia. The bush felt denser and more uninterrupted. It surprised me how unpopulated this area was, only two days' walk from the coast. I realised I wasn't walking towards remote inland Australia as I had anticipated; I was already *in* remote Australia. I felt as though I'd been instantly thrust into the depths of the Outback.

I was hot and annoyed. I had come up against a cattle grid in the fence line and couldn't find a gate to lead the camels to the other side. After walking for two hours south along the fence, I eventually found an old gate, which I battled to open with a pair of pliers I had luckily packed. All this before I could start heading east again, in the right direction. Grids were not marked on the map and I had never thought to ask Sam the owner where the gates were.

I was now on Woodleigh Station, following an old bore track that was clearly disused, with wheel ruts interrupted by established vegetation. It wasn't the track I had planned on taking, but at least it was leading east. It ran along a fence line, which had fallen down in places, adding to the feeling of isolation. Woodleigh, Carbla and Yalardy Stations were all owned by Sam Fenny and his father, Rick Fenny, a well-known Western Australian vet, and together the stations spanned over a million acres. These mind-bogglingly vast outback stations are not at all like farms. Too dry for crops, they are pastoral leases rather than freehold land. The country here is wild and difficult to manage, and the livestock that ranges across it is often equally wild. I couldn't help reflecting on how much of this land was rarely set foot on, away from the thin web of vehicle tracks that connected bores sunk as water points for cows, sheep and sometimes goats.

I had decided to use these bore tracks to cross stations, as they would lead me to gates through fence lines, and also to watering points for the camels—at least, if the bores were working. The track I was following now seemed completely abandoned.

I kept looking behind with concern, hoping the camels wouldn't tangle a leg in bits of fence wire that lay strewn across the ground. Mac was about eight metres behind me at the back and it was impossible to control where he placed his feet.

I passed a windmill that creaked eerily and the whole place smelt like death. I picked my way around bones in the sand, kangaroo carcasses and mounds of emu feathers—signs of a harsh land that should never be taken for granted.

Growing up on the eastern seaboard, the Outback felt like a mythical place, and no one seemed to know exactly where it began or ended. It had held little appeal to me or my friends; destinations overseas were far more exotic and exciting. The Outback was for the 'grey nomads', oldies on winter odysseys towing huge caravans and a hell of a lot of stuff. It wasn't until I moved to Adelaide with Sam in my mid-twenties that it beckoned for the first time. The movie *Tracks* had recently been released, and the fact that it was about a woman on an adventure on her own resonated with me.

Sam had recently introduced me to multi-day hiking. Having never done much camping or strenuous hiking, and having never had to push myself physically, I discovered a passion for it. I felt safe with Sam. With his Army training, he was extremely capable in the bush. He knew how to survive, to navigate, to make fires, to use all the right equipment.

'I want to walk the Heysen Trail,' I announced one day to Sam. 'The upper section, the part in the Outback, on my own.' I had seen markers around Adelaide for the 1200-kilometre trail stretching up into the Flinders Ranges. I had never camped solo, but walking for nine days along the upper and most remote section of the trail, from Hawker to Parachilna Gorge, seemed the perfect way to experience my own woman-in-the-bush-alone fantasy, exploring this strange and unknown Outback.

After much trepidation—'I don't know Sophie, even lots of Army guys I know have never done a hike like this alone'—Sam surrendered to my determination and kicked into military instructor mode, putting me through drills in the local park. He taught me how to create a shelter, light a fire, plot a GPS position on a map, use a satellite phone and bandage a snake bite. The more I learnt, the more I realised how little I knew, and how out of my depth I was for the environment I was heading into in a few days' time.

As I drove five hours north from Adelaide to set off on the Heysen Trail, I felt as though I had landed on a foreign planet. I had never seen the sky so big. The red-brown flatness of the landscape accentuated the huge blue dome of sky above. But what shocked me most of all was the dryness of the land—barren and unforgiving, with barely a tree for shade. Crumbling stone ruins reinforced the seeming impossibility of anyone, or anything, surviving out there.

When I got out of the car at the small, quiet, outback town of Hawker, into the hot, crackling, dry heat of the Flinders Ranges, millions of small black flies descended on me, crawling persistently into the corners of my mouth, nose and eyes, anywhere there was a trace of moisture. Sam had insisted I bring a fly net, and now I didn't care how silly I looked wearing it on my head. Without it I looked like a living corpse from a horror film.

As I began my walk the following day, the beauty of the landscape momentarily made me forget the bone-crunching weight of the pack I was carrying. The mountains rose from the red earth like the giant spine of a crocodile, folding in waves, revealing ancient layers of earth compacted over millennia. But a splitting headache from heat and exertion brought me back to the present. The sweat evaporated instantly in the dry, making my head pulse as if it was about to explode.

The first three days were gruelling. The pack was heavy, I was anxious I didn't have enough water, the heat and flies were intolerable. To top it off I had to smash a rock into the head of a hairless, screeching baby kangaroo that had been abandoned from the pouch and was being eaten alive by ants. After putting the poor thing out of its misery, I walked along sobbing for the rest of the afternoon, wondering what the hell I was doing this for, and who would ever want to visit this hostile land.

Looking across at a severed goat's leg caught in the wires of the fence I was following, the Outback seemed just as hostile and brutal now as all those years ago on the Heysen Trail, and I wondered again why the hell I was doing this. Considering that up until five years ago I had no affinity with the Outback, it seemed a huge leap to go from a nine-day solo walk to a nine-month one. But after I had made it through the first few days on the Heysen Trail, I had felt stronger, fitter, and more determined and capable. I didn't care that I was dusty and dirty, because I felt awakening within me a muscle of endurance that I had never known existed. I had never had to overcome physical hardship, and finally doing so felt good. After nine days on the Heysen Trail I felt like a superwoman. That feeling was addictive, but I had no idea back then what that desire to challenge myself would lead me to.

The flies were here as well, a black blanket crawling down my legs and across the sweaty shirt on my back. They hung about my face as well, but this time I didn't wear a fly net—a 'tourist net' as we called it in Uluru. I still hated the flies, but I had developed an ability to tolerate them. I let them crawl over my face with Zen-like acceptance.

The bush was still dense down the track and didn't open up all day. By the afternoon I was forced to camp in the suffocating scrub. The dull grey-green vegetation was all made up of varying species of acacia. Hardy short trees that looked dormant, as if they were in a state of survival rather than flourishing renewal. As I let the camels off to graze, I realised they weren't that fond of the landscape either. They stood around not eating, huddled together like scared children. It took me several days to work out the cause of this fear: they were used to the wide open spaces of the desert and had never been in a landscape where they could not see the horizon. They liked to be able to see out around them and view potential threats, even though camels have no natural predators in Australia. Despite their placid, chilled-out facade, and slow swaggering walk and dopey expression, camels share a level of fear and anxiety innate to all herd animals—one that seems disproportionate to their size.

During our first week, the camels spooked at everything. They careered over a fence, getting tangled when they baulked at a solar panel attached to the pump at a water trough. Clayton almost flattened me when he took fright at seemingly nothing as I was putting his hobbles on. I was furious with Delilah when she jumped over a metre-high corrugated iron fence, startled by some goats, as I was giving the other camels a drink; for a moment I was convinced she would break a leg. Having worked with so many docile, domesticated camels, I had no idea mine would be so dangerously terrified. I began to make a list of all the things they were afraid of: shadecloth, tanks, solar panels, sheep, goats, structures of any kind, ant hills, and anything possibly hiding in dense scrub.

After four days of walking, at another dense, lifeless-looking bush camp on Woodleigh Station, the camels wandered off in their hobbles in search of feed. I knew how well adapted camels were at eating tough desert fodder and had naively assumed that there would always be abundant feed for them. I had never anticipated walking through areas that would be this devastated by drought. Beneath the monotonous maze of bowgada bushes there was not a morsel of feed. I would later learn how marginal this swathe of country that I was traversing was. It was a sandplain, stretching from the coast inland to the Murchison district, an area devoid of natural water catchments. The bowgada had upward-facing needles for leaves, like quills on an echidna; it was completely unpalatable except for the seed pod. With the lack of rain there was not a pod in sight. The camels reluctantly attempted to eat the quills of the harsh bush but quickly gave up.

A worrying thought crossed my mind. I realised we were wandering further from camp, the camels disappearing into the bushes. In this landscape, it would be so easy to lose my bearings and get lost in a sea of scrub, wandering around unable to find camp and get back to all the equipment I needed to survive. I was also terrified of losing the camels themselves. Without stopping to graze, even in hobbles they were moving quickly through the scrub on a quest to find food—and maybe a way out to an imaginary horizon beyond—and the sound of their bells only stretched so far. I rushed back to camp and retrieved my phone, marking a waypoint in the app where I had placed our gear. I felt safer having my phone with me, staring at the orange dot that was me moving further away from the little flag that marked camp. I vowed to carry my satchel packed with a few essentials—my sat phone, water and snake bandages—every time my camels grazed far from camp, which it turned out was most days.

From time to time, beyond the thick bush, I could hear vehicles in the distance. It was nice to know I was not completely on my own: Greg was still nearby, mustering goats. With the border restrictions, he had decided to stay in Western Australia and take a job as manager of Woodleigh Station, rather than return to Uluru where the pandemic had forced all tourism operators to shut.

Later that afternoon, when I was still tailing the camels as they grazed, I heard a car pull up in the distance. Like an apparition, Greg appeared out of the scrub. He'd found our tracks. He strode over, looking like a handsome Aboriginal cowboy in his boots, jeans and big Akubra. The top buttons of his shirt were open, revealing a glimpse of raised scarring on his chest. Greg was from Rockhampton, but had spent time in Aboriginal communities in the APY Lands and could speak Pitjantjatjara. The scars, he had told me, were from initiation ceremonies for Aboriginal men.

He beamed a huge smile at me and I burst into tears. It felt like he was the only person who knew where I was or what I was going through. He had become my sounding board in the weeks leading up to my departure. I had barely begun and already I was tired and frustrated, scared of the dangers of dealing with 700-kilogram animals that seemed more afraid than mice.

Greg passed me an ice-cold beer he had brought. It was bordering on frozen; the coldness felt and tasted unbelievably good. As we followed the camels together, he sipped his beer quietly and let me vent. When he left on dark and I brought the camels back to camp, the bush pressed in closer around me.

At the following night's camp, I tied the camels to scrawny acacia bushes commonly known as 'dead finish'. Their tiny rows of needle leaves barely filled an ice cream bucket when the camels stripped them with their lips. It wasn't much of a meal, but it was the only thing they were interested in eating in this landscape. They were losing weight rapidly and it had me worried. I hadn't expected this. I also looked a state. I appeared as though I had a bad fake tan from the red dirt that clung to my skin, and my hands were becoming scratched and rough from threading the rope through the pincushion of leaves to tie the camels up every night. After walking all day, then walking all afternoon tailing the camels as they grazed, I was exhausted.

I launched my drone to take some aerial pictures of the landscape. The images revealed a scene that was both beautiful and sickening. Endless, uniform bush, with no land features or buildings in sight, stretching off to the distant horizon, with one red road cutting through the middle. What had I been expecting? I wasn't naive about how vast Australia is. When the journey had remained purely in my imagination, it had been easy to see it through rose-tinted glasses, but I was staring at the hard truth of it now. It would be many months of continuous walking through flat, monotonous bush.

When I finally sat down to feed myself, I could barely summon enough energy to wash my pot afterwards and roll my swag out for the night. But with my hands growing more callused and scratched, and my legs more sunburnt and caked in dust, I reminded myself that I had wanted to see how much I could strengthen my muscle of endurance. After the initial gruelling phase of getting used to the trek, I hoped there would be a turning point, and it would be smoother and more enjoyable from there. That time was still a way to come.

At the end of my first week of walking, I arrived at a set of goat-trapping yards with the camels. I'd arranged for Greg to pick me up from here and drive me to the Woodleigh home-stead for a day's break. I unsaddled the camels and let them off in the yard, relieved they could enjoy a bale of hay and I didn't have to babysit them. They tucked into the hay, the five of them bunched together, warily eyeing a pair of tiny baby goats in the corner of the yard. I made a mental note to add 'cute baby goats' to the ever-growing list of things the camels were afraid of. As time went on, I would add other suspects such as 'adorable miniature ponies'.

Greg arrived to collect me and suddenly we were barrel-ling through the bush in the station ute, the wind from the open window whipping about my sweaty, dust-encrusted hair. We listened to American country tunes as Greg dodged goats running across the road from the thick bush on either side. After a week of sedately walking at three kilometres an hour, it felt like we were travelling at death-defying speed. Seeing the bush blur past so quickly only accentuated what a long way it was on foot.

The shower at the homestead washed away my apprehen-sion and the hardships of the first week. I watched the water turn red as it was sucked down the drain. Afterwards I joined Greg with a beer and he showed me around his new station home—a beautiful homestead, made of bricks quarried from the compacted tiny white shells on the beach I had walked across at Carbla. The outbuildings, shearers' quarters, cook's cottage, kitchen and meat house stood decaying, with old metal bedframes and mattresses covered in a layer of dust. I was filled with a yearning to bring it all back to life, to wipe the dust away. I felt almost clucky, wanting to nest and put down roots.

I'd had these feelings with Sam from time to time, a craving to carve out a home, but I was never quite ready. I wanted one more big adventure first, and this was it. I needed to do this for myself before my thirties crept on and I was weighed down with the commitments of a family or career. But in my quest to achieve this, I had fucked up, and was now truly free of any such future. I was single, with seemingly no prospect of having children, walking into the Outback for a year with little chance of meeting anyone.

I picked up an enamel mug and wiped the dust off it, staring out the window to what would have once been a garden patch. For a second, I imagined Greg and I living here together, restoring the place. Through the long truck trip to Western Australia, and with the isolation we both felt so far from home, we'd grown so close. A hint of chemistry often seemed to bubble below our friendship. Did I want this settled life more? A home, a family? The first week of my adventure had been hard; it would be a relief to give it up. In my fantasy, I would stay here with Greg and we would manage the station. But these were mere imaginings, born of a desire to avoid the loneliness ahead.

I knew I would never forgive myself if I stayed. I had to keep going.

Several days after I had left Woodleigh homestead I watched as the camels drank deeply from an old sheep trough—the last drink they would be having for a while. The population in many parts of the Outback had dwindled drastically since the heyday of wool, when Australia 'rode on the sheep's back', and now many of the bores marked on my map had fallen into disuse. The sheep troughs we would be passing on our two-and-a-half-week walk between here and Wooleen Station would be decaying like the abandoned outhouses, relics of a bygone era. I didn't think my camels could last that long without water. Camels are capable of going weeks, if not months, without drinking, but their ability to go without depends on how hot it is, how hard they are working and the moisture in their feed. It was hot here, and the feed was dry. After three days without water, they were gulping it down as if dying of thirst. Luckily Greg had agreed to tow a tanker of water to us in a week's time.

I also made the most of the trough, taking off my shirt and splashing water over my face and body. The flies buzzed around my wet skin. It was a moment of cool relief from the heat of the day.

I crossed a cattle grid that marked the end of Woodleigh Station. It hadn't been used in some time and was completely filled in with sand. I walked the camels over it, and couldn't help laughing as they lifted their feet into the air, taking huge, exaggerated steps like they were walking on the moon. My laughter petered out as I scanned the long sandy track that crossed this swathe of unused country. There wasn't the faintest sign of a wheel mark. I'd likely see no one for a week, until Greg dropped off the water for the camels.

For the first time, I felt truly lonely.

The days seemed to be getting harder rather than easier. The scrub was still dense and claustrophobic, the camels were still spooking and running away from camp, it was mid-April and the heat of summer was still packing its last punch. The vegetation was getting drier and drier, with less for the camels to eat. Desperate to get more food in their bellies, I took every opportunity to stop whenever we found something edible.

Early one morning, I noticed a patch of gidgee trees, which I knew the camels liked. The leaves were broader and slightly greener than the dull bowgada bushes that surrounded them. I pulled off the track and meandered from gidgee to gidgee, allowing the camels to feed, then slowly made my way back to the road through the uniform scrub. *But where was it?* I was sure I was heading in the right direction, but it still hadn't reappeared. It seemed ridiculous to consult my phone map when we had literally only pulled off the road ten metres, but I had now been walking for half an hour with no sign of it. I could no longer see the gidgee trees and all the bush looked the same. I began to doubt my sense of direction. Finally, I conceded that I was completely lost, and took out my phone. I was horrified to see that I had walked in completely the wrong direction, away from the road.

Once we were finally back on the road, the heat of the day radiated in every direction. The sun beat down and reflected up off the red sand of the exposed road. I wanted to stop and make camp already. I was hot and over it, but I had wasted time and lost ground wandering around disorientated. If we couldn't make our daily ten kilometres, how would we ever reach twenty-five?

I played some podcasts on my iPhone to pass the time. The road was dead straight, and the bush either side unchanging and boring. As I walked, I constantly scanned each side of the road for places to camp. I looked for clearings in the bush where I could sit the camels down, and where there were feed bushes for the night. Slowly, ten kilometres came and went. It had just gone midday and the temperature felt close to forty degrees. I turned to look at the camels and heard a buzzing as a hundred flies that had hitched a ride on my sweaty back rose into the air, disturbed in unison.

The rope I was holding pulled back, and I felt Delilah sitting down. She had already done this three times today, protesting that she was tired and over it as well. I moved back past Jude and growled, 'HUP, Delilah!' She roared back at me with indignation but got up. Like me, she wanted nothing more than to sit in the shade on this hot afternoon. I pulled off the track into the bush. We hadn't found anywhere good to camp in the last two hours. If I carried on, would we get to something better, or would we walk for several more hours and still not find anything? I stared at the topographical maps on my phone, wishing for a crystal ball that would show me the vegetation to come.

While I paused, wondering if I should go on or stay, Delilah sat down again. I looked around, disappointed but resigned to this nondescript camp. As I unpacked the camels, my back ached from the repetitive strain of lifting some 500 kilograms of gear on and off the camels' backs, morning and afternoon, for the past two weeks. I was like a little old hunched-over lady, wandering around like a half-shut pocketknife.

I bent down and opened my food boxes to fish out an electrolyte tablet. I barely waited for the tablet to finish fizzing before downing it in one hit. While the camels were enjoying the shade, I ventured off to find out if there were any bushes for them to eat. I walked into the bush on the other side of the track, and thought I could see a change in the height of the vegetation ahead. As I got closer, I realised it was a patch of gidgee trees, like the ones I had seen that morning. I cursed, rubbing my forehead with my hands. This was a far better camp, with actual food for the camels! *Why hadn't I looked around more before I unsaddled?* This new spot was only 500 metres away—but still too far to carry so much heavy gear on my own.

I heard bells tinkle in the distance and rushed back to camp to make sure the hobbled camels weren't wandering too far. When I arrived, Clayton had his head in my food boxes, and Charlie was pushing around an object on the ground with his lips. They had raided my supplies! I moved Clayton aside to assess the damage. All my sweet potatoes were gone, a couple of apples had been stolen, and one of them had even been game enough to take a bite from an onion. They looked at me innocently, as if surprised that I would be so shocked. They were obviously hungry. I summoned up all the energy that I could. I was going to have to saddle them up again and move the gear to the better camp.

The camels looked horrified and confused when they were made to *hoosh* again and I began to rush around like a madwoman, throwing gear on their backs as quickly as I could. If I was going to do this whole process for a second time today,

I was going to do it as fast as I could! It felt like someone had hit the rewind button as I reassembled all the gear on the camels' backs in the same order that it was unpacked only two hours ago.

When I unsaddled for a second time, not just my back but every muscle in my body ached. But I felt satisfied that finally I had a good camp with feed for the camels. They happily rolled in the dust and went about eating the wide leaves of the big gidgee trees. I leant against Jude, using his big body as the camp chair that I had decided not to pack, while I read a book. Delilah had found the perfect little node of wood on one of the trees to scratch a very specific spot on her chin. She moved her head back and forth on the branch, and with every motion her bell clanged obnoxiously. She seemed oblivious to the disruption she was causing to the general air of relaxation.

That night I stared up at the Southern Cross. I traced a line with my finger through the long axis of the cross, then pretended I was kicking a ball through the two pointers (Alpha Centauri and Beta Centauri), found the spot where these lines intersected and brought my finger down to the horizon. South. Sam had taught me this. There was hardly a part of my daily routine that did not remind me of him and something he had taught me. Sam had been my compass point, and I had wanted to navigate my life around him—until I veered wildly and irrevocably off course.

4

The Loneliness of the Road

BUTCHERS TRACK TO
WOOLEEN STATION—117 KM

I had seen no one for a week. I was now walking along Butchers Track, a public dirt road that connected with stations and towns to the east. Because of the Covid-19 travel restrictions, not a single car passed me. I daydreamed as I walked, wondering what might be happening in the outside world. Would I walk into Byron Bay at the end of the year to find a scene from a zombie apocalypse film, with vines growing through houses and upturned burnt-out cars? I imagined the camels and I as the sole survivors of this pandemic that had ravaged the world. It was strange to be so disconnected that I wouldn't have had a clue if World War III had broken out.

The days blurred into one; I had little concept of what day of the week it was. My waking hours were an endless cycle of packing, walking, unpacking, chasing camels around the bush, cooking dinner and getting into my swag so I could get just enough sleep to do it all again. A haze of worry hovered around me as I walked. *Will there be feed for my camels? Are they thirsty? Are their loads too heavy? Are their loads sitting evenly? What will spook them next? Will we ever be able to walk twenty-five kilometres per day?* Once I had exhausted my worries, the monotony of the bush around me would bring my thoughts back to Sam. I wished, once again, that he was here with me and we were doing this adventure together.

How had it all gone so wrong? The fairytale relationship I had always wanted, with the guy I had fallen in love with at eighteen. Our joyful time living in the campervan and surfing the Americas together had eradicated every bit of estrangement we had felt while Sam was at war in Iraq. As the hours of walking ticked slowly by, I retraced and relived in my mind every turn our relationship had taken. It had started to unravel when I had decided to keep travelling and he returned home to Australia. As I stood at the Santiago Airport departure gate in Chile, where we finished our overseas adventure together, on my tiptoes hugging Sam goodbye, kissing him deeply with tears welling in my eyes, I'd had an almost fatalistic gut feeling that this would be the most in love we would feel for a long time. I was right. My passion for camels was driving a rift between us. When I chose to journey onwards, too many long-distance separations compounded one another. Our lives were moving in different directions, and I was having experiences with camels and cultures overseas that Sam could not relate to. When I returned to the Sunshine Coast to work at the camel dairy, Sam had taken a job on the Gold Coast, and it was no longer possible to live together. The two-hour drive that separated us made the chasm that had already formed between us grow wider. It was like being in a slow-motion train crash. After feeling so directionless, I finally had a focus, a fascination for camels, which was blinding me to the fact that my relationship was falling to pieces.

In a last-ditch attempt to save our relationship, we moved back in together on the Gold Coast. I could remember it vividly, how I cried when I first saw the apartment. Sam liked it because it was close to the surf, but I felt trapped and hemmed in, the family downstairs swearing loudly at one another in constant domestic disputes, barely drowned out by the highway one street away. The only thing that kept me sane within the claustrophobic walls of that apartment was planning my escape to learn more about camel trekking.

Only a week after moving in together again, I flew to Adelaide and caught a bus to outback South Australia to spend a month volunteering with Camel Treks Australia, run by Paul and Karen Ellis, whom I had randomly met when I walked the Heysen Trail. Meeting them back then now felt fortuitous, and I was excited to be returning to the Flinders Ranges, where I had taken my first steps into the Outback. I reasoned again that a little more long distance wouldn't matter; I would go back to the Gold Coast after this.

The first few treks I assisted with took place on Clayton Station, roughly 300 kilometres north of Hawker, on the Birdsville Track. It was the furthest into the Outback I'd ever been, and it opened up my world. The sky was even bigger here, and the landscape a diverse range of gibber plains, wide coolabah-spotted creek beds with hot, artesian bore water filling waterholes, and the sand hills of the Tirari Desert stretching out to Lake Eyre. I drank it all in. I fell in love with the Outback, and fell in love with sleeping next to camels under the stars. It was here that my own camel trip took form in my mind: a crossing of the entire country from westernmost point to easternmost point.

One of the guests on an eight-day trek told me she had read *Tracks* as a young girl and had always wanted to do a trip like Robyn Davidson's. But she'd married and had kids and life had got in the way. 'That's why I came on this trip— it was the closest I could get to doing a camel trip,' she said as I led the camel she was riding through the dunes. I knew in that instant that I would not let the idea of my adventure slip away. It was a grandiose scheme, but like this woman, I would always regret it if I didn't seize my chance.

I called Sam from a lonely payphone in Marree on the edge of the desert. The bleak scene matched the coldness in his voice. I hadn't called in over a week, prioritising camels over our relationship. And then, as I pressed the phone into my cheek, I unwittingly drove the final nail into the coffin. I told Sam that Karen had offered me a further month's work, on Beltana Station in the Flinders Ranges, where they would be situated for the remainder of their winter trekking season. It was only one more month, with a week's break beforehand—but one more month when a relationship was already on rocky ground was too long.

When I flew back to the Gold Coast to take the week off, Sam picked me up from the airport. It was a quiet drive home.

I was miffed he hadn't asked me anything about my time away, or the camels. I was brimming with stories and excitement that went untold. There was no lustful sex as we burst through the apartment door, no staying up late with a glass of wine and catching up on one another's lives. Sam went straight to bed. I climbed into the cold space beside him and felt lonelier than I had ever felt.

We barely saw one another in the week I was home. Sam had to work, and again we were on opposite schedules. On the final morning before I was due to fly back to South Australia, we went body surfing together. Dipping under and soaring across the face of a wave, we were once again united by our love of the ocean.

'It's going to be okay, Soph,' Sam told me with his steady, reassuring voice when we emerged from the surf and shared a salty kiss, dripping sea water onto the sand. But I could see our relationship shattering in my hands, and didn't know how to save it. I wanted desperately to do this one big adventure, before 'life got in the way'. And I wanted Sam to be part of it, too. I had pleaded with him to join me in South Australia, but he had work commitments, and it was becoming clear to me that I was forcing him into something he didn't want.

In the end, our undoing was an act of cruel self-sabotage. I didn't know how to fix my relationship so I blew it up, from the inside out, with a French chef who worked on the camel treks. He was everything Sam was not: emotional, foreign, passionate, intense. He had a crazy sense of humour and a temper to match. He loved the camels, and it felt like we wanted similar things from life. I was seduced by the notion of falling in love again, rather than having to fix something that was broken. We drew close in the bubble of our unusual working environment, in the closed confines of the Outback, in an alternate world. One night, I whispered his name outside his swag, and when he answered, I crawled in.

I never intended to cheat on Sam. I guess no one plans to cheat in a relationship. I thought I was in love, in a fantasy relationship, which the Frenchman fostered. But it could never work in the long run; he would forever be the man I cheated on Sam with. And Sam, no matter how much I cried over our relationship, and for all its highs and deep lows, would always be the love of my life.

I returned to the Gold Coast choked with betrayal. I couldn't face telling him—so instead I broke up with him. It was a hideous conversation, filled with sadness rather than anger. We both knew we were moving in different directions. Deep down, I knew I was making the worst decision of my life, but I didn't know how else to deal with it. After the initial shock and devastation, I hadn't expected Sam to accept my decision so readily. I hoped our split would be temporary, that someday we would find our way back together once my trip was over.

But now, in outback Western Australia, as I walked with the camels through another hot day, I wondered what the fuck I was doing. What had I done? Why had I given him up for this? Painful images haunted my steps. I squinted against the glare with no focus, remembering the time I drove out of our street on the Gold Coast for the final time, leaving Sam sitting on the bed with his head in his hands. I was sobbing so much I could barely drive, distraught at my own actions.

I remembered the time he messaged me while I was in Uluru, to tell me he had a new girlfriend, and how I collapsed in the sand gasping for breath, enraged that he could move on so quickly. Images then flashed through my head of the woman I had stalked on Instagram, the two of them laughing in the snow, how I'd been stricken with poker-hot jealousy. And then I remembered the moment I told Sam the secret that had been eating me up inside—that I had cheated. He had asked me for details on the phone, hatred emanating from his voice: exactly where and how many times had we slept together? He sent me a package filled with all our old trinkets and photos of one another, accompanied by a note that I could barely read, telling me how selfish I was. I burnt the letter in the backyard at Uluru, but I kept the photos of us. I still couldn't let him go. Then, there came a softening, when he forgave me, even though I could not forgive myself. But our conversations always ended painfully until we agreed it was best not to speak. I deleted his number and unfriended him on social media. But then he messaged just before I began my trip to wish me luck. It was the first time I'd heard from him in twelve months, and I had thought of him every day since.

We walked all day without finding a trace of camel feed. I picked a desolate clearing in which to camp. After unsaddling, the camels wandered around forlornly, searching for something to eat, and, finding nothing that they liked, sat back down in the shade looking dejected. I had lost my Zen abilities with the flies and resorted to wearing a fly net for the afternoon. I lay on my tarp in a foetal position, bawling into the black net coated in flies.

'I'm sorry I've taken you on this awful adventure!' I gasped between sobs to my camels. I didn't want to do this anymore. I felt broken and inconsolable. I had fucked up everything . . . and for this! I wanted someone to make it better. I wanted Sam. I opened my phone and re-read his message from the day I left.

> Hey Soph it's Sam, it's been a while hey? Probably too long to be honest. I just wanted to touch base again. I know you're almost ready to embark on your journey—and I really just wanted to wish you good luck and let you know I'll be thinking of you and keeping tabs as best I can on your progress. It really is such an epic thing you're doing, I can't even fathom how far you've come since the humble days of learning to put up a hootchie—Jesus Christ I can't imagine your navigation sheet right now!

With that one message he was back at the forefront of my mind, and I was cursed with obsessing over my massive screw-up. I looked over at the camels and took a deep breath, reminding myself that I had chosen this. Every decision I'd made that had led me to crying in a foetal position on my tarp had been my own. No one forced me to come on this adventure; it had been a choice. I had to let my obsession with the past go. I was no longer turning out of our Gold Coast street sobbing; I was here in the bush in Western Australia, alone with my camels. I sat up, leant against my swag, took out my journal and wrote Sam a letter. We had sent many love letters to one another in the past, since we were so often apart. But

I knew I would never send this one; I just needed to write it for myself. It was a statement of regret, for everything I had done, how I had cheated, and how I had not appreciated what we had between us. I finished with, *I still love you and always will.*

I put down my pen and packed away my notebook. Sam was always quoting from the documentary *180° South*, especially his hero Yvon Chouinard, the founder of the outdoor store Patagonia: *Adventure is when everything goes wrong. That's when the adventure starts.* He liked the description of adventurers as 'conquerors of the useless'. I felt like that now—on a useless mission to conquer something I could not yet define. The adventure had started and everything had gone wrong, but when I boiled it down to the basics, we were all okay. No one was hurt or injured. Most of my worries had all been in my head. So often I had taken my feelings of anxiety and instability out on everyone around me. Here, I was on my own. I had no one to blame, and no one to console me. I was the only one who could pick myself back up off this tarp and keep going. I looked over at the camels again. They looked thin and dejected; they had no feed and I had to keep moving forward.

That night I lay in my swag, staring up at the crystals my friend Keirin had given me, which I had hung from a loop in the swag directly above my head. There was a tiger's eye for strength and willpower, and an amethyst for peace and protection. I reached up and touched them, feeling their cold jagged forms in my hand.

'Strength and power,' I repeated to myself, willing the crystals to imbue me with these qualities. Cocooned in my swag, physical tiredness won out, and I was asleep within seconds.

Still, not a single car passed us along Butchers Track. The stillness fed my imaginings of the apocalypse that was unfolding in the outside world. The weather felt spooky. It was overcast and the clouds were threatening rain. I made camp early in a small patch of stunted bullock trees that were only in this one spot, forming a bit of a fairy ring, surrounded by the usual dry, inedible scrub, and wandered after the camels as they grazed.

I looked up from tailing the camels and realised we were a long way from camp. I turned in a full circle, completely disorientated. The thick uniform bush and overcast day meant it was virtually impossible to tell which way was north, south, east or west. I felt for my phone in my pocket, knowing I would need it to navigate my way back to camp.

The sky was gradually getting darker, so I linked Jude, Delilah and Charlie together and tied them to a bush. Clayton and Mac were grazing a little way away. I hooked them to one another and headed back to link them with the other three camels. But as I wove through the bushes to Jude, Delilah and Charlie, all I could see was thick scrub. My heart pounded. *Where were they? Where had I tied them?* It felt like the bush was closing in around us, choking us. I heard the soft chiming of a bell and rounded one more shrub. The first three camels came into view and I breathed a sigh of relief; the bush had momentarily loosened its grip on our throats. I headed back to camp quickly, stumbling over logs and under overhanging branches, staring at the light from my phone and the little flag that marked camp in the growing darkness.

Back at camp, the fairy ring of bullock bushes had taken on an eerie feeling. I made a fire to cook dinner, but couldn't shake the feeling that someone or something was watching me beyond the glow of the flames. Greg had often spoken to me about spirits in the bush, being so attuned to the energy of the land. I had felt it too, in my time at Uluru, Kata Tjuta (the Olgas) and Rainbow Valley near Alice Springs—as if certain landscapes held power, a palpable, thrumming energy that spoke of ceremonies that had been held there for thousands of years.

The feeling that evening wasn't overly pleasant. I put another large log on the fire, remembering Greg's instruction: *The smoke from the fire will blow away the bad spirits.* With an unsteady voice I spoke into the darkness. 'I just want to let you know that we are just passing through. I'm asking you for one night's rest. We will be gone by the morning.' The darkness felt thick, and I dreaded stepping into it to check on the camels.

The wind picked up through the night, and by morning the clouds were gone. The day was cool and clear. There had been a shift in the energy of the place. I packed up camp, but before I left, I stopped by the ashes of the fire and said softly, 'Thank you for letting us rest here safely. We'll be off now.'

We carried on along Butchers Track that day, and by the afternoon had picked a new camp with a large gum tree for shade.

While the camels sat resting, I strung a length of paracord between two bushes as a clothesline and washed my clothes in a bucket I carried for giving the camels water. Rather than detergent, I washed them with lemon juice and apple cider vinegar, as I planned to give the camels the water afterwards; it seemed criminal to waste any water in this dry landscape. Once I was done, I offered the bucket to Jude. His slurping woke the other camels from their dozing and they were immediately up and all pushing to get their heads in the small bucket. I tried to offer a small slurp to each of them, but one of the others would reach their head in, tipping the bucket and spilling more than they were drinking. The water was quickly finished, and they looked questioningly at me for more. Charlie picked the bucket up with his teeth and shook it as if he hoped more water would appear. I took it off him before he could break it.

'One more day, guys. Greg will come tomorrow with the water. Hopefully . . .' They hadn't had a drink in a week, and seemed to be so thirsty. I hadn't expected to have water troubles so early in the trip.

I picked out bushes nearby to tie the camels to—a process made harder by the fact that they suddenly noticed my temporary clothesline and decided it was the devil himself. I added 'clothesline' to the list of things that made no sense for them to be afraid of.

I cooked dinner, then stripped down and washed my filthy body with less than a cup of water. I used a car chamois as a washcloth, a trick that had been suggested to me because it absorbs water readily and dries quickly when wrung out. I called this nightly ritual my 'shammy shower'. I stood, naked, enjoying the warmth from the fire on my bare skin. I wandered around camp, checking on the camels, still fully naked, except for my boots and head torch. I was getting used to this, I thought. Why bother with clothes when no one was around? Then I heard the sound of a vehicle. *Shit!* A car was coming, and I was camped right next to the road. I raced around, tripping over as I tried to pull my jeans and a shirt on. I had felt invisible in the bush, and was now in a state of panic about seeing another human being. Thoughts of notorious outback murders and movies such as *Wolf Creek* streamed through my head. I was a woman alone—and naked until a moment ago—in the bush, at night. I cursed lighting the fire next to the road and quickly tried to kick some sand over it. Its glow still shone out like a beacon in the dark. The roar of the approaching engine woke the camels, and they all stood up with a clanging of bells. I flicked my head torch off and crouched behind a bush. I saw lights hurtle by and breathed a sigh of relief. Then I heard brakes. Air brakes. It was a truck. *Shit, shit, shit!* Ivan Milat in seedy truckie form. For a split second I wondered if I should get my guns out.

Then, above the idling of the truck, I heard a familiar voice.

'Soph!' It was Greg, in my old Hino camel truck. I emerged from my hiding place, my heart returning to its usual rhythm. It was stupid to be so scared. Who would find me out here, other than Greg? I had more chance of being raped or attacked in a city. I would give the Outback more credit from now on.

'You scared the shit out of me! I didn't think you'd be here till tomorrow,' I said, walking towards him in the dark. He gave me a huge hug, squeezing me tight. It felt nice to be held. I hadn't seen anyone except the camels in a week.

I took the next day off with Greg. In the morning, we tied the camels to the truck and topped up my little red bucket with water from the tanker Greg had brought. The camels downed bucket after bucket. Jude drank ninety litres, his belly expanding before my eyes. While the camels ate hay around the truck, Greg cooked Johnny cakes and I sucked the honey that dripped off them from my fingers while I brewed several rounds of coffee. I felt like I was on holiday. No saddling up, no walking, no deciding where to camp.

After breakfast I stood behind the truck in my bra and undies and Greg used the remaining water to shower me. It felt strangely intimate, but also not. I couldn't stop giggling at the oddness of the situation, standing on a dirt road in the middle of nowhere, buckets of water being thrown on me like an animal. I shampooed and conditioned my hair and changed into a set of fairly fresh vinegar-smelling clothes. I felt like a new woman.

By early afternoon, it was time for Greg to go. I was in tears as he enveloped me in a last great bearhug. This was the final goodbye. I would now be walking too far away for him to visit, and I wouldn't see him until the end. I sat in the sand on the edge of the track, watching the cloud of dust from the truck disappear as the engine noise faded.

I was met again by the silence of the bush and the never-ending buzz of flies. I kept on staring, once the truck had disappeared, down the long stretch of road I had walked.

Then I turned my head and stared along the endless stretch of road I still had left to walk. Without Greg, Western Australia felt vast, lonely and unfamiliar.

When I was a child, my dad and I would fly to the United Kingdom to visit my grandparents. We always booked the window seat, and I'd gaze down at the vast red land passing below us. Dad said it was remarkable that you had to fly for five hours from Brisbane before you even left the Australian land mass. From above, it looked like there was nothing down there except swirls of red and brown hues merging into one another. Now, on the ground, walking with my five camels, I pictured us from that same bird's-eye view. Like a tiny dot walking alone amid this infinite wide brown landscape.

I turned off Butchers Track and took a series of old station tracks to Wooleen Station. They were disused, barely distinguishable in places, and I felt intrepid, not knowing if I'd be able to connect the dots. It was nice to leave the monotony of a dead-straight road. The country opened up, and I felt like I could finally breathe. It was wonderful to see this new variety in the landscape. The old vehicle ruts we followed crossed saltbush flats, claypans, small dry creek lines and rocky escarpments. My spirits buoyed, I chatted away non-stop. I had always talked to my camels, but having been alone on the road with them for close to three weeks, I now had full-blown conversations with them. I also sang a lot. Jude and Delilah had been named after songs—'Hey Jude' by the Beatles, and 'Hey There Delilah' by the Plain White T's—and I always joked that I wanted camels I could sing to. 'Hey Jude' seemed a little sad, though, so I resorted to another favourite. In the solitude of this abandoned landscape, I belted out Elton John's 'Tiny Dancer' at the top of my lungs, pretending I was singing a duet with Jude.

'Come on Jude, sing it with me buddy!' I would urge him, carrying on, unperturbed and out of key, as Jude smiled and chewed his cud nonchalantly behind me.

The feed situation for the camels had become much better and we were all starting to relax into the routine of the days going by. When we arrived at the Murchison River, the scene before our eyes was an unaccustomed delight. Green, succulent creek flats lay before us, packed with tonnes of delicious fresh camel feed, leading down to a line of large river gums in the distance. The green seemed luminous after the endless brown landscape we'd been traversing. I waded through this sea of camel feed, pausing to let the camels put their heads down and take big, succulent mouthfuls. Two emus appeared on our left, curious about our little procession. Cows came running in too, jostling one another to get a look at the odd long-necked animals I was leading. The camels tore their heads away from the greenery at their feet to look up at the emus and cows. Their chewing stopped, their bodies and lips taut with fear at being surrounded by these spectators. Charlie was walking quickly up against

Delilah's side; Mac had started to shove and push Clayton in front of him. Jude's speed had also increased, and I held the rope firm, trying to steady him.

By the time we reached the giant gums of the creek, my string of camels had descended into pandemonium. The back camels were running, and I was having to hold Jude's head to the ground to keep him steady.

Why did they have to be like this, when we had found the most beautiful spot to camp?

'Steady!' I yelled. *Didn't they realise that all I wanted to do was camp in a nice spot with lots of food for them?* I found a pretty area by the creek to make camp and sat the camels down one by one. Every time I made them sit, they would jump back up again. They all had diarrhoea running down their legs, a sign they were terrified. *What was wrong with them?* The cows and emus were now out of sight, but the camels seemed petrified of the whole area.

I sat them all down again, placing two leg straps around each of their front legs to stop them getting up. Still, they circled around, crawling on their knees like commandos. I tried to get Jude to stay still, so I could remove the string of his nose line from around the peg on his nose. He roared and threw cud up into my face. I stood, covered in hot stinking cud, shaking with rage. I grabbed his rope and shoved his head to the ground. I yelled in his face, my exhaustion and worry from the past month bubbling up from inside me. Jude looked wide-eyed and terrified at me and I let the rope go. I was still shaking, shocked at my own anger. I needed to walk away before I lost my temper at any of the other camels.

I left the camels saddled and walked up the creek. There was a small waterhole obscured by bushes around a bend from where we had camped. It was the first natural body of water I had seen since the ocean. I stripped down and squatted in the shallow pool, dunking my head under the water to abate my anger. I contemplated how I could be so mad at animals I loved so much. Their behaviour seemed irrational and was frustrating. I got out, putting the same dirty clothes back on, and walked back around the bend to where I had made camp. One, two, three, four camels, I counted. *Where the fuck was Mac?* I walked down into the creek and looked around. Sitting on the opposite side of the creek, 100 metres from where I had last left him, with leg straps around both front legs and the row of jerry cans still on each side on his back, was Mac. I blinked. It was as if he had teleported. He must have crawled, with both front legs bound, through the thick bushes, down a steep embankment and across the creek.

The next day was like leading a tightly coiled spring that was ready to burst and unravel at any moment. The camels swung out, pulling one another off a steep embankment in the creek, and walked all day at double their regular pace. I struggled to keep up and keep my five wild animals under control. I could not have been more relieved to see the tall palms and radio tower of Wooleen Station come into view.

David and Frances Pollock, who were as warm and friendly as they had sounded on the phone, greeted me as I unsaddled and settled the camels into the homestead yards. Normally they operated the station as a tourism venture, with guests staying in the beautiful historic homestead, but because of Covid-19 restrictions there was only me. Frances had put me up in a converted relocatable hut. She apologised profusely that it didn't look like much from the outside, but she thought I would like it best as it was nearest to the camels. After the way in which the camels had acted over the last two days, I was in fact looking forward to time away from them, but I appreciated the sentiment.

I pushed the hut door open and felt as though I had been transported to a luxury five-star hotel. Beautiful plush white linen dressed the bed, and at the foot was a folded towel with an assortment of small soaps and boutique moisturisers.

After a shower, I let my aching body sink into the white fluffy bedspread, staring up at the ceiling. I was one tough month into my trek. It was going to be very hard to leave this place and keep walking.

5

A Home in the Bush

WOOLEEN STATION TO
SANDSTONE—385 KM

I woke a little disorientated and groggy from a sleep-in, cosied up under a white cloud of doona at Wooleen Station. I was content; I had relished the social interaction with Frances and David the previous night. I hadn't realised how starved I was for conversation.

I dragged myself out of bed, bleary eyed, to check on the camels. I found them sitting around their hay bale contentedly chewing their cud. I slipped through the railings of the yards and approached each one of them, greeting them face to face. When I reached Jude, I noticed his back leg was on a strange angle. I looked again and saw a piece of old fencing wire protruding from his knee cap. The warm fuzzy feeling I'd had when I woke up quickly vanished, replaced by familiar surging waves of worry about the camels' welfare. I touched the wire and Jude immediately stood up. It was wedged in the callused section of his upper back leg. He must have sat on it in the night, and pushed it right into the flesh with his own weight. Calling a vet wasn't an option in this remote area; I'd have to remove it myself. The wire was in a terrible spot. I assessed the cattle yards and realised quickly that Jude was far too big to secure in the crush. I put a halter on him and tied him to the rail, scrutinising the wire and trying to work out how deep it had been embedded. I stood by his shoulder, running my hands over his body, patting him gently.

'It's all right, mate,' I told him calmly. Then I took a deep breath, prepared myself, and with as much speed and confidence as I could muster I grabbed the wire with both hands and yanked it as hard as I could. WHACK. Jude's back leg shot forward like lightning and I went stumbling backwards, victoriously holding the wire in both hands. I rubbed my own leg, where the kick had landed and Jude's toenails had scratched me. A little swelling, but I was okay. I wasn't angry at him; it had been a natural reflex because it hurt. I examined the wire and the blood showed it had been submerged ten centimetres into the skin. I sprayed the wound with antiseptic that I was carrying in my kit and walked Jude around and, thankfully, there were no signs of him being lame. I didn't know what I'd do if something happened to one of the camels. This had only been a minor incident, but a camel injury would basically mean the end of the trip for me. I could never leave one camel behind.

I walked back to the homestead feeling far more awake than I had half an hour before.

After cleaning and repacking my food boxes for the month ahead, I hopped in the ute with David and Frances. They took me to an area of the station they had fenced and were experimenting with growing native grasses in. I gazed out the window at the bare red dirt and gum trees, thinking of nothing in particular. David noticed my gaze and commented, 'It's not meant to look like this. The landscape. Everyone's grown accustomed to seeing bare ground and we all think that that's what the Outback is like.'

He was right. I hadn't thought there was anything wrong with the landscape; it just looked like the Outback to me. Frances piped up, 'There are diaries from early explorers that talk about men wading through knee-high grass on horseback.' It was hard to imagine the land looking any different to how it did now. I had thought of it as a static thing, until David and Frances explained that arid landscapes are particularly delicate environments, and the Western Australian rangelands, as this area is known, had been overstocked in the wool boom era and the country had never recovered. Sheep and feral goats had eaten down the slow-growing desert flora, leaving the ground bare and susceptible to erosion. The kangaroo population had also exploded. Soil erosion caused channelling, which in turn meant that the precious little rain that fell flowed quickly away, rather than being dispersed across the dry ground. It was a vicious cycle. There were very few cattle on Wooleen.

Frances and David had instead turned to tourism, to allow the land to rejuvenate.

We pulled up at a fence that encircled a patch of long billowing native grasses. David and Frances walked among them, examining the health of different varieties. I followed slowly, running my fingers through the stalks. This couple were unlike any other station owners I had met; they were young, with new ideas and a passion for regenerating the land. I was fascinated. It was only a small area of grassland—less than an acre—but they were inspired by the radical idea that perennial grasses could one day cover the red soil of the rangelands again.

I dreaded my departure. The longer I stopped for a break, the harder it was to get going again. I didn't want to leave my cosy room, regular showers and delicious dinners. Most of all I didn't want to leave the company of David and Frances. I would miss their friendship and the stimulating discussions on pastoralism and the state of the land. After a week, I gritted my teeth, saddled up the camels and hit the road.

I took a track that passed behind the homestead. Now that it was May, the weather had finally started to cool down, and I planned to do fifteen-kilometre days in my quest to cover more ground. But that first day back on the road, we only made eight kilometres. Delilah was feeling the heavier weight of the newly packed food boxes and kept sitting down. I didn't feel like fighting with her, so I gave up and made camp early on a dry lake bed. The lake was within a small paddock and, after checking exactly where the fence line ran, I decided I'd be able to let the camels off without having to tail them.

I collected some dry logs from the gums and lit a fire, reclining on my swag with the billy on the boil. I opened a pack bag and took out the books David had given me before I left: *The Wooleen Way,* his memoir, in which he describes Wooleen's regenerative ethos, and *A Guide to Plants of Inland Australia.* Since spending so many hours with the camels watching them graze, morning and afternoon, I had discovered a passion for plants. The vegetation was so different here to the east coast, and learning what plants the camels did and didn't like to eat drew me to discover more about them. I bent down to examine a type of bluebush Clayton was nibbling and flicked through the plant guide to identify it. I already knew many of the desert plants from living at Uluru, but every day I was learning more. It amazed me how ancient a humble little shrub could be; this bluebush could be over a hundred years old. Clayton moved on to something else. The camels never ate continuously at a single bush; they love variety in their diet, just like humans. They seem to have an innate knowledge of exactly what they need to eat for perfect digestion. Camels have three stomachs, and are the ultimate engines of efficiency. They absorb every ounce of nutrition and moisture from their food, and expel only small dried pellets of dung, disproportionate to their size. I had grown to respect and admire how camels survive in this terrain, and they, in turn, had introduced me to the incredible variety of plants that were also adapted to this landscape.

There was a purity about it: fewer weeds existed here, and only the toughest specimens survived.

Later that afternoon, I took photos of the sun setting, its rays piercing between the big, knotted trunks of the gums. I was enjoying having a camera in my hands again. I turned the lens to the camels, adding to the hundreds of photos I already had of them, sitting, grazing, rolling. I captured them as a group, and individually, as if adding their experiences to our holiday album. They felt like family now, and I felt like I was part of their herd. They were part of where I went, and I was part of where they went. Because they outnumbered me, I even wondered whether they thought they were on their own adventure, pondering this strange human who was following them. I coined my own phrase as I hung out among them: *Home is where the herd is.*

As the sun set in the west, a huge glowing full moon rose in the east. I clicked away frenetically, capturing the beauty of the scene. The purple hues of late evening lingered, without a breath of wind. The moon cast its light across the dry lake while the camels rolled, kicking up dust. I marvelled how the arrival of the full moon was timed with the setting of the sun. From now, it would rise later into the evening, revealing a star-studded sky before I took to my swag. It seemed strange that I had never paid attention to the patterns of the moon night by night. I stood on my tarp, my home in the bush, staring up at its round familiar face as a dingo howled in the distance. A Wooleen dingo. Despite criticism from many neighbours, Frances and David didn't cull dingoes on their station, considering them a critical part of the ecosystem, keeping feral goats and kangaroo numbers in check, allowing the low-level shrubs that prevent erosion to regenerate. The dingo howled again, sending shivers up my spine. Haunting and beautifully eerie, it made me feel intensely alive. It was the sound of the wild. A wild land that I was gradually getting to know and understand.

It had been hard to leave the comfort of Wooleen Station, but in that moment, outdoors under the moonlight with my camels was exactly where I wanted to be.

On the road to Meka Station, I paused to stare at the carcasses of two dingoes strung up in a tree on the side of the road. The sunken eye sockets glared down at me, their bodies a medieval warning to other dingoes, akin to a human head on a spike. Clearly most station owners did not feel the same way about them as David and Frances.

'They're not dingoes, they're wild dogs and they're psychopathic killers!' Bob declared vehemently at the Meka homestead. I was sitting around the dinner table with him and his wife Trish, having been invited for 'tea'. The intensity of Bob's statement was at odds with his soft nature. He had kindly put the camels up in his yards, giving them a great big bale of hay and refusing to take any money for it. Now, we sat around their wooden dinner table discussing the large role camels had played in the wool industry in the early pioneering days. Jude, Delilah, Charlie, Clayton and Mac's ancestors had been imported from India, Pakistan and Afghanistan, as they could carry more and survive longer distances without water than bullock and donkey dray teams. I imagined camels out the front of Meka Station, pulling wagons full of supplies, or a string of seventy camels carting wool for export overseas. They say Australia's economy rode on the sheep's back, and in these arid areas, the transporting of wool from the sheep stations relied on camels. Bob explained how there had once been a Cobb & Co. staging post on the road next to the woolshed, with a market for fleece to be bought and sold. But that was in the old days—before motorised transport superseded camels and they were released into the Outback, where a wild population had survived and thrived. It was also before the wool industry had collapsed, and places such as Meka and Wooleen stations, which were once the size of small towns, supporting all the labour that was needed for producing wool, had shrunk to being run by a couple of people. It was the same on every station I passed through. Trish and Bob managed their entire property of a million acres virtually on their own. It was a tough and isolated existence.

Bob told me that with so few people living in the bush, it was impossible to keep the dingoes in check, and there were now so many wild dogs that it was impossible to run sheep in Western Australia, so everyone had turned to cattle. It was the reason I had passed so many abandoned bore points. Fewer cattle numbers than sheep meant less water needed.

I found these chats at homestead kitchen tables fascinating, offering insights into the landscape I was walking through. But given that dingoes were a contentious topic, I didn't mention to Bob how I had seen one several days prior. The lean blond dog had cautiously approached my camels from behind, raising his head to sniff the air as I tailed them through the bush while they grazed. The camels seemed not to have noticed his presence, and the dingo didn't seem to notice mine. After the many sinister stories I had been told—like the recurring tale of a pack of dingoes that had chased a man up a windmill while he was checking on the water—I wasn't quite sure how to react. I watched him, but he didn't crouch or bare his teeth or raise his hackles; he seemed simply curious about these new visitors to his territory. As I moved towards the camels, my boot crunched on a dead branch. The dingo's head snapped towards me, his focus on the camels broken in an instant. His tail shot between his legs as he took off into the surrounding scrub. The camels looked up from their respective bushes but seemed unperturbed; they were far too big a prey for a dingo, and they knew it. Unexpectedly, dingoes would not be added to the list of irrational things that camels were afraid of.

I could understand Bob's hatred of dingoes—the sport they could make of killing sheep, wastefully mauling multiple ewes in a night rather than eating what they needed. But I also couldn't help feeling that the dingo had its place, and it had been somehow nice to see this one.

I woke to the soft beeping of my watch alarm, which I set for an hour before sunrise every morning. My routine with the camels was regular now. It was a strange feeling, as I had rarely had a routine in my life. I had skipped from job to job and home to home, working irregular hours, so I had never allowed time for one to manifest. But now, even though my home was always on the move, the camels lent a consistency to my days. In the huge scope of this big adventure that I had embarked on, the routine made it feel manageable. Every day, all I needed to do was get up and walk. I could do that.

I crawled out of my swag and looked up at the blanket of stars above me. The moon had set several hours ago. Frances from Wooleen Station had shown me how to find the Dark Emu in the night sky, and now I couldn't help but see the dark space between the bright cloudy stars of the Milky Way that resembles an elongated bird. The sky felt more familiar; I had been learning to recognise other stars using an app on my phone at night before nestling into my swag. I knew more than the Southern Cross now. I could name the stars in the constellation of Orion and could identify Canopus, Sirius and the twins, Castor and Pollux.

I shivered, my naked body exposed to the cool night air. I pulled the tarp off my saddle bags and stood on it to get changed into warm clothes. I pulled on my favourite big green jacket that Sam had bought as a present from an op shop. I had considered throwing it away because it reminded me of Sam, but I couldn't bring myself to do it. I was resigned to the fact that everything would remind me of him.

I lit a fire with sticks and branches collected the evening before and rolled up my swag, ready for the day. I placed my blackened percolator coffee pot on the fire and waited for it to warm up. I liked having this extra time in the morning.

It was my time. I knew that as soon as the light crept over the horizon, the camels would begin to get restless and my entire day would be dedicated to them. I imagined it felt similar to being a mother, enjoying a few precious seconds of peace while the kids were asleep. This was the time I gave myself to prepare for being mentally and physically 'clocked on' as a camel carer until dark. Drinking my coffee as I leant against my swag reading my book was also one of the few occasions where I was able to sit down for any length of time. Once I got going, I didn't stop, not even for lunch—not until I lay down exhausted in my swag at night.

As the day began to break and the light became bright enough for me to switch off my head torch to read my book, I heard a new sound: the distant braying of a wild donkey. Like the howl of a dingo, it was wild and beautiful. Just like camels and goats, donkeys were introduced to Australia, strangers with a knack for survival in this harsh and foreign land. It made me wonder who really belonged here, in this vast desert. As humans were retreating from these places, the animals were proliferating. Some species—especially feral cats—were doing huge damage to the native flora and fauna. Camels could not be absolved from fault, either, although at least they are a soft-footed animal, less damaging to the fragile soil than the hard hooves of donkeys, goats, sheep and cattle. Yet 'feral' species such as the camel and donkey had been in part responsible for building white settlement in the Outback. They were still here because they were hardy survivors. I, too, was learning to understand and survive in this land, and I couldn't help but feel respect for anything, and anyone, who was willing to live out

here. Did I belong out here? The landscape, in all its unforgiving wildness, was sucking me in.

The donkey let out another loud *eeyore*, waking the camels,
who stood up from their resting position with a clanging of
bells. I put down my book; it was time to let the camels off to
graze and get going for the day.

I followed donkey tracks all day, tiny hoof prints in the sand
leading towards Lake Austin. There were also the paw prints of
a dingo and pup. I realised with a sudden epiphany that after my
gruelling first month, I was actually starting to enjoy my adventure. Walking at such a slow pace, I observed every detail in the
land, like reading the sentences of a book. Gleaning its secrets
and patterns, and how the parts connected with one another.
I was noticing where various plants grew, the communities and
soil they grew in, how they changed as the landscape changed.
How many varieties of ants there were. Who knew there were
so many species of ants? I looked at tracks and scats as evidence
of the creatures who had been here before us, details that would
not have been visible whizzing by in a four-wheel drive.

The track petered out and I found myself face to face
with the huge expanse of glittering salt-encrusted lake that
had been marked on my maps. I decided to leave the station
tracks and follow the shoreline to the far side. Taking the
road around the lake would be longer, and boring. Besides,
I needed to make up time. I was drifting behind schedule and
had to pick up the pace if we were going to cross the centre
of Australia before summer rolled round again.

In the foreground different shades of brown and pink and
white indicated the varying degrees of thickness of the salt.

There were zigzagging tracks, little brown dotted lines where animals had broken through the palette of white into the brown mud below. In the distance the heat haze melded with the sky, and it was hard to make out where the land ended and the sky began. I held Jude by the end of the rope and stepped ahead of him out onto the white surface. My boot slipped, and I looked down at the brown skid mark I had made. The surface looked solid, but not far below was sticky and slippery brown clay.

We stayed clear of the salt, making our way around the lake's edge. We reached an unexpected inlet filled with water, where black swans gracefully sailed along its surface, dwarfed by the large red sand dune behind it. The combination of harsh desert and this pleasant lake scene struck me as incongruous.

I realised then that this inlet also posed an issue. I would need to cross it somehow if I wanted to keep circumnavigating the lake towards its eastern edge. The thought of backtracking after I'd been walking for several hours seemed entirely unreasonable. *Surely there must be somewhere solid enough to cross.* As I neared the spot where the inlet joined the lake, the water dried up and became salt. I could see tracks where other smaller animals had crossed, and the bank on the other side felt so close; the inlet was no more than fifty metres across. A narrow chasm of deceptively innocent-looking white salt stood between us and the solid bank of sand on the other side—the salt a veneer hiding the treacherous, bottomless mud below. My mind flashed back to Clayton Station in South Australia, and trekking with Paul and Karen, when we found the skulls of two wild camels that had been caught in the mud in Lake Eyre and perished. I knew from accounts of early explorers whose expeditions had been brought to a halt by impassable salt lakes that this terrain spelt bad news. The soft and smooth round pads on camel's feet become like ice skates in mud, slipping and sliding beneath their weight. I remembered reading in *Tracks* that one of Robyn Davidson's camels had slipped and fallen in the mud and she was forced to take a month-long break. But still, the far bank felt so close . . .

I hesitated, shuffling nervously. I weighed up the options. I desperately didn't want to regret my choice, but once again, there was no one but me here to make the decision. I forced my trepidations aside and decided to cross.

I looked for where the salt seemed thickest and pressed my boot down, standing on one foot to see if the surface would hold my full body weight. It did. I carried on tentatively, one slow step at a time. As Jude set foot on the salt, he hesitated. I gently encouraged him with a small niggle of the rope, and he followed.

'It's all right buddy, we will just take it slow, we've got this,' I cooed, trying to muster a tone of confidence in my voice.

All five camels were now on the salt, and we were making fairly stable progress across the inlet, with only a small slip and slide of a foot here and there. I kept stomping the ground, testing its thickness, then turning to walk backwards so that I could watch the camels' progress. Just as we came to the middle of the inlet, I noticed the slight change in the hue of white, a slight transparency that should have betrayed what would follow next.

All of a sudden, the salt cracked beneath Jude and he sank down to his knees in mud. He looked at me with fear in his eyes and I glanced frantically across at the far bank. It had seemed

Setting off from the beach near Carbla homestead: Shark Bay, Western Australia.

Jude and Delilah tentatively getting their legs wet: it was their first time in the ocean.

Sunrise illuminates my first night's camp, seven kilometres down the Carbla driveway.

Delilah, exhausted after carrying the food boxes after only a few days on the move.

Mac and I comparing footwear. I am sporting a prominent sock tan while Mac is wearing hobbles; even hobbled, the camels would wander many extra kilometres each day in search of food.

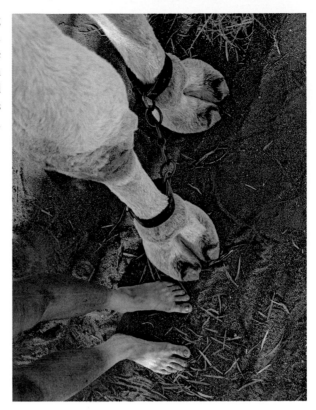

The camels grazing at dawn near the edge of Lake Austin, a huge salt lake.

Murdoch re-engineering my pack gear out the front of the Nambi homestead.

Cameleer and owner Noel in front of White Cliffs Station, the last outpost before the true desert began.

Keeping an eye out for wild bull camels while my herd grazes in the Great Victoria Desert. After the camels stampeded, I always made sure I carried the yellow EPIRB on my belt.

Filling my little red bucket from the hand pump at the abandoned homestead at Yeo. The camels are eagerly awaiting a drink of water.

The largest of my camels, Mac carried most of our water and brought up the rear of the string.

Summer hits early in the Great Victoria Desert. Sheltering from the heat of the midday sun after walking, Charlie and I lie flat out, with Clayton and Mac resting nearby.

Leaving Western Australia behind and crossing the dry Serpentine Lakes in the Great Victoria Desert, following the Anne Beadell Track.

In the shade of a mulga with members of the ranger team from Oak Valley Community—without the support of the Anangu I would not have made it through the waterless desert.

Two weeks later, the desert was transformed by heavy rain. Jude is eager for his tenth drink of the day, determined not to miss any opportunity.

Emerging from the desert, I walked the final five kilometres across the bare gibber plains that surround Coober Pedy with my dad—a wonderful way to finish the first half of my journey.

so close, but now that we were sinking into the bottomless clay, it looked much, much further. Jude struggled, trying to free himself from the mud, unaided by Delilah, who had now sunk as well and was pulling back on Jude.

'Walk up, Delilah!' I yelled. 'Come on buddy, keep coming,' I urged Jude. I was in a panic: should I turn around or keep on pushing forward? To turn around would risk entangling the camels in their ropes. My heart was in my mouth as I watched Jude free himself from the mud, pulling Delilah forward as he complied with my plea.

'That's it, mate, keep moving forward.' I looked behind him, worried about Mac at the back. The others had created a muddy mess, and he was the heaviest. He tried to avoid the worst of the quagmire, but the other camels were pulling him forward against his will. His back foot slipped from underneath him and he sat down in the mud.

'Come on, Jude buddy—you've got to pull them all through,' I shouted. With a look of dread in his eyes, Jude seemed to heed my words and continued to struggle through the mud. Mac heaved himself back up off his stomach and I held my breath, praying for them all to keep their cool. We slipped and slid our way to the far bank, and only once we were on solid ground did I allow myself to breathe. Relief that we had made it washed over me at the same time as I berated myself for having been so risky with my camels' welfare. How could I have been so stupid!? If anything had happened to them, I would have never forgiven myself.

'Thank you for trusting me, Jude,' I said as I stroked his muscular neck. 'I promise I'll never make you do something like that again.' Jude dropped his head and began feverishly eating some green roly poly weed from the sand. He took big, panicked mouthfuls, chewing with great gusto, like someone stuffing their face with chocolate after a stressful day.

That night I camped by the edge of Lake Austin, watching the pink hues of sunset illuminate that seemingly innocent white salt. Since day one, I had conducted a final nightly check of the camels, making sure no ropes were tangled before I clambered into my swag. This time I stopped and lingered with Jude, who was chewing his cud contently. I stroked his cheek, then slowly lowered my face so it was resting on top of his head. I breathed in deeply. Jude paused his cud chewing and let out a deep sigh that melded with my breath. I felt his head relax into my arms.

'Night, Jude,' I whispered into his ear. 'Thank you for being a great leader. I'm so proud of you, buddy. Tomorrow we've got to keep leading the team forward to the other side of the lake. We've got this. Thank you for trusting me today. I love you. Goodnight.'

These pep talks with my leading camel became a nightly ritual. I had always felt there was a bond between us, but now I felt that bond strengthening with the trials of our every day. Jude made me laugh with his loopy personality and goofy smile, and he made me want to scream with frustration when he led the team astray or wouldn't sit still when he was told. But he was my favourite lunatic, my leading boy, and I loved him all the same.

6

Unravelling

SANDSTONE TO LAVERTON—400 KM

'This is my new wife,' said Kerry, introducing me to the locals out the front of the pub in Sandstone. I glanced at him sideways, only just catching his grin and wink, which were so smooth you could easily miss them.

Kerry was the manager of Black Hill Station, where I had pulled in for a three-day break, and he had driven me five minutes down the road to the National Hotel in Sandstone for happy hour. He was a wiry old man with an innocent cheekiness, and I liked his sense of humour. One morning on the station he handed me a mug of coffee with naked porn stars on the side. Their big boobs bulged in my face every time I took a sip.

'Hi, I'm wife number three,' I told the locals with a smirk, laughing along with Kerry.

Inside the pub I perched on a bar stool with Kerry and his friends. There were old black and white photos on the walls of wool wagons, horse and bullock drays. At the turn of the twentieth century, Sandstone had been a bustling goldrush town supporting 6000 to 8000 people. In an area littered with ghost towns, it had managed to survive in its own quiet way. The tidy little one-pub town with its eighty or so residents seemed like a friendly and manageable place to walk my camels through when I left Black Hill Station.

The couple who sat with us were prospectors. We were on the edge of the Goldfields region now and talk quickly turned to gold and tales of murder and bodies hidden down mine shafts.

'The locals will sometimes pay their tabs here in gold,' the barmaid told me, placing a weighty nugget the size of a twenty-cent piece in the palm of my hand. She passed Kerry and the prospectors stubby coolers with their names written on them in felt-tip pen. It was clearly a tradition among locals to leave their stubby coolers here, on a shelf above the bar. Before I left, I bought one for myself. The barmaid wrote 'Camel lady' on the side of my cooler, and placed it on the shelf.

'I'll keep it here for when you come back,' she said.

When I left Sandstone, all I could think about was needing to cover more ground. I had one more month of walking before I reached the desert. I needed Mac to be able to carry ten full jerry cans of water for this stretch, and I needed all of us to be covering twenty-five kilometres a day. Otherwise, there was no way we would make it across the country in the cool of the winter months.

Twelve kilometres out of Sandstone, Mac sat down. He was tired, even though he was only carrying six full jerry cans. How the hell was he ever going to carry eighty kilos more over twice the distance? I urged him up and onwards.

The camp I found that night was average. The camp I found the second night was worse. And the camps I found the third, fourth and fifth night after that did not improve. The feed was bad again and the country felt dense and closed in. The camels were spending more time wandering than grazing. They needed more time to get food in their bellies—but we didn't have that time. The days were getting shorter and I was pushing us to walk longer distances. All I could think of was speeding our pace up.

By the sixth day, low clouds brought a drizzling rain. I knew I should be happy for the slight relief that this would bring to the drought-stricken land, but it made walking miserable. It was the first rain I had experienced for over two months.

I found a shallow dry creek bed with some measly feed and made camp early to get out of the rain. As soon as I had unsaddled the camels and set up my lightweight tarp as a lean-to shelter, the rain stopped. I was angry we had made so few kilometres that day. We had walked too few kilometres the past week! As I shovelled spoonfuls of Nutella into my mouth in an attempt to make myself feel better, I sat under my pointless shelter feeling morose. I dreaded letting the camels off to graze.

I knew the small amount of feed in the creek bed wouldn't entertain them for long and I would soon be chasing them through the bush again.

As predicted, they completely ignored the feed in the creek and made a beeline into the bush beyond, headed for god knows where. *What was going through their heads?* It was so infuriating. I ran to catch up with them, collected them all, removed their hobbles and walked them back to camp, where I reattached their hobbles and released them in the creek bed again. Again, they charged straight out of there.

'What the fuck is wrong with camp?' I yelled at them. 'Where the fuck are you going? You've just walked past all the fucking good feed bushes!' I waved my arms in the air like a lunatic. 'You need to eat!'

I had never considered myself short-tempered. Who was this angry person? Sheer exhaustion or fear of failure, or both, were bringing out an almost primordial anger in me. I felt like belting the camels, and then immediately felt horrified that I could have such a thought. Again, I stomped about unhobbling them, tugged them back to camp, and this time, tied them to some bushes. They ate for a short while then stood there, looking at me unhappily as if to say, 'What do you expect us to do now?' I walked out of the dry creek bed and onto the road, looked down its long empty stretch, closed my eyes and screamed at the top of my lungs. It felt good, better than I expected. It was all I could do to release the twin weights of anger and worry I felt for the camels. I wondered again if this is what motherhood sometimes feels like.

I pulled out my satellite phone—my expensive but necessary

connection to the outside world—and sent Chris, my boss at Uluru, a short message.

'Do you have a scotch in hand? Can I give you a call?'

Chris phoned back immediately. 'What's going on, darl?'

I vented all my frustrations and worries to Chris in a torrent of emotion.

'I just don't know how we're going to make it across in time,' I finished with desperate exasperation.

Chris paused and then said, 'You might have to think of splitting the trip into two years. It's baby steps, darl, but your camels will get there. You have to think, only a year ago they were running wild. You have to make sure you give them enough time to eat—that's the most important thing. Don't worry about what other people think, it's your trip. Don't worry that you told everyone you'd do it in nine months. No one is going to begrudge you if you say you had to take it slower to look after your animals.'

When I got off the phone to Chris, I let the truth of his words sink in. I would have to find somewhere to wait out the summer heat, then finish the following year. An immense feeling of devastation washed over me. In reality, if I didn't finish the trip in nine months, it would become a two-year endeavour— a long time to put my life on hold. I vaguely thought of Sam and the hope I was secretly cherishing that one day we might get back together; I had discovered he was single again now. But with this new time frame, that hope was suddenly even more distant. I hadn't realised until that moment how attached I was to finishing by the end of the year. Whenever a day felt hard, I reminded myself that I'd be done by Christmas. Now, a journey of two years seemed to stretch out before me like a gaping abyss that was too long and deep for my psyche to comprehend.

I crawled into my swag and stared up at Keirin's crystals. 'Strength and power,' I whispered. The decision to split the trip into two years had been made, but the weight of the decision hung heavy over me.

The next morning, I woke in the dark to a thin layer of frost coating my swag. The clouds had cleared overnight, and a cold snap had frozen the moisture from the previous day's rain to ice. It was June, and well and truly winter.

I saddled the camels in the dark, figuring there was no point in lingering at this average campsite. The steel racks that held the jerry cans and food boxes felt like blocks of ice. Just before the sun rose, the temperature dipped to a new low, forcing me to stuff Jude's lead rope into my jacket pocket to keep the tips of my fingers from freezing, as I led the string out into the frosty morning.

Despite the cold, and the decision I had been forced to make the evening before, I vowed to change my perspective and to view today in a new and positive light. It was a peculiar morning, with low mist lifting and the rays of cold sunshine piercing through, lighting up the bushes covered in dew and spider webs like bejewelled Christmas trees. It was still, peaceful and bliss-fully quiet. I was now on a two-year adventure. I turned the thought over in my head. It was all about changing my perspective. Just like I was enjoying the sparkling dew in the morning light rather than letting myself be annoyed that I had packed up in the cold and dark and that all of my equipment was damp and dirty from the previous day's rain. *I could do this*, I vowed. *I could do this shifting-of-perspective thing.*

I was in such a state of bliss enjoying the morning that when I checked my maps two hours later, I realised that I had missed a turn and walked an hour in the wrong direction. Determined not to let this blot out my good mood, I reconsidered the maps. If I turned left into the bush and went cross-country for a day, then I should reconnect with the track I was meant to have taken and cut off a corner in the process. I turned left into what was luckily fairly open scrub. My positivity undampened, I walked for several hours through the bush, singing at the top of my lungs and casually holding my string of camels by the end of the lead rope.

And that's when it happened. A sharp tug on the rope woke me from my pleasant daydream, and out of the corner of my eye I noticed a black cow in the bushes. Jude had been suddenly roused, too, and had launched sideways to escape this unexpected and terrifying creature lurking in the shadows. In quick succession, the lead rope was pulled out of my hand, I fell flat on my face and gear tumbled down around me while I lay sprawled in the dirt. My camels took off galloping into the distance.

Picking myself up, I ran and ran, my heart thumping and lungs exploding for want of oxygen. The camels disappeared out of sight. Everything I needed to survive out here was strapped to their backs. How had I been so stupid! What was the point of an EPIRB (emergency beacon) if I didn't carry it on me? Why bother with a satellite phone if it was packed away? I felt naked and naive for thinking the camels would always be safely at my side. In a wild state of all-consuming terror, I crested a ridgeline and narrowed the gap between us, lunging forward with my knife as I got closer to desperately try to cut Clayton's rope and regain some form of control. They took off again and I ran like my life depended on it. And it did. *Fuck, fuck, fuck . . .* I had never thought about what I would do if I lost my camels, because I never thought I would. My lungs were on fire, and I felt like I was having an out-of-body experience, looking down at this terrible scene unfolding from above. I spotted the camels again in the distance and pushed myself forward, ignoring the pain in my body. As I made it closer to where they had stopped, I slowed down and tried to regulate my breathing. I didn't want to scare them more, and thought I'd collapse if I kept running. Jude's rope was caught around a bush he had circled, and the other camels had spiralled in on themselves, anchoring Jude and preventing further escape. I slowed even more to a limping part-walk, part-jog in a futile attempt to reach them in a calm manner. I needed to grab hold of Jude before they got out of this tangle and kept running. The camels were all puffing like maniacs too. My hand reached out and I took hold of the glorious safety of Jude's rope, followed by the nose line, which I had hooked around his neck. I untangled the string and faced Jude, suddenly shaking with rage as I quickly tied him to a tree.

'*HOOSH*, Jude!' I yelled, in a deep thunderous roar. He didn't comply. I yelled at him again and tugged downward on the nose line. I knew this would hurt him but I was overcome with rage. Jude sat down and I placed the two leg straps on his front legs. His eyes were wide and white foam streaked down from the corners of his mouth. Clayton had broken his halter and it sat skewiff across the front of his face, and one of his green pack bags was dangling low on his side. I scrutinised each of them in turn, checking their legs to make sure they weren't injured. Once I was satisfied that besides some broken and lost gear, the camels were all okay, I collapsed on the ground in a fit of tears, gasping for air amid long guttural sobs. Jude, unhappy about being made to sit, crawled around on his knees beside me.

'*Hoosh*, Jude, *HOOSH!*' I screeched again. I was so mad at him. I had trusted him and thought he trusted me. *What an idiot to spook at a COW, of all fucking things!* I retrieved my sat phone from Jude's pack bags, desperate to have its safety in my hands again. I was convulsing as I sobbed. I needed someone to know what had just happened, and someone to make me feel less alone and less in danger. I pulled the phone's antenna up and dialled Sam's number. I knew Mum and Dad would panic if they heard me in this state. Sam was my next go-to person. I didn't remember in that moment that he was no longer my boyfriend.

'Hello? Soph?' The unmistakable crackle of what Sam knew to be a sat phone gave me away.

'What's wrong? Is everything okay? Are you hurt? Are you hurt?' he repeated urgently. Between sobs and an uncontrollably shaking voice, I managed to stumble through the gist of what had happened. It was as if no time or pain had come between us; there was only concern and care in his reassuring voice.

'Shit, Soph, that's so scary. Are you sure you're not hurt? Do you have water on you now? Do you know where you are?' I didn't know where I was. I had dropped my phone when I was pulled face down in the dirt at the beginning of this mess. I assured Sam I was okay and that I'd go looking for the lost equipment. Hearing Sam's voice was immensely calming, although I could tell I had worried him.

When I hung up reluctantly, I was still shaking. I suddenly remembered Bob Cooper's book *Outback Survival*, with his 'ABC' for survival. Although I couldn't remember what the letters A or C stood for, I had remembered B for its unusual advice in an emergency situation: B was for brewing a cup of tea. Making a cuppa gave you an opportunity to calm down, take the time to plan what to do next and operate with a rational mind.

So, with trembling hands, I unpacked my billy can. It now resembled more a piece of scrap metal, crumpled where two pack bags had banged up against one another. Luckily it was malleable, and I was able to remould it into something vaguely circular by hand. I drank a cup of tea and ate a chocolate muesli bar and quietly sobbed some more. I boiled the billy again and drank another cup of tea. The camels' breathing and my own slowly returned to normal. I wiped my face and tipped the last of the tea into the red dirt. I wanted to call Sam back, but I knew I had to get out of this situation on my own.

I calmly packed away the billy can, adjusted the broken pack bags, dug out a new halter for Clayton and stood Jude up to leave. I scoured the ground painstakingly for the camel's tracks, retracing their prints back to where it had all gone wrong. It took over an hour, proof of how far they had run. At a large expanse of submerged rock, I lost their tracks completely, but eventually found them trailing off on the other side. Disturbed dirt and a scramble of prints finally led to a cluster of miscellaneous equipment in a clearing of scrub. On the ground lay my tube of paper maps, my water canister, jacket, lunchbox and phone. I picked my phone up and inspected it, relieved when the screen lit up normally. I still felt shaken, horrified by what might have happened if Jude hadn't got tangled in a bush or if I hadn't been able to find my lost navigational equipment.

I wanted to be done with the day and make camp here, but to do so would only make the camels more tense and on edge. They would remember the cow that had frightened them here in the first place. At least I knew where I was now and could keep moving forward.

I gripped Jude's rope and nose line firmly. 'It's going to be a long time until we're friends again,' I told him.

We walked for four more hours through the bush, scrabbling up and over low hills and weaving through thick trees and undergrowth, searching for the track I had intended to connect with by cutting cross-country. The camels were still frightened and walked quickly; I was fuelled by my anger and a determination to find my way out of this rugged bush to the path I was meant to have taken that morning.

As the light of the day waned, so did my anger, overtaken by pure exhaustion from the day's events followed by traversing such rough terrain. At sunset we emerged out of the bush and onto the track I was looking for. And by dark, I had already forgiven Jude. I would always forgive him; I loved him too much.

The next day it was clear that we had to live by Chris's motto, 'Baby steps, darl.'

Everything had unravelled and we were back to square one. Throughout the morning some invisible presence would spook the camels and all five huge animals would come thundering up behind me, threatening to plough me down and trample me to death. It was unnerving, but they always pulled up at the last minute. It was futile to be mad at them; they were only scared half-wild animals. Instead, I practised the art of completely ignoring their behaviour. By lunchtime I had perfected walking without even flinching or turning around when four tonnes of camels came galloping up behind me.

By lunchtime, though, another worry had come to the fore-front of my attention. Delilah was lame.

That evening I unloaded Delilah and inspected her foot while she was sitting down. There was a small round hole in the pad of her left front foot. I pressed it and she flinched. There didn't appear to be any foreign objects in it, but she had clearly staked it on something. I got out my medical kit and tried to fashion a boot made of cotton wool and gaffer tape. It was a clumsy attempt and I couldn't get it to stay on her foot. The other camels were getting fidgety and I let them off to graze. I released Delilah without hobbles to make it easier for her, and watched as she limped along, trying to keep up with her friends. Her pad needed rest to heal, but there was no way I could stop her walking on it—and we were still a week away from the yards at Weebo Station.

After beginning the month pushing hard to make more ground, we were now reduced to a painfully slow pace of two kilometres per hour. I urged Delilah onwards, hardly daring to turn my head to look at her; it was unbearable to watch her wincing with every step. Two days out from Weebo, I couldn't handle the sorry sight any longer, and reneged on the advice I had been given not to mask her pain unless absolutely neces-sary. I rummaged through my pack on the side of the road, looking for my stash of Bute, an anti-inflammatory pain relief medication in powder form. I must have underdosed her, as it made no difference.

Two days later, we limped up the driveway to the Weebo homestead.

'Come on sweet pea. We're almost there,' I cajoled her. 'Go girl, you've been a mother, this is nothing compared to child-birth.'

Bryan and Shannon, a young couple in their thirties, came out to greet me with their two sons, Tanner and Maitland, and their governess, Olivia. I unsaddled the camels in a lovely set of large open yards and Bryan brought over a huge bale of nutritious-looking hay. They said there was no problem staying as long as we needed for Delilah's foot to heal. I liked the family instantly; they were comfortable to be around, and it quickly felt like we'd known each other for a long time. For several days, while the camels rested, I forgot about my troubles. I slept in, watched morning TV and shared meals with Bryan and Shannon. I helped with some cattle work, drafting, branding and castrating. Watching this dynamic couple working as a team in the yards, I realised I was a little envious of their relationship. Since the day the camels had bolted on me, Sam and I were messaging and talking regularly again. In my head I played out scenarios in which, once my trip was over, we would get back together. Just this one trip, and I would give it all up, and do whatever it took to have this kind of partnership with Sam.

In the safety of Weebo Station I relaxed, and the camels' wild side softened too. I watched Charlie lay his head on the ground as Tanner cuddled him and Mac patiently allowed a giggling Maitland to place his cap on Mac's head. But between these endearing moments of family life on the station, the looming desert stretch cast a shadow over my days. The events of the previous weeks had left me feeling rattled and ill-prepared for what lay ahead. I was about to cross Australia's largest desert, the Great Victoria Desert, with camels that were underweight, inexperienced and half wild. I was effectively entrusting my safety to four lunatic teenage boys and a highly strung mum. I was in a state where ignorance was no longer bliss.

After a week, Delilah's foot appeared healed enough to push on. Though there was now more time, as I was splitting the trip across two years, with all the unexpected delays I would still be hard-pressed to cross the width of the Great Victoria Desert before the heat returned.

Seven-year-old Tanner could barely reach the floor pedals or see over the dash of the ute as he confidently drove me around to the rainwater tank so I could fill up my jerry cans. I filled only six again, soberly thinking that this would be one of the last times I'd be able to do this before I needed all twelve jerry cans full.

It was incredibly hard to say goodbye to the family at Weebo, but I knew that the longer I stayed, the harder it would be to hit the road again.

Several days out of Weebo, as I bent to unlatch a gate that led to the next station, I noticed a concerning print on the ground: the fresh outline of a camel pad. Disturbingly, this camel print did not belong to my own camels.

I had entered Nambi Station and was now in the bounds of wild camel country. The foot imprint was huge, much bigger than the pad marks of my own camels. It could only belong to a large lone bull. In winter, the wild bull camels would be coming into season, or rut. At this time of year, when their testosterone is high, they will stop at nothing to get to female camels or to fight with other males. My camels, smaller and encumbered with ropes and hobbles, wouldn't stand a chance. Everyone I spoke to or read about who'd done camel trips had

had to shoot wild bull camels—which is why I was carrying my rifles. Even before setting off, I knew it would be a case of not *if*, but how many.

I closed the gate behind me and walked the camels into Nambi Station.

Later that afternoon, I sat on the front porch of the station's cottage drinking tea with Murdoch, the caretaker. I wasn't quite sure what to make of him. He was rough in appearance, his dark hair stood on end and his serious expression only lightened as he passed me his phone to show me the wild camels he'd shot the day before. This didn't surprise me, although I shifted in my seat uncomfortably. Only moments before we had been discussing the feasibility of mustering wild camels for meat. I had learnt from station owners in Western Australia that because there was no abattoir for camels in the state, mustering them was not financially viable. Station owners and caretakers like Murdoch were left with no other option.

'I managed to shoot three before the rest spooked,' Murdoch said, in no way perturbed by how bloodthirsty this might have made him sound. I handed back the phone and admitted I was nervous about having to shoot wild bulls out in the desert.

'I'm a terrible shot.'

'Are your rifles sighted?' Murdoch asked. Embarrassingly, I didn't know exactly what this meant. Until I bought my rifles while I was living at Uluru, I'd had no experience with shooting or hunting. A local gun enthusiast had taken me target shooting, but he'd been so focused on precision and the different makes of scopes and rifles that most of the information had gone over my head, and I had never really learnt the basics. Taking the time to comfortably position oneself, don earmuffs and shoot a still target seemed a world away from shooting a live animal that was charging towards you in the heat of the moment. Not only that, but I didn't know if I could shoot a camel—an animal I loved so much. Everyone seemed to give me different advice about shooting, and not knowing any better I had heeded it all, good and bad.

'Someone told me it would be easier to shoot a camel at close range if I took the scope off my rifle,' I told Murdoch. I went to retrieve my gun from my gear so I could show him my .308.

'Who the fuck told you to take the scope off? You don't even have any sight on this! How the fuck are you meant to know what you're aiming at?' Murdoch was really worked up. 'I'm sorry, I mean it's not your fault—you didn't know any better. But I'm really pissed off at whoever would tell you to do that.' His intensity startled me.

Sharing dinner with Murdoch that evening revealed a softer side. There were photos on his mantelpiece of three girls—his daughters, he told me with pride. He didn't get along with his ex-wife and he enjoyed living out here. It was quiet and he could do what he wanted after leaving the Army.

'What did you do in the Army?' I asked. I knew a little about the various divisions from Sam.

'I was an infantry sniper. I wanted to be on the front line shooting shit,' he grinned. I smiled back. This explained his enthusiasm for guns.

The next day we raced along the property tracks in one of the station's LandCruiser utes. I had only planned on staying at Nambi for one night, but Murdoch offered to drive me further ahead on a scouting mission so I could identify which track I needed to take. Murdoch's rifle sat propped on the dash of the car. I felt the same unease I experienced in all vehicles now, the sense of overwhelm, seeing how quickly the kilometres flashed by compared to how slowly I would cover the distance on foot.

We found the turn-off to the next station, and I marked it with a waypoint on my map. When we stopped to have lunch and a cup of tea, Murdoch bent down to examine some dingo tracks near the car.

'Dogs are the hardest pest to kill. They're so smart. These tracks are about a week old.'

'How can you tell?' I asked.

'You have to look at what sort of surface the track is on. Is it clay or soft sand, are there any other tracks covering it? I'll also look at the poo to see how old it is. Next time you stop somewhere, have a look at your camels' poo and see how it dries out over several days. It will give you an idea of how old wild camel tracks are.'

We finished our cups of tea and Murdoch squeezed out the used tea bags, wrapping the string neatly around the bags and placing them in the back of the ute.

'I don't like to throw any rubbish away. Old habits of being a sniper. Leave no trace,' Murdoch said. I had lots to learn from this man whom I'd wrongly judged. I thought guiltily of the times I had shallow buried or only partially burnt my tuna cans and tea bags, hoping no one would find them in the bush.

On the drive home, Murdoch offered to lend me a scope to fit on my rifle and get it sighted properly for me. I was keen to get going, anxious about crossing the desert—but when else was I going to receive help with my rifles from an ex-sniper?

With his tattered T-shirt and untamed beard, Murdoch seemed an unlikely drill sergeant. His appearance, however, belied his wealth of knowledge and ability as a teacher. Drill practice began the next morning, and Murdoch covered everything from the ground up. How to hold the rifle comfortably, how to carry it when I wasn't shooting, where to aim when I shot the camel, how to approach the dead camel, how to check if the camel was dead, how to store the rifle safely locked but loaded, how to look through the scope, how to steady the rifle—and, most importantly, how to breathe when I took a shot. The .308 was a big gun for me. My arm shook from its weight when I lifted it to my shoulder, and the deafening BANG it produced left unmuffed ears ringing. Once at Uluru, the recoil was so fierce that the scope hit me painfully in the eye. But I needed a rifle this big if I was to take down an animal that weighed close to a tonne. Still, I was terrified of it, and had avoided unpacking it since my days of target practice at Uluru.

'It's all about getting comfortable with your weapon,' Murdoch told me. 'In the Army you are constantly made to do drills so that your gun becomes an extension of your arm.'

Murdoch emptied the bullets from the rifle's magazine onto my canvas tarp, which we were sitting on behind his cottage.

'Every day while your camels are grazing, I want you to get the gun out, load and unload the magazine, lift the rifle to your shoulder and practise looking through the scope. You can even practise finding the target on your camels. Look for the spot behind the foreleg, where you'll be aiming for the heart.'

I lifted the rifle to practise; the bullets were loaded, but the bolt was locked and the chamber empty. I nestled the stock into the hollow of my shoulder and looked through the scope, pointing the rifle at Clayton grazing in the homestead paddock. It felt very disconcerting to point a gun at my own camel; Clayton looked so innocent and oblivious. But shooting a wild bull camel would be for the protection of my own herd.

All afternoon we practised shooting a target and adjusting my scope, so that what I saw through the rifle's optics matched where the bullet would land. Murdoch urged me on, calling out, 'I want you to get the next five shots in a cluster next to one another.'

It was dark by the time we finished sighting both the .308 and my smaller .22 rifle. Murdoch was pedantic and relentless until he felt both rifles were accurate and I was shooting to his satisfaction. It had been an overwhelming amount of information to take in and I was tired, but I now had tools in my kit that would stand me in good stead later.

I called Sam that evening to tell him everything I had learnt.

We were both excited talking about it, since Sam could relate to my experience from his time in the Army.

'I can't believe how much this guy is helping you. What a legend, he deserves a medal,' Sam said emphatically. I couldn't believe it either. It was like Murdoch had magically appeared when I needed him most.

I was up early the following morning to pack up my gear and saddle my camels. Murdoch came out to see me off. He scrutinised me as I awkwardly picked up Jude's heavy leather bags, slung them over my shoulder and lumbered towards him in the sideways crab-like motion that I used to deal with their weight, then fiddled to get the bags hanging evenly and attach them to the saddle.

'Can I give something a go?' Murdoch asked. He adjusted a strap on the saddle bag that made it hang lower and allowed room for another bag on top. Before long, he was systematically going through the arrangement of the load on every camel. His meticulous packing reminded me of Sam. When I thanked him, he said, 'I've packed too many heavy Army packs; you learn pretty quickly how to make it easier on yourself. Who's carrying these jerry cans?' he asked, pointing to the twelve canisters I had lined up.

'Mac. The steel racks fit five on either side, and Charlie will carry the other two. But Mac's struggling. I don't think he can cope with 200 kilograms, plus the weight of the saddle and racks. He gets too tired,' I said.

'Well, then, we need to distribute the weight onto the other camels. You're going to need all twelve jerry cans full for the desert, aren't you? Let's go from the start of the string and work out what each camel needs to be carrying. But first, let's start with you. You need to work out what you need on you to survive if your camels take off again.'

I paused for a moment to consider what my most crucial items would be.

'Water,' I said. 'Phone with my maps, sat phone, EPIRB and pocketknife.'

'And I would add one more thing. A lighter, so you can start a fire for warmth. So, every day, I want you to check those things off: water, phone, EPIRB, sat phone, knife, lighter. They must be on you at all times,' Murdoch drilled me.

We carried on down the line of camels, working out how to distribute the jerry cans and rearrange the saddle bags. By the end, I had agreed to spend two more days on the station so that Murdoch could weld me new, lighter racks for the food boxes, as well as jerry can racks that fitted only three jerry cans either side—a load I guessed Mac would be able to carry.

Five days later than I intended to leave Nambi, I finally set off down the road. It was a cool, crisp morning and I walked with an added enthusiasm in my step. I felt like my camels and

I had been part of an episode of *Extreme Makeover* and were now setting off on a completely new journey, infinitely more prepared and organised. I was fitted with an orange Camelbak that Murdoch had given me so I could carry water on me, and the camels were decked out with new freshly painted racks and a different order of saddle bags. For the first time, I felt a glimmer of confidence about setting off into the desert.

That evening as the camels grazed, I took out the .308 and practised unloading and loading the bullets, like Murdoch had coached me. As the sky turned purple, I heard a car approaching. In the back of Murdoch's ute was the remainder of a bale of hay, a small camp barbecue and camp chairs. For my first four nights out of Nambi, he had agreed to meet up with me. 'Soon you're not going to have any support in the desert, so if I can make this little stretch easier on you and the camels, then I want to help,' he told me. I felt guilty that he had already done so much, but the offer was too tempting to turn down.

I sat contentedly sipping tea, in the delicious foreign comfort of a camp chair, while Murdoch cooked me dinner and the camels happily gathered around the hay. I could not believe the extent to which he had helped me. That a total stranger could be so generous was almost beyond comprehension. Meeting him had a profound impact on my entire trip.

7

Into the Desert

LAVERTON TO ILKURLKA
ROADHOUSE—543 KM

'It's pretty brave doing what you're about to do,' Trevor told me over dinner.

It was nice to be back at Laverton Downs Station with Trevor. I had met him several months prior, on our journey to the coast of Western Australia in the camel truck. Amid the multitude of new places that I was travelling through and new people I was meeting, the familiarity was comforting. I didn't feel brave at all, though. I felt like I was about to leap off a precipice.

The Great Victoria Desert stretched out before us, spanning an incomprehensible 422,466 square kilometres—almost twice the size of the UK land mass. Laverton would be the final town until I reached Coober Pedy, if all went well, in around three months' time. Once I started along the Anne Beadell 'Highway', a rough four-wheel drive track that was the only road that traversed the desert, there would be no way for a truck to pick us up and rescue us. The scale of isolation in this desert would be vast. There would be no fences whatsoever. No yards every couple of weeks where I might rest my camels. No night off from the relentlessness of watching them. If one of my camels became injured, I would have to leave them behind— or worse still, shoot them.

I had two more weeks until I arrived at the turn-off for the track. Once I was in the desert, there was no turning back. The nervous anticipation of the unknown made me feel sick.

'Why don't you see how you go over the next two weeks, and if you don't feel you or your camels are up to it, give me a call and I can pick you up in a truck before you hit the Anne Beadell?' It meant a huge amount to hear Trevor say this. I couldn't believe, yet again, that a stranger would be so helpful. He had no prior vested interest in my trip; I was simply a girl who had called him out of the blue and asked if I could rest my camels at his station. Now he was offering to drive an eight-hour round trip if I needed help.

The following morning, Trevor drove me into town to pick up a mountain of packages that had arrived for me at the post office. On our way back to the station we stopped to talk to a local whose family had lived in the area for generations.

'It's dry out there at the moment,' he said ominously. 'Even the gnamma holes are dried up.' Gnamma holes are natural hollows in rocky ground that hold fresh water in a land where only salt lakes exist. The fact that I would be heading into the desert at the tail end of a long drought, made the precipice I was about to step off suddenly seem especially deep.

Back at the station, I suspended my feelings of trepidation by opening my packages as if it were Christmas. Mum had sent me fresh socks made of alpaca wool, which promised to be warm, but seemed a little too fancy to survive daily walking. My friend Nikki had sent me home-made Anzac biscuits with a heartfelt note, which made me instantly cry and miss home. Dad had sent mostly excessive emergency items. He followed my day-to-day progress on his own mapping apps at home, and had been incredibly worried after the camels took off on me. Now that I was heading into the desert, his anxiety was mounting, mainly born of the fact that I wasn't crossing the desert in an ordinary year, but during a pandemic. There would be no cars on the road. No one around if I needed help or if anything went wrong. The Anne Beadell traversed Aboriginal land, and all permits had been revoked to stop the spread of Covid through communities, except my own, which was granted on the basis of the slow mode in which I was travelling. Out in the desert, I would be conducting my own form of self-imposed isolation.

On my final evening at Laverton Downs Station, a wind whipped up and brought with it clouds. The gusts harried the plastic wrappers from bags of rice, lentils, pasta, barley and four kilograms' worth of muesli as I packed them into cotton drawstring bags to place in my food boxes. The clouds brought only a few spots of rain, not enough to dampen the dust. The drought's grip was firm on the land.

The next morning, the moisture in the air had created a thick layer of fog that shrouded the camels' yards when I saddled to leave. Clayton, still with his persistent fear of being touched, made an ordeal out of having his halter put on, throwing up his cud, roaring and making a spectacle. The fog had well and truly lifted and the day was clear and sunny by the time I had finally haltered him.

'There's always one problem child in the bunch,' Trevor laughed. He waved me off quietly and then headed back inside.

As I walked away from the station, my phone pinged with an email. I was still close enough to Laverton to receive a signal.

Hi Sophie,

I never seem to be able to find the right words during goodbyes, so this is what I really wanted to say. I think you are really inspiring with your guts and determination and passion to do what you're doing. You will always have a place in my heart. Thank you for letting me be involved with a little piece of your great adventure. All the best with the rest of the trip, until we cross paths again, good luck.

Trevor.

I began to type a reply, but before I had time send it, I had walked out of phone range.

There was one more station at the edge of the desert before I hit the Anne Beadell and the true desert began. White Cliffs Station seemed like it belonged on a movie set. It was a dilapidated wooden homestead with a large wraparound verandah that looked, in its state of disrepair, to be on a worrying angle. Noel, the station owner, was equally as characterful. A camel man from Coolgardie, he greeted my camels just the way they liked when they met new humans—not patting them, but leaving his hands by his sides and allowing my camels to smell his lined and weathered face and long white bushy beard.

I left the camels in Noel's ramshackle yards. The house was dark inside, with only shards of afternoon light reaching beyond the wide verandah and illuminating fragments of dust hanging in the air. The whole place seemed abandoned, except for the central room in which Noel cooked, slept and ate, and which had a clutter of old furniture. There was no power, except for a loud old generator that ran for a few hours in the evening, and no running water. Noel showed me to the outdoor toilet with a bucket next to it for flushing, followed by his shower facilities: a bucket hanging from the back verandah beam, with holes punched in the bottom. I looked at it dubiously. I had been hoping for one final shower before I set off into the desert.

'I'll heat up some water. It's lovely showering out here watching the sunset,' Noel said.

When I tried it that evening, I had to agree. I stripped down on the back deck of the run-down homestead on the edge of the desert. The spot offered no privacy—but so far away from the reaches of society, it didn't need to. I looked down at my angular naked body. My stomach was completely flat, almost hollow, and there wasn't an inch of fat on my hips. I had never been fat, but I had also never been skinny like this. It didn't seem to matter what or how much I ate, the weight kept falling off me. I scoffed Nutella and drizzled loads of olive oil on every meal, and still my body burnt it off. I hoisted the bucket up onto the verandah beam easily; I was lean but strong, my muscles toned from walking and slinging saddles and bags around on a daily basis. I let the water rain down on me, watching the sunset colours fade in the reflection of the dam that glimmered in the camels' yard. The thick bush lay just beyond.

Afterwards I dressed in my thermals, jacket and beanie and went inside. It was July now, and midwinter. Although the place had felt abandoned during the day, the one central room felt quite cosy with the fire going. A couple of dim lights were on, and I could hear the hum of the generator next to the camel paddock, no doubt keeping them awake. I always felt sorry for them when we arrived at a station. I was sure they preferred sleeping in the peace of the bush.

Noel rolled another smoke—his second or perhaps third since I had arrived that afternoon. We drank a glass of his surprisingly smooth home-made whisky, then Noel served up camembert and kiwi fruit on biscuits, an unusual combination. There was an old deep-backed TV in the corner of the room, the type that predated flat-screen devices. He loaded a VHS of Pink Floyd live in concert and we sat drinking moonshine, listening to the other-worldly instrumentals and watching the psychedelic stage show. I felt like I was tripping out, and I hadn't smoked a thing. It was a surreal final night indoors with an old hippy in a crumbling homestead on the edge of the desert.

It was good to be back on the road. The desert stretch that I had spent weeks stressing about was now upon us, and the act of daily walking, as always, helped to ease my apprehension. The country opened out and looked more like the desert I knew from Uluru. It was unforgiving, hardier, more waterless and less palatable for stock than where I'd come from, and yet its untouched nature made it appear softer and more alive, with hardy spinifex and desert heath myrtle greening the landscape. In this area of even lower rainfall, we were beyond the range of cattle, goats, wild horses, wild donkeys and even kangaroos. All their tracks in the sand had disappeared, leaving only wild camel tracks crisscrossing the road. Camels were the only large animals that could survive out here.

I followed a service road for a gas pipeline that ran through the area, making my way to the Anne Beadell track that would take me in a direct line east across the Great Victoria Desert. I felt as though I was on the edge of civilisation; wild country surrounded us and beckoned me into its heart. Despite my misgivings, I was looking forward to experiencing a desert that few of my friends even knew existed, or could place on a map. This is what I had come for. It was less well known than the Simpson Desert; some people even assumed it to be in the small state of Victoria, and almost no one knew it was our largest desert. Its mystery and solitude were even more enticing.

Now, though, standing on my tarp with my few possessions, in that afternoon's camp in an island of mallee and mulga within a sea of spinifex, exposed to the elements, the untouched, raw wilderness all around me was terrifying in its endlessness. The pipeline, despite its man-made ugliness cutting through the land, felt like a safety net, a tangible thread connecting me to the human world. I didn't want to leave it. I felt like I was flinging myself out into this vast wilderness, vulnerable and naked, like a piece of meat left to dry out in the sun and be picked over by crows. Nature had always been comforting to me, but this was a new level of wild.

Late that afternoon I walked with the camels as they grazed, rifle slung over my shoulder, like a soldier defending our remote island outpost from potential attackers. I saw no wild camels, although evidence of them was everywhere. The sun was setting earlier now that we were in the thick of winter, which left the camels little time to graze after our day's walk. I let them wander until the last light had faded and we were plunged into darkness.

Up until now, wherever I had camped at night, there had always been a faint glow of light on the horizon—the distant light of a town or remote mining camp carrying for hundreds of kilometres across the flat landscape. Now there was nothing.

Like all the light in the world had been extinguished. Blackness blanketed us, and I could barely make out the shapes of the camels right next to me. I flicked on the new ultra-bright head torch Dad had sent me. Its beam was far more powerful than the old one I had been using, but it made the darkness that surrounded us seem even thicker beyond its light.

The silence was different, too. There were no longer any sounds of the flies and insects that came with summertime. The camels were quieter, not wanting to lose the warmth of their folded *hooshed* position to stand and graze in the night. They had grown thick winter coats to deal with these freezing desert nights. I slept deeply in the swag next to them, under a layer of two polar sleeping bags and a woollen blanket, dreaming vividly. It had become common for my unconscious mind to wander actively at night, summoning up images of people and places present in my life but far away from me now. The time and space that I had alone while walking allowed forgotten memories to resurface. Each night I would dream of a different friend, as if conjuring their presence, bringing each of them with me into the lonely expanse of desert.

Reaching the turn-off for the Anne Beadell felt like a huge moment—the real point of no return, beyond which Trevor would not be able to rescue us with a truck. It was another milestone that was pivotal for me, yet made no difference in the lives of the camels.

'This is it guys, we're setting off into the Great Beyond. Only 1200 kilometres to Coober Pedy!' I called. The camels simply looked back at me, curious about why we had paused if it wasn't for them to eat.

With my mind and days vacant from everything other than walking in solitude, obsessions took hold. My mind grappled with numbers, turning water quantities, load weights and the number of kilometres to the next water point over and over in my head. On the Western Australian side of the track, water tanks were placed roughly 175 kilometres apart, as emergency water for tourists who might get into trouble on the road. Once I entered South Australia, there would be nothing. I would be relying on the local Aboriginal community who had agreed to deliver me water so that I could make it across. It was important to think about how much weight each camel was carrying, how much water I had reserved for myself and how much could be given to the camels to drink, but I began to turn these thoughts into an unhealthy addiction. I went back over the calculations again and again, grasping hold of the figures as if, in this wild land of unpredictability, they were the only certain thing in my life.

The next water point marked on my maps was Yeo, a former homestead, now a simple two-room hut. I tied the camels to a mulga tree and had a look around. This building in the desert was upkept for tourists, and had none of the colourful character and decrepit charm of White Cliffs Station. Around the back was a bucket attached to a pulley that could be used as a shower. This did remind me of Noel's place. It would be a full moon that evening, and I imagined sneaking back here for a shower in the desert under the moonlight—a rare luxury that could only be had where there was water to spare.

Off to the side of the hut I found the well with an old hand pump connected to it. I leveraged the handle up and down and the water flowed out in short gushes into my little red bucket, from which the camels drank. The action of the pump was not without effort. It would be a time-consuming process filling all twelve jerry cans and lugging them 500 metres back to where I had decided to camp for the night. I left them empty next to the pump, deciding that was a job for later.

I let the camels off to graze, walking next to them, turning more numbers over in my head. I was shaken from my obsessive thoughts by a rumbling sound. It was disconcerting, at odds with the silence of the desert, but I quickly realised vehicles were approaching. I was shocked; I had expected not to see a soul out here. Suddenly a convoy of motorbikes, buggies and four-wheel drives came tearing up to the hut, the roar of the engines shattering the quiet. I watched cautiously from the bushes as nine young guys stepped out. They were a little rough-looking, a couple of them sporting mullets, and all of them with a tinnie of beer in hand. They chatted and swore at one another, clearly believing that they were the only people around. *There goes my full moon shower*, I thought, stepping out of the bushes to reveal myself.

'Where the fuck did you come from?' one of them exclaimed, looking around for my car.

'Oh, um, hi, I'm on a walk, I've got some camels out here,' I said.

The boys looked confused. 'You're bullshitting?' another boy said. 'You're really here all by yourself with camels?' There was no way to convince them other than to show them the camels themselves. They cracked more beers and walked with me into a clearing behind the hut. As soon as they saw the camels, they stumbled over one another in a rapid fire of questions.

'You're walking all the way across Australia? Where did you start from? Why would you want to walk that far—didn't you ever think of driving?'

The camels arched their necks away from the boys who reached hands up to pat them, unsure of the onslaught of this loud beer-swilling group. I felt the same way, if I was honest, but I was polite and calmly answered their questions.

The boys left to set up their camp and drink more beer, and I collected the camels to tie them to the bushes for the evening. When I arrived at my modest little tarp, all twelve of my jerry cans sat filled to the brim in a line. The boys had painstakingly filled each one up from the hand pump and had delivered them back to my camp. They handed me a beer and invited me to join them for dinner. With the jerry cans full and ready for the morning, a beer in my hand and steak on offer for dinner, things didn't seem so bad.

But the prospect of being surrounded by nine blokes suddenly made me aware of how feral and haggard I must look. I hadn't seen my face in a long time; my appearance had been completely unimportant out here. I changed into my good jeans, usually reserved for station stops, and put away my tattered walking pants—brown slacks covered in tuna oil stains with holes in the knees, stitched patches in other places and flecks of dried camel cud stuck to them.

The guys were blasting Yothu Yindi through the speakers of a car at their camp, a band I liked. As more drinks were downed, they shot a potato gun, whooping and laughing into the night sky. They admitted slightly sheepishly that they were on a boys' hunting trip, out here to shoot wild camels. They handed me beer after beer, but I paced myself, sipping slowly, knowing I would have to be up early to walk all day. Still, I ate my steak like a half-starved animal. While the boys got drunker and louder, I called it a night at 10 p.m. One of them followed me back to my swag, clearly hoping I might invite him inside. I firmly said goodnight and he walked away like a deflated balloon. I wondered if he might return, fuelled by more alcohol, but as I lay in my swag, I relaxed. I thought about all the times I had been alone with men in the bush on this trip. Not once had anything happened that made me uncomfortable. Considering one of the questions I was frequently asked before I left was *Aren't you worried about weirdos?*, it felt nice to acknowledge that I had so far only encountered the best in humanity. All the men I had met had been nothing but good to me. These young blokes might be a little rowdy, but they had been kind and thoughtful enough to fill my jerry cans. I didn't feel unsafe with them.

Except at 2 a.m., when I wondered if they might run over my swag in the darkness. I could hear the engine of the buggy revving as it tore around the bush at top speed, obviously being drunk driven. I could hear the camel bells: Jude, Delilah, Charlie, Clayton and Mac were also all awake, kept up by the blaring techno beats that were booming at full volume from the boys' camp. I finally drifted off to sleep as the party died down, but it wasn't long before my alarm sounded.

In the morning while I saddled, the boys came by my camp, with sore heads and bloodshot eyes, in a vain attempt to help out and say goodbye. I walked away from camp that day weary and heavy-eyed. I could have been annoyed at being kept awake, but instead I laughed to myself: never in a million years had I expected to listen to an all-night rave in the middle of the desert.

The camels' pace was slow and their eyelids drooped. They were tired too.

Plains of old dry spinifex covered the ground in a thick spiky mat. I had passed nothing for the camels to eat all day except lone stands of desert poplars—small, bright green, spindly trees that seemed too soft and tender-leafed for the desert. The camels enjoyed the nuts that grew at the top tips, but the leaves smelt strongly and must have been partly unpalatable. I made do with a stand of these for camp. The camels were restless and agitated as I unsaddled them and, again, their mounting anxiety led to my mounting annoyance. *Why won't they just chill out!* I released them to graze and quickly found the source of their disquiet. Just upwind from where I had placed my equipment were *one, two, three, four, five* decomposing camel carcasses. My camels must have been able to sense them, but as a dumb oblivious human I had not, and now I was camped right next to them. My gear was too heavy for me to move camp, and it would take too long to resaddle the camels and relocate; I had done that once and would never do it again.

The camels shuffled at a nervous speed in their hobbles, and I walked quickly to keep pace with them. As I did so I found more wild camel carcasses—another fifteen scattered in close proximity. *What was this place, a wild camel grave-yard?* I paused to look at the piles of bones with patches of taut leather skin. Camels in the wild are usually naturally healthy, so these ones had likely been disposed of by local rangers, or shot by hunting parties like the boys I'd just met. Surrounded by all this death and destruction, I thought of the part I would have to play in all this. I didn't want to have to shoot a wild camel, 'pest' or not, but with evidence of their presence all around me it seemed inevitable.

I brought the camels back to camp for the evening. The wind had shifted, bringing with it the smell of death, wafting through camp. There was an eerie feeling in the air. I tied the camels to the poplar trees, but they didn't eat, or sit to chew their cud. They stood shifting about uneasily, making horrible high-pitched squeaks as they ground their teeth—a sign they were truly scared. I wondered about camel spirits. I believed in human spirits, and had experienced that creepy sensation one night at camp during my first month, but I had never thought of the spirits of dead animals. Without anyone to reason me out of it, my mind ran rampant with superstition. I had picked up a well-preserved camel skull the previous day while walking. It was slightly morbid, but I thought if I painted it, it would make a nice souvenir. Had I invited bad luck? Was it haunting me with the souls of the decaying camels that surrounded us?

I slept badly and so did the camels, tossing and turning throughout the night. In the morning I woke earlier than usual and saddled in the dark, wanting to be away from this place. I couldn't finish my muesli so I emptied it onto the ground next to camp. Without thinking I said, 'This is an offering to the spirit of the camp.'

It was a strange thing to say, and I laughed a little at myself. But alone in the desert, many strange things were taking hold of my mind, and from that day forth I continued the bizarre ritual of the morning muesli offering. The desert had made me too superstitious to stop.

The camels' heightened nerves meant we made good progress during the day. In the late afternoon we stopped at another island of dense mulga nestled within an open plain of old spinifex. It was the beginning of August, the sun had just set, and the short twilight of midwinter was fading quickly. I unhobbled the camels and led them back to camp for the night in their string.

That's when I heard it: the unmistakable sound of a burbling bull camel, a noise like a blocked sink bubbling as the water struggles to drain through a plughole. I stopped in my tracks. I couldn't see the bull, but the sound came from a line of thick mulga forest across the spinifex plain. My camels stood alert. They had heard it too.

I tied Jude to a bush and re-hobbled him as another means of restraint, so he didn't bolt off again. I didn't have time to hobble the others. I ran the short distance back to camp and grabbed my .308 rifle. I paused for a moment. *Remember what Murdoch taught you. Breathe,* I repeated to myself. I needed something to steady the gun. I looked around camp and knelt down beside a jerry can, resting the rifle upon it. I saw the bull striding out from the mulga. He threw back his head and again burbled as he blew out his dulla—the pink bullfrog-like sack male camels have in their mouth. The sound carried across the spinifex plain, loud and clear. Even from a distance I could see the white foam covering his mouth, which, along with his inflating dulla, showed he was clearly 'in season'. The bull camel was looking directly at my camels, coming towards them with clear intent.

I loaded the rifle and looked through the scope. *Breathe, breathe . . .*

The bull started to trot, covering ground quickly as he made a beeline for my camels.

Wait, breathe. Don't shoot too early.

He was now less than 100 metres away.

Breathe. He was fifty metres away. I had to do it now. I squeezed the trigger, the rifle fired, and the recoil momentarily made me lose sight of him through the scope.

I reloaded without thinking, like Murdoch had taught me. The bull had stopped in his tracks and was staggering. I was breathing heavily. *Had I killed him—or just injured him?* I ran towards him in a panic and, from a standing position, I shot again twice, missing both times. But the bull had now fallen to the ground. The first shot must have hit him.

I put down the .308, grabbed the smaller .22 rifle and approached the bull with caution. I could hear Murdoch's voice in my head: *Always approach from the hump side, never his*

legs, just in case he's not dead. Don't forget the nerves will also
make them twitch for a while. And always, always approach
with the gun loaded, just in case he gets up.

I held the .22 at the ready. The bull's feet were twitching a
little, but his eye was still. I pointed the gun point-blank at his
temple and fired a shot to make sure, then bent down and rested
my index finger on the dead animal's eyeball—another practice
Murdoch had taught me. It was still. The wild bull was dead.

I was surprised at how unemotional I felt. I had prepared
myself to be devastated at this moment, but I felt fine. I had
known this day was coming, and the adrenaline of the moment
had helped to focus my mind on carrying out the steps neces-
sary to get the job done quickly and humanely. I looked at
him lying on the ground. A beautiful animal, he was big,
strong and muscled, with a healthy thick coat. He was a camel
that I would have loved to train as part of my own string.
But I had known the realities of walking the desert during the
camel rutting season before I came out here. I didn't feel good
about what I had done, but it was a case of protecting my own
herd—my own means of survival—and I felt a certain relief
that the inevitable situation had played itself out and found
me capable.

We camped that night with the dead bull lying less than
100 metres away. Again, we were up early to saddle in the
dark and leave this site of death before the sun peered over
the horizon.

Only a couple more days went by before I shot my second and third wild bulls—both on the same day. It was windy, and neither my camels nor I had noticed the wild bull until he was almost upon us. The wind must have favoured his line of smell and he was trotting towards us through the bushes. I rushed to tie up Jude, then struggled to grab my rifle butt, which was poking from my swag, high on his back. Pulling it out, I shot the bull before I even knew what was happening. The adrenaline was pumping so strong the BANG from the rifle sounded like a distant whisper. I carried on walking a few minutes later, shocked by the violence I was capable of.

I found a spot to camp and was unloading the camels when I noticed their heads had turned to stare in one direction. Another wild bull was staring back at us. He blew out his dulla and foamed at the mouth and, without hesitation, I took the shot that would end his life.

My camels didn't flinch at the sound of a gun—even the bang from a .308. That was why I could never fire a warning shot to deter the wild bulls, as they took no notice of it. I also knew they would simply come back during the night, a situation that would be much worse for me. I couldn't risk it.

My camels were scared, however, of the large dead bull that now lay only metres from camp. I led Jude around while he grazed, hoping that my presence by his side would help calm him. We found an area where some patches of green feed had come back after a fire. Slowly Jude's manic state began to relax, and he dropped his head to eat for longer periods at a time. Food was always therapy for him.

Once I had tied the camels for the night, I walked back to the dead bull in the darkness. I flicked on my head torch and took out my foldable pocketknife. I wanted desperately for this bull's life not to have been wasted. I stared down at the body blankly. *Where do I start?* An old camel man had told me to take the backstraps, but where exactly were they? I poked my knife at the hide on the back leg. The skin was tough. There was no way my small pocketknife would be able to pierce it. I wouldn't be eating camel meat that night. His body would become yet another wasted camel carcass left rotting in the desert. I returned to camp and ate my vegetarian stew.

Several days later I sat sobbing silently on my canvas tarp again. It saw all the ups and downs of my trip, that tarp. I had stopped early in the day to make camp at a large clearing that I hoped would provide a relaxing afternoon's break, and seemed like an easy area to keep an eye on the camels. As I attended to washing my filthy clothes and socks, all of which now contained holes (alpaca wool ones included), I took my eyes off the camels for one moment. The next time I looked they were nowhere to be seen. I ran flat-out across three football fields of open ground to reach the scrub that they had disappeared into. I caught them just before their tracks were lost across rocky ground. I was straining for breath by the time I reached them, scared and furious, feeling betrayed by Jude, who had led the charge. We were meant to be a team!

I could tell in his eyes he was scared; the tension among the herd had been building. The smell that wafted up from the carcasses of dead camels strewn around the bush, combined with my own wild camel encounters, had added to Jude's mounting anxiety.

Back at camp I tied him and sat down on my tarp, hung my face in my hands and cried. I took out my phone, knowing that it would only fuel my feelings of hopelessness. Checking the map continually, ten to twenty times a day, had become my new obsession. The orange dot that marked us had barely moved since yesterday. I zoomed out and felt so overwhelmed I sobbed some more. On the map there was nothing around us. No markers with names of towns, no river systems, no roads turning off—only thin parallel lines marking the maze of sand dunes stretching out like a sea to our north, south, east and west.

The following morning my feelings were only compounded. I was saddling in the dark, each of the camels had a leg strap around one leg, and I was laying the blankets down on their backs. Some unknown silent-to-humans sound spooked them, and all five launched into the air in perfect herd unison and took off into the darkness on three legs. I stood holding a blanket, dumbfounded with terror as I watched them disappear into the black surrounds. I shone my head torch into the darkness and followed the trail of blankets into the centre of the clearing. They stood huddled together, standing on three legs and looking as terrified as I had looked moments before. It was amazing how they'd been able to move so quickly, even on three legs with a foreleg pinned in a bent position.

Would they ever settle? I wanted to scream at the top of my lungs. But what sort of leader was I if I remained constantly angry? They were only as scared and overwhelmed as I was. I took some deep breaths and picked up the trail of blankets one by one. I heard Chris's voice echo in my head: *Baby steps.* I had to compartmentalise.

When I eventually resaddled and was ready to go, I was no longer thinking about crossing the desert in its entirety; I was simply thinking about getting to the next water point.

That was it. That was as far as I would allow my mind to stretch.

Baby step by baby step, my camels did slowly begin to settle, the consistency of our routine playing a crucial role. As we carried on eastward, the height of the sand dunes began to increase. We were walking parallel to them, along dune corridors, making walking easy. Unlike photos of the Sahara Desert, in which a barren sea of sand fills the frame, this desert was full of vegetation. Patches of country had been burnt by wildfire, but in these areas where spinifex had not had a chance to regain its chokehold on the sand, new growth from a variety of ground-cover plants found some space to flourish. We made camp in one of these areas and the camels spent a contented afternoon eating what I looked up in my *Plants of Inland Australia* book as scarlet creeper. I nicknamed it Camel Spaghetti as I watched Delilah devour it, sucking it down with pouted lips like the scene from *Lady and the Tramp*. Jude's favourite was another perennial that grew in the sand hills. As he grazed, I walked by his side, picking his favourite treat from the sand. I had forgiven him again and we were back to being a team.

'Jude,' I called. He looked up and came shuffling over in his hobbles, eyes wide with expectation, his soft lips gently taking the plant from my fingers.

I climbed the nearest sand dune at sunset and sat gazing down, watching my camels eating. It was nice to gain some elevation, as it made it much easier to track the camels, and I had walked for over three months across a mainly flat landscape with often thick bush. I could see across the swale behind me—and the dune behind it, and the next one behind that, and another dune beyond. I had felt overwhelmed by the vastness of it all, but now, something stronger was taking over. I felt alone, tough and alive.

Up on the sand dune, I flipped open a book I had brought with me to read before sunset—*Spinifex and Sand*, David Carnegie's account of his expeditions across the goldfields and the Gibson Desert with camels. The perfect book to read in a place such as this. I pondered what it would be like to do such a trip without camels. It was a full-time job caring for them, but without them, an unsupported crossing of the desert would be impossible. Whenever I wondered what the hell I was doing out here, I always came back to the camels. As much as they frustrated me, they had become a guiding force in my life, gifting me with a focus and passion I had never experienced before. No matter how I felt, they drew me into the present. Working with them consumed all of my attention, and their company was like a form of meditation. I had always felt like I was looking for 'more' in my life. I couldn't quite define what this 'more' was, but I knew the camels were part of it. They taught me patience and persistence. They were my guides in this desert territory that was new to me, connecting me more deeply with nature, and teaching me about the beauty in the detail of this landscape that, without them, I never would have set foot in. They had become my best friends and travelling companions.

I closed my book and took big strides down the dune, sinking into the soft sand. In a half-conscious experiment I went around to each camel, plugging their bell with the excess leather around their neck collars that I used as a bell stopper. There was dead silence. The desert felt empty and suddenly lonely without the tinkling of their bells. I didn't like it one bit. I definitely couldn't imagine doing this trip without them.

That night I was woken by the sharp clang of the camel bells, a familiar signal that something had disturbed them and they'd all stood up suddenly. I heard an unmistakable burbling again. *Fuck, it was a bull camel at night!* A situation I had been dreading. The cold barrel of the rifle lay next to me in the swag. I grabbed it, groped for my head torch and unzipped the canvas at record speed. I searched about with the beam of my head torch and finally the light fell on a pair of fluffy, spindly, baby camel legs. My body relaxed. I could see a bull in the torchlight, too, but I knew if there was a baby there, there must also be females in the mix. It was only the lone bulls that would bother us. If I could scare the females, the bull would follow.

I pulled on my boots and jacket, and with the rifle slung over my shoulder, ran at the camels in the darkness, shrieking out crazy banshee noises. I heard a commotion as they turned and took off into the night, back into the darkness beyond the beam of my head torch.

I crawled back into my swag, relieved. I stayed awake until I heard the sound of my camels' bells as they sat back down again, relaxed now that the danger had passed. My travelling companions, my only friends in this vast expanse of desert, were safe.

8

Transformation

ILKURLKA ROADHOUSE TO
COOBER PEDY—729 KM

I turned up the Yothu Yindi album on my phone and danced as I walked along the sandy track to the beat of the didgeridoo. I hadn't listened to music in almost a month, and after the silence of the desert, this small amount of stimulation seemed more emotive, more intense. A couple of weeks out of Laverton, the Spotify app on my phone had failed and I had been left without music for a month until I connected to the wi-fi at the Ilkurlka Roadhouse. I danced like no one was watching, because of course, no one was watching . . . except the camels, who looked on, unperturbed by my silly dance moves as they chewed their cud and took in the surroundings.

I had left Ilkurlka the previous day with full food boxes and water jerries. The roadhouse was my only resupply point in the Great Victoria Desert. It was more of a remote light-house in a sea of sand than a traditional greasy truck stop: a small collection of buildings on Aboriginal land, with one fuel bowser. It had been great to have a shower and put on a load of washing, but the site had no good feed for the camels, and no yards to contain them in. There were also the dirty traces of previous human camps everywhere—old dried bits of toilet paper, aluminium foil and unburnt tea bags sitting in the extin-guished coals of prior camp fires. It made me keen to get back to the untouched purity of the desert.

A huge wildfire had swept through the area a few years before, only missing the buildings and fuel tank at Ilkurlka by metres. The burnt-out remains of a campervan told the story of its ferocity. Large trees such as marble gums had survived and were resprouting, but the burnt carcasses of acacia bushes and lack of spinifex made the bare ridgelines of the dunes more visible, their peaks surging like lines of swell rising into the distance. Not long ago an expanse like this would have terrified me, but now I felt a prickling excitement at being alone in the desert's endlessness. Its staggering vastness made my heart pound harder with a feeling of freedom like no other. There was not the faintest sign of a wheel mark on the track ahead of me, only clean rippling sand that the wind had carved.

I was drawing deeper into the heart of the desert.

A week and a half later, the final water tank beside the track came into view within a swale of unburnt mulga forest—a nice

shady place to make camp and take a day off with the avail-
ability of water. Beyond this spot I would be relying solely on
the help of Oak Valley Community, the traditional owners of
the Maralinga Tjarutja Lands in South Australia. When I had
applied for a permit to pass through, they had called me,
asking if they could bring the community to meet me and the
camels on the road. They had also offered to bring water for
the camels. I was excited by their visit, but I felt uncomfortable
about relying on their goodwill. For them it was a round trip of
several hundred kilometres to visit me, and I didn't know how
much water they would be able to bring on rough roads. Even
with their water drop, it would be a long stretch on either side
for the camels to go without a drink. And since leaving Ilkurlka
at the end of August, it was as if a switch had been flicked from
winter to summer.

The afternoon was hot again. I tied the camels by the tank,
filled my little red bucket with water and ferried it over to
them one by one. To let them drink together would mean
chaos and water spillage. They were all desperately thirsty
and couldn't fit their heads in the bucket at the same time.
Back and forth I went with the bucket, eight times to each
camel, until slowly they had stopped straining desperately
at their ropes for a drink when it was another camel's turn.
Jude and Clayton, with their dark coats, always seemed to be
the thirstiest, while Mac, despite carrying the heaviest load,
turned out to be the most water efficient. It was a worry to
see them drink so feverishly; it had only been three days since
their last drink. Their thick winter coats were not helping
them in the sudden hot weather.

The dunes beyond our camp in the mulga seemed bare, scorched by the fire. But on closer inspection as I tailed the camels while they grazed, I could see they were dotted with new life. As in other burnt patches, sprigs of succulent, water-retaining greens were shooting through the sand. Tufts of wild parsnip hid beneath the charred skeletons of bushes, and Jude's favourite perennial was also present. The desert was in a constant cycle of death and rebirth, it seemed. It was a good place for them to fill their bellies and regain strength for the road ahead.

I climbed the crest of a sand dune and called Dad on the satellite phone.

'You must be only a day away from the border,' he said. It was comforting to know that thousands of kilometres away, Dad was tracking exactly where I was on the map. He was the person who most knew what was going on day to day for me.

He added, 'I've looked up the weather and tomorrow will be thirty-eight degrees, followed by forty degrees on Thursday and strong winds.' It wasn't good news.

I hung up, troubled, cutting the invisible tie to the outside world. Silence. I lingered on the dune, not wanting to push the antenna of the satellite phone down for fear that loneliness and isolation might swamp me.

I hesitated, then dialled Sam's number. I had spoken to Sam several times after I shot the wild bull camels. He had been keen to hear about my growing aptitude with a rifle, and I had told him every detail of my wild bull encounters. Sam's enthusiasm and regular communication had bolstered my hopes. *Maybe we could get back together? Maybe he might want to see me arrive in Coober Pedy?* But this time on the phone was different. Sam seemed distracted as I tried to unburden my water and weather worries onto him. I could hear him typing on a computer; I had called him at work.

'Um, sorry, I have to go. I can call you back later,' he said absent-mindedly.

When I hung up, I was annoyed at Sam for not listening to me—but more annoyed at myself for calling him. He was no longer my boyfriend. It wasn't his job to listen to my problems. I was using him like a crutch to prop me up and support me. That was not what this trip was about. This was my time alone in the desert, where I had to learn to support myself. I pushed down the antenna for the satellite phone and returned to giving my attention to the camels. Present in this moment.

The following morning, the familiar beeping of my watch alarm sounded at a new early-morning record of 1.30 a.m. It was partly set so early because I was still on Perth time, even though I was only ten kilometres from the South Australian border. The other reason was that walking in the dark was a better option than under the heat of the midday sun. With tiredness threatening to pull me back to sleep, I forced myself up and out of the swag.

The night was still, and the moon was high in the sky. It had risen during the night. My head torch shone out like the high beams on a car when I flicked it on, accidently catching Jude in the face. I saddled quickly and efficiently. I had a system and a routine now. There was an order in which everything went on the camels' backs, taking the least amount of time. The camels sat quietly, but I still placed a leg strap on each of them, wise to how unexpectedly they could take fright. I worked from the front to the back of the string, then from the back to the front, working up and down the line of camels. Brush, brush, brush, brush, brush. Blanket, blanket, blanket, blanket, blanket. Saddle, saddle, saddle, saddle, saddle. I had surprised myself by how quickly I could do it now—just 45 minutes, compared to two and a half hours when I first set out.

We left camp in the moonlight. I had saddled in the dark many times before, but it had always been light once we set off; this was our first walk in the dark. I positioned my head torch around my Akubra and we followed the light of its beam. The moon lit up the mulga trees either side of the track, casting eerie shadows. We passed the water tank and I joked to the camels, 'I hope you've topped up your tanks.'

We paused for a moment. Jude spread his legs and a stream of urine trickled out into the sand. The others followed suit, all five peeing in unison.

'Don't do that. You're going to need that water!' I pleaded. But it was futile—it always happened after they'd had a big drink and eaten green feed. They became like sieves, stopping to pee every ten minutes. Rather than stand and wait for them, I pulled my own pants down and squatted in front of them, and all six of us peed together. I had become comfortable dropping my daks and peeing on the spot whenever I needed to go; it was one of the great advantages of being in the middle of nowhere.

It would be strange and almost inconvenient, I thought, to have to adapt to using a toilet again once the trip was over.

I switched off my head torch and allowed my eyes to adjust to the moonlight. I hadn't expected the camels to be this well behaved and calm in the dark. Jude reached forward to grab a mouthful from a bush as we passed, and I marvelled at how good their night vision must be. It was a beautiful time to walk—still and cool—and as the moon slid closer to the horizon, I watched the sun rise, illuminating the land-scape that surrounded us and extinguishing the moon's glow. After all these months and all these kilometres covered, I still enjoyed the simple act of walking. It felt like such a fundamental action for both humans and animals, walking under one's own steam.

The time passed quickly, and by mid-morning we were there: at the South Australian border. There was no large 'Welcome to South Australia' tourism sign. Just a small metal plaque that had a longitude and latitude marker, a visitor book with a pen in a waterproof box, and a few signs saying, 'Laverton Shire' and 'Welcome to Spinifex Country' in the direction we'd come from, and 'Welcome to Maralinga Tjarutja Lands' in the direc-tion we were going. Still, to me, this nondescript patch of scrub was a momentous milestone: Jude, Delilah, Charlie, Clayton, Mac and I had now walked across the entire width of Western Australia. So much pride in our accomplishment welled up inside me that I wanted to cry. It had been the hardest thing I had ever done. Western Australia was the biggest state and the most remote. We had cut our teeth on this leg of the journey and made it through. The camels looked as nonchalant as when we'd reached the Indian Ocean five months and seven days ago to begin our great journey. To them, we had paused for no reason at some signposts.

There was no other way to mark the occasion except to write in the visitor book. The last entry was in March 2020, almost six months ago, by a man driving the Anne Beadell before Covid-19 had hit. I flipped back through the pages and noticed that if it had been a regular year, I might have passed two four-wheel drives a day. The pandemic had given me the rare opportunity to have the desert to myself—something I'd always hoped I would get to experience so many years after Robyn Davidson's trip, in a much busier world.

I signed the visitor book: *Crossing Australia with my five camels, Jude, Delilah, Charlie, Clayton and Mac.*

I wished I could have lingered longer, soaking in the moment, but the day was heating up and I needed to push on.

The track crossed a string of salt lakes, marked on my map as the Serpentine Lakes. I paused briefly to pull out my camera, set it up on the tripod on a self-timer and loop the camels around in a circle so I could take a picture of us walking. We were out of focus in several shots and not where I wanted us in the frame. I would just have to settle with a memory of the beauty of the salt lakes. I stuffed the camera back in the saddle bag, the heat radiating from the bare ground contributing to a sense of urgency. My priority was to make camp early so the camels could rest and conserve water and energy.

By early afternoon we were a mess of limbs and body parts, camels and human, spread limply in a small patch of shade, almost on top of one another. Clayton and Charlie lay flat on their sides, their necks arched back towards their humps and heads resting on the sand, in an odd position that can only be comfortable to a camel. I lay between them. We were six; I was definitely part of the herd now. We shuffled uncomfortably, sweating with the stillness of the day and adjusting our positions to move with the constant travel of the shadows. It wasn't until evening that the sun's bite had dissipated enough for the camels to graze. We had been travelling in and out of burnt country as we walked and it was always a gamble where we made camp. Today there were no moisture-giving plants for the camels to eat, only salty vegetation around the salt lakes, which I guessed would only contribute to their thirst. I let the camels graze into the dark.

Now that we were in South Australia, I had changed the time on my watch, but my alarm still sounded in the very early hours of the morning. We were up and walking back into the burnt landscape.

The moon was still close to full, illuminating the open dunes and mottled marble gums with their gnarled limbs and fuzzy new growth, looking like comical, friendly monsters in the dark. The camels walked rhythmically, chewing their cud in time with my step . . . I needed no light; the moon was enough. It was hauntingly beautiful, peaceful, as though we were the only beings in existence. It felt like the silence when you dip under a wave. Even though a vast emptiness surrounded us, for me everything felt sucked inward, still and concentrated on my breath and the camels chewing.

It was exhilarating being in this wild place. It felt as though we were walking while the desert slept, but I knew beyond the light of the moonlit path the desert was in fact awake, many little reptiles and marsupials busily creating tracks in the sand that I would find in the light of day. While I meditated on the rhythm of our steps, a glimmer of dawn crept into the sky, lingering for a while, slowly lighting up the world around us and revealing the landscape, soft and full in its true form.

And then the fierce shining ball in the sky rose, casting its harsh light across everything. Suddenly it felt like a race against time. The desert inhabitants escaped underground, but larger beings like us could not. The heat was rising, and by midday the wind had picked up too. It was hot and strong in my face and I pulled my Akubra down tightly on my head. The desert felt harsh and dangerous again; it was amazing how quickly my opinion of the place could change. I wanted to make camp and hide.

I unsaddled in the sand, trying to squeeze into the shade of a few meagre cypress pines that were billowing and swaying in the wind. The camels weren't keen on napping. They were hungry and set off in their hobbles with me tailing them, leaning into the strengthening wind. Scanning the ground for feed, I could see this was the most barren landscape we had encountered, with no new growth beneath the charred stubs of bushes. I thought of a passage I had underlined in *Spinifex and Sand*:

Nothing is more heartrending than to be forced to camp night after night with the knowledge that one's poor animals are wandering vainly in search of feed. To tie them down would have given them some rest, but at the same time it entailed their certain starvation; whilst, wandering about, they stood some chance of picking up a mouthful or two. How anxiously each ridge was scanned when camping-time drew near—no feed—on again another ridge or two, no feed—just one more ridge, and, alas! 'no feed' is again the cry.

The wind raged stronger as we crested another dune, the camels searching desperately for feed. I could see the angles of Charlie's hip bones, and his hump had withered virtually to nothing, the fat deposit used for survival times all but gone. The other camels didn't look much better, all of them lean. I wanted to let them wander longer in the hope that they could gain a few more mouthfuls, but the weather felt increasingly danger-ous. The sun was now hidden behind a brown haze of dust and sand kicked up by the gale-force winds across the naked dunes. Brown as far as the eye could see, the desert looked like a nuclear waste land. I felt panicked that we were now several dunes away from the visible safety of the track, exposed in the dust storm. I gathered the camels urgently and made my way back, walking double speed, buffeted by gusts. The camels walked calmly while the wind raged around us. They could be nervous and spooky about many things, but wind did not scare them. When I reached camp my equipment, which I had wrapped in my tarp like a burrito, was barely visible under a layer of sand. This was no place for us to hide.

Battling the wind, I led the camels a little way from camp to a tiny patch of unburnt mulga. The soil had more clay in it here, and the trees provided a little protection. The camels sat down with their backs to the wind and I used Jude's large form to shelter me. We all waited. There was nothing to do but wait for hours until eventually the wind's force subsided and the sky brightened.

Jude stood up, shaking his body with a clanging of his bell. The others stood up too. We emerged from our shelter to find the apocalyptic brown haze lit up by the setting sun—like a phoenix rising from the ashes. The stillness after the wind felt palpable.

As the camels searched for mouthfuls, I found life after the nuclear sand blast: a beautiful little thorny devil lizard, like a miniature dinosaur with spikes and a patchwork of colours, chocolate brown, rust red and sand. I lay on the ground, watching it slowly conduct its staggered walk, swaying backward and forward as if unsure when to place a foot on the ground.

The desert was such a land of extremes, filled with wonder and brutality only moments apart. The temperature had dropped with the change of wind, and the sky was filled with soft pastels.

The weather had developed into a pattern. Days of increasing heat built up into another dust storm, which brought a momentary cool change, before the temperature rose once more. Everywhere we camped, the feed was dry, and the camels could glean little moisture from it. We continued in this altered routine, rising and walking in the dark, waiting out the burning ball of the midday sun, and allowing the camels to graze into the cool of night. My sleep had been reduced to six hours—not long enough for me to recover from the rigours of each day.

As the heat of another day finally subsided and we were all huddled in the shade, Clayton stood up to make the first move. He nibbled at a small piece of saltbush where he had been resting, then shuffled over towards camp. He lowered his face and sniffed the top of one of the water jerry cans. His big dark eyes looked wide with sorrowful longing.

'I need you to hang on a little longer, Clayton. Two more days and you can have some water from the jerry can.' I knew even then, with the meagre water rations I was carrying for the camels, it wouldn't be enough to properly quench his thirst.

It broke my heart to deny him. For all of Clayton's unsociability, he was such a smart camel and knew exactly where the water came from.

Once all the other camels were foraging a little way away from camp, I got up and filled my Camelbak with water from the jerry can. I instinctively turned my back to them so they couldn't see what I was doing. I knew if they heard the slightest sound of water being decanted, they'd come running back, hoping for a drink.

I followed them, stopping with them while they ate the tough, sour feed. I was so incredibly tired that I sat down in the sand of the track. The sand was warm and comfortable, and I felt my eyelids drooping. I woke with a start, looking around dazed and confused. How long had I been asleep? *Fuck, where were my camels?!* I glanced around and breathed out; they were only fifty metres away.

I walked over to them, then sat back down. I just had to rest my eyes for two minutes. Before I knew it, I woke up again, panic washing over me, looking around for the camels. It happened several more times: lying on my back in the dirt, beneath the shade of a meagre shrub, I would nod off into a microsleep, unable to keep my eyes open.

Eventually I forced myself to stay awake, terrified that if I let myself go deeper into the realm of sleep, I might not wake for hours, and the camels would be gone.

The cycle of sleepless nights and water-conserving days continued. I needed to push the camels ten days without water before reaching Voakes Hill Corner, a feat that was proving harder than I anticipated with the hot weather. This afternoon we were again waiting out the heat, hiding under the boughs of a patch of black oaks off the track. I was worried about the camels. Even with the meagre water rations from the jerry cans they had become increasingly lethargic and less inclined to graze, their thirst causing them to preserve energy. I was lying on my tarp, boots off, with my eyes closed, surrounded by them, when I thought I heard a noise. I stood up quickly, feeling a little giddy in the heat, and listened intently. Yes. It was a car. There were voices, excited talking, then a throng of ten people suddenly appeared from behind a clump of bushes. I was still standing on my tarp, barefoot and a little stunned. I hadn't seen another human in fifteen days. There were four Aboriginal men and four Aboriginal women, followed by a white couple who strode over and shook my hand. They introduced themselves as Sam and Shane.

'We're the ranger team from Oak Valley Community. The guys spotted your tracks in the sand and we figured you must be camped somewhere in the shade,' Shane said. They were on the road checking sacred sites as well as marking GPS coordinates for quandong trees, a traditional source of bush tucker that was being decimated by wild camel herds.

Shane honed straight in on my camels. 'Do your camels need a drink? We've got some spare water in the vehicles.' I could not have been happier. Shane and Sam picked a path through the bushes and drove the fully laden dual-cab utes into camp.

'Shall we have lunch here? *Kuka* [food]?' Sam asked the group, speaking partly in English and partly in Pitjantjatjara.

Before I knew it, Shane and some of the other men were filling buckets up with water. My camels shuffled over to them eagerly, taking long desperate gulps.

'Looks like they were pretty thirsty,' Shane said kindly.

It was a hive of activity. Someone had got a fire going and put a large billy can on for tea. Sam set out a table and boxes with plates, cutlery and leftovers from the previous evening's camp meal. And in the whirlwind, I was given a can of ice-cold Coke, offered a camp chair and handed a plate of food. I sat between the Aboriginal ladies, sipping the deliciously cold, bubbly black liquid. I didn't normally like soft drinks, but here, in the desert, it tasted like the best thing in the world. I listened to the women speaking in their own tongue, a language that belonged to the land that I was passing through. It was nice to hear it. I hadn't realised that Pitjantjatjara would be spoken this far south of Uluru. It was a surprise to recognise some of the words that Greg had taught me, and to now be able to use them. The oldest of the ladies, a small woman wearing an over-sized T-shirt with the Maralinga Lands logo and a long skirt, pointed at my feet and said something I didn't understand.

'Cindy is worried about what happened to your feet,' Sam explained. I stared down at my ankles, which were covered in dirty, sand-covered strapping tape.

I laughed. 'Oh, nothing's wrong, it's just that all my socks have holes in the heels.'

Sam was instantly up and rummaging through the ute. She handed me a rolled-up pair of socks.

'These are the ones the rangers get issued. They're bamboo. You can have them.'

'Thank you,' I said gratefully, turning the thick, durable socks over in my hands.

'It's lucky we caught up with you,' Shane said. 'Tomorrow is meant to be over forty degrees. There's a stretch heading east from here that has been very badly burnt, with absolutely no shade for at least twenty-five kilometres.'

I thought about this predicament. Shane said the thick bush we were in now lasted another five kilometres before it petered out. I'd cover that short distance tomorrow, and have to wait out another day in the shade before I tackled the barren section.

'We'll catch up with you tomorrow on our way back,' Shane told me.

'And then party at Voakes Hill!' said Sam enthusiastically.

'I've got a thousand-litre tanker that I'll bring up. Will that be enough for the five camels to have a drink and for you to fill up your jerry cans?' Shane added.

I was amazed. Their community was 160 kilometres south of the Anne Beadell—a big distance on sandy tracks and up and over dunes to haul so much water. I thanked them all profusely. In another hurricane of activity, everything was packed away again, and the ranger team was ready to leave. They were pros at making and breaking camp.

'Before we leave, we have something for you,' Sam said, handing me a little packaged salad through the car window. 'We heard on the bush telegraph from Phil at Ilkurlka that you were craving fresh food.' I watched them leave, refreshed from the social interaction. It seemed I had made a new group of friends.

That evening I sat savouring every mouthful of my fresh salad. Living on a diet of dehydrated food, it was the best salad I had ever tasted.

I caught up with the ranger team the following afternoon as I sheltered in the last meagre patch of mulga before the fire-ravaged dunes.

'*Palya!*' we shouted at each other as the ranger group pulled into camp that afternoon—Pitjantjatjara for 'welcome'. Their faces were becoming familiar now, and I got to know them all a little better on this second visit. Shane and Sam were a fascinating couple who had worked in many Indigenous communities and had spent time in every desert in Australia. There was Cindy, the oldest of the aunties, Lance, who seemed to like wearing AC/DC merchandise, Gloria, a reserved lady whom I was told was a very good artist, Hilary, a squat, friendly woman and Clayton, her husband, who loved the fact that I had a camel that was also called Clayton, and who insisted I take photos of the two Claytons together. The team made themselves at home, all of us sitting together on my 'house' tarp beneath the shade. I commented on the hot wind that was blowing up the dust storms.

'*Pirriya*,' Cindy said.

I shook my head, and Sam interpreted for me. 'It's the name for the hot wind that blows from the north, straight from the Gibson and Tanami deserts.' That resonated with me; I liked having a word for it, in the language of this land. Being able to name it gave me a greater sense of connection and understanding.

When it was time for the rangers to head back to the community, the women huddled around me and Cindy grasped my hands in hers. She spoke to me fervently and the others interpreted her meaning. They explained that I was on Anangu land, and my safety was now their responsibility—one they took deeply to heart. They would be looking out for me.

'If you need anything, don't hesitate to call on the sat phone,' added Sam. Cindy began to sing and clap a protection song, and the other women joined in. They were still singing and clapping as the car drove away.

The following day I crossed the barren dunes, walking in the dark hours of the early morning. Without the tyre tracks from the rangers' utes, it would have been impossible to make out the Anne Beadell. The fire combined with the numerous dust storms had eradicated all evidence of the road.

Five days later we arrived at the area known as Voakes Hill Corner, where a road turned off to Oak Valley Community, 150 kilometres to the south. There was another flurry of 'Palya! Palya!' as the women rangers, community nurses, families and kids arrived to meet me. Unsaddling was a community effort, with kids pairing up to carry the camels' saddles.

In the shade of the mallee trees, a camp had been set up, and I settled myself down with the women. The men were on their way; they had stopped to check sacred sites. I asked Sam about this, as I had passed a sign on the track that read 'No camping next 50 km'. Of course, I couldn't cover such a distance on foot, and had no other option but to camp in the middle of the area.

'The community Elders actually did lots of consultation about your visit,' Sam said in a hushed voice. 'The men discussed you needing to camp in that area and gave their permission.' I could tell she meant it was a secret men's business site. She had a deep respect for the culture and I felt a bit like a blundering tourist, not realising I'd be passing through sacred ground. Still, it was good to know that Aboriginal lore was very much alive out here in the desert.

The male rangers returned, and throughout the afternoon the rest of the community began to arrive. Several of the school-teachers had driven up for a visit, and finally Jeremy, the chair of the Maralinga Tjarutja Lands Council, whom I'd initially spoken to on the phone, arrived, driving the school bus with more children and families. I was touched and lost for words when the ranger team presented me with a beautiful gift basket filled with presents. There was an Oak Valley Arts T-shirt with one of Gloria's artworks and *Tjanpi* (spinifex) printed on the back, a pair of handmade quandong seed earrings, a book titled *Maralinga: The Anangu story*, punnets of fresh strawberries and blueberries, and a small collection of toiletries—moisturiser, shampoo and conditioner.

'The ladies thought you might be wanting to take a shower,' Sam said.

In the bushes beyond sight, Shane had strung up a tarp for privacy and had boiled a huge pot of water so that I might bathe. It felt fantastic to wash my hair. I bucketed the water onto my body, trying to work out how long it had been since my last shower at Ilkurlka. It was around three weeks. I looked out onto the mallee trees and thought of all the strange forms of showers I had taken since living on the road. Afterwards, I put on my new *Tjanpi* T-shirt, with my best jeans and my new quandong seed earrings.

In the evening, everyone gathered about, feeding the camels treats they had brought—sweet potatoes and oranges. The kids laughed and squealed, dropping the oranges when they pulled their hands away too quickly for fear of the camels biting them. I picked the orange segments up from the ground and dusted off the sand. I showed them the camels' soft lips, and how gentle they were when they used them like fingers to take hold of the food. Everyone then gathered to help me fill my jerry cans and watch the camels drink water, the kids squealing some more when they were showered by the camels shaking the excess liquid from their lips.

One of the teachers had brought a guitar, and that night we all sat around the fire, in a mess of camp chairs, swags and inflatable mattresses, singing or gazing silently into the flames. It was nice to be among new friends under the desert night sky.

Pirriya, the hot wind, was blowing from the north. I knew its name now, and I knew it well. I'd watched the rain clouds accumulate on the horizon, good at judging these weather patterns now. Hot days would lead to grey skies that looked ominous, but would only produce a handful of raindrops before the wind changed, bringing with it cooler weather and pushing away all possibility of rain. All the same, Jude felt like a coiled spring as I led the camels back to camp, the sound of thunder making me doubt my pessimism about the possibility of rain. The camels could sense the weather coming in. I tied them to mulga bushes and donned their hobbles, then rushed about stringing up my lean-to shelter. Underneath it I placed my swag, book, gas burner and camera, thinking I'd peacefully watch the storm roll in with the comfort of a good book and a cup of tea. The camels were tethered, gear wrapped, and I was sitting comfortably under my shelter leaning against my swag.

Suddenly I heard the roar of the wind funnelling through the dunes, and every bush in sight was alive with violent movement. The wind ripped out the tent pegs pinning my shelter, and instantly my tarp was flapping above my head like a wild animal trying to escape. A second later, the sky opened up and it poured with rain. All my gear was getting drenched. I frantically began stuffing my camera, book and other items into my pack bags. By the time I was done, I was drenched from head to toe. My tarp was still flapping about wildly, refusing to be tamed, so I crawled under the mulga bush Delilah was tied to and looked out upon the scene of destruction as the rain fell in curtains. *So much for watching the storm in comfort!* I laughed hysterically. *Who gives a shit?* It was pouring! I let out a hoot of joy.

'It's raining in the desert!' I yelled at the top of my lungs. The camels looked at me bewildered, but I didn't care. I hadn't seen proper rain like this in over five months.

It rained into the night, and more the next day, and the day after that. I was now skirting around huge pools of water that had formed on the track. I squeezed the camels between the bush on the side of the track and these flooded ruts, trying to prevent them slipping and sliding on the wet ground. They all followed my line except Mac, who charged straight into the water with his thick stocky legs, apparently thinking he was an amphibious vehicle. Jude insisted on stopping at every single body of water to have a drink. It didn't seem to matter that he was now peeing every five minutes—there was no way he was going to miss an opportunity.

The Oak Valley rangers messaged me on the satellite phone to say that they'd had sixty-five millimetres of rain—almost half their annual rainfall—in a single night. Shane had even phoned my dad to let him know that if he didn't hear from me, it would be due to the bad weather inhibiting the satellite signal.

Within days I watched the desert spring to life. Parakeelya, a ground-covering succulent, appeared out of the bare sand, coating the dunes in a blanket of purple flowers. Birds were singing everywhere, and I saw my first wild budgerigars flying overhead.

We were now making camp in areas abundant with camel feed. Tall clumps of Jude's favourite perennial grew everywhere, making parts of the dunes look like green fields. This flush of new feed also brought with it more wild camels. I was forced to shoot two more bulls—but thankfully, not all these encounters resulted in death. Some were even comic.

At a camp packed with good feed, I climbed a dune and spotted several female camels grazing. I grabbed my rifle, but the bull was nowhere to be seen. With no clear threat obvious, I decided to let the situation play out. My camels got closer and caught sight of the wild girls. It was as if three good-looking ladies had suddenly walked into a bar. Mac's head snapped up from grazing, he threw back his neck and blew out his dulla, making the familiar deep burbling sound. He seemed to have forgotten the removal of his balls and switched to being an instant Casanova. He was going to ask these ladies for a date. Full of bravado, he started shuffling towards them at top speed in his hobbles, looking a little less cool and collected than he imagined. Jude and Clayton decided that the boys were out on the town and followed Mac's lead. Charlie, who was too young and innocent to even understand what sex was, didn't want to get left behind, and followed too. Delilah paused for a moment, then with a look of indignation that her boyfriend Mac was chasing after other women, followed suit. All five of them looked ridiculous, falling over their own feet as they shuffled at top speed towards the new girls at the bar. The wild camels looked up startled, wondering what on earth these strange camels were doing, charging towards them in fancy dress with their halters, ropes and hobbles. They took off. Mac pulled up looking crestfallen.

'Mac, you might have to play a bit harder-to-get next time. Your approach was a little bit too keen, mate,' I laughed.

Cindy stood over the fire, leaning on a shovel with a cigarette hanging from her mouth, while Hilary knelt in the sand folding the dough for damper. Cindy made a hole in the sand and Hilary placed the dough within it, covering it with the coals from the fire. Kangaroo tails wrapped in foil were already cooking in the underground oven. I watched Cindy as she sat down by the fire, running her dark bony hands through the red sand.

We were at a spot marked on the map as Emu, and this was my last visit from the Oak Valley rangers. A natural variation within the dunes and mulga forests, this area was a huge, open bluebush plain—one that had been chosen by the British Army as a test site for detonating atomic weapons in 1953. Two bombs, codenamed Operation Totem, were exploded here. The first, weighing 9.1 kilotonnes, was detonated in weather conditions that contravened the criteria for safe firing. Hilary told me about the ensuing 'black mist', as it was called—the nuclear fallout that swept over Wallatinna, a property to the north-east of Emu Plains, where Anangu people were camped.

'Many people got very sick. Coughing, sore eyes, rash. Many people died.'

I'd had no idea about the destructive history of the area. But I was brought to tears when I began to read the Anangu account in *Maralinga: The Anangu story*, which the rangers had given to me in my gift pack. It looked like a book for kids, with its brightly coloured artwork, but the history of these people who called this desert home was tragic. They had been removed from their land for the top-secret testing of long-range atomic missiles by the British. It was a classic case of a race of people with no connection to Country deciding that this was a region devoid of anything useful—a disposable wasteland. The area was so large, however, that it was impossible to ensure all Aboriginal people had been safely relocated. Many wandered back to their Country only to be met with the devastating effects of radiation poisoning. Hilary herself had visited a contaminated site with her mother as a child and now had long-term health issues. The Anangu who were sent to the Yalata Mission on the South Australian coast found the land there totally different. The pale limestone soil made them feel sick and they longed for their red dirt Country.

It wasn't until the mid-1980s that the Anangu were given back their traditional lands and Oak Valley Community was formed. I thought about the valuable work the rangers were doing, looking after their beloved Country, which as I had seen on foot was far from an empty and disposable wasteland. It was quite sad to be meeting the rangers here for the final time, but I was thankful that the care of the land was now rightfully back in their hands.

As I waved and yelled *Palya* (a word also used for goodbye) to the ranger team as they drove off the following morning, I thought of how I had begun this trip determined to be self-sufficient. I thought I would be on my own, but I had found that whenever I needed help, it seemed the right people would appear at the right time. I felt alone at times, but I had actually received the support of many—and without Oak Valley Community, my camels and I would never have made it through the most waterless stretch of the country alive.

It was 4 October, my birthday. I rose in the dark to saddle my camels. As first light appeared I could see the sky was heavy with rainclouds, and we made it less than an hour down the road before it began to pour. As the raindrops steadily fell from the rim of my Akubra, I contemplated pushing on, but the rain was too heavy and all my gear was getting soaked. I needed to pull up and quickly make camp.

As I unsaddled the camels, I noticed their heads turn in unison, looking into the distance. *Shit!* There were seven wild bull camels looking back at us. *Why did this have to happen now, while it was raining, and on my birthday?* There were too many of them for me to shoot. I squinted into the rain and noticed they looked like younger males. Hopefully they could be deterred. With the gun slung over my shoulder, I picked up a stick and ran at them.

'Fuck off!' I screamed at the top of my lungs. The wild camels turned, ran for a short distance, then stopped to look back at the crazed human pursuing them.

'Fuck off, leave us alone!' I yelled again, throwing the stick in their direction. They turned again and loped off into the rain.

When I arrived back at camp, wet and looking like a mad-woman, my own camels barely batted an eyelid. They had become used to my wild and erratic behaviour by this point. I set up my tarp and sat beneath it, trying to light a fire from wet wood to keep me warm as my shelter flapped violently in the wind, slapping against my back. The pathetic fire only smoked out my shelter, so I smothered it and sat looking at the rain, shivering. I laughed to myself; it was such a ridiculously miserable birthday it was funny. I stopped railing against the weather and the unpredictability of the landscape, and found I actually enjoyed being part of it.

I was now down to the last portions of rice and lentils in my food boxes, and even my muesli was about to run out. It had taken me three months to cross the Great Victoria Desert, something I could have done in a four-wheel drive in a matter of days. But I wouldn't have wanted to thunder through in a metal box, shielded from the desert's many moods. Even as the rain beat down on my tarp, I loved the fact that I was out here exposed to the elements. I had seen and experienced it all with my eyes and ears and skin. My camels and I had been connected to it and become part of it—the wind, the heat, the dust storms, the fire-ravaged country and the bare dunes at night under the full moon. We had experienced the rain and the new life that followed.

It was a miserable birthday, but I wouldn't have swapped it for the world.

In the afternoon the rain cleared and the camels bucked and chased one another, delighted after sitting all day with their backs to the weather. I was reminded that nothing lasts forever: everything is in a cycle, a state of constant transformation.

The end of the desert felt within sight. My dad and a family friend, Andrew, had arranged to drive to Coober Pedy and meet me along the Anne Beadell for several days camping before I arrived at my final destination before the summer—Mount Clarence Station, about fifty kilometres north-west of Coober Pedy.

I was counting down the days, excited to finally share with them what my life on the road with the camels had been like—but the spring storms had made the tracks impassable by vehicle. Dad called on the sat phone to say he wasn't sure if they would even be able to make it to Mount Clarence Station, let alone down the Anne Beadell. The station's driveway was dirt, and it only takes ten millimetres of rain on the clay soils of the Outback to make driving impossible.

I was devastated. First Covid-19 had prevented Dad travelling to Western Australia to see me off as I started my trip—and now the rain was washing away our chance to connect along the way. It felt like everything kept conspiring against us.

I could hear the desperate determination in his voice on the sat phone. 'Even if we have to chopper in, we'll be there!' Dad said, only half-jokingly.

Meanwhile, I had also been waylaid by the rain. I was now walking close to thirty kilometres every day to reach Mount Clarence in time for Dad's hoped-for arrival. The rain carried on, but my resolve outweighed it and we pushed forward. The dunes had now petered out and the sand had been replaced by clay soils and gibber stones. In our wake, the ground was punctured with sink holes where the camels had slipped and sunk in the mud. Their pads were becoming soft and swollen.

The sky cleared on my final night. Dad and Andrew were meant to be here camping with me. I felt let down, as I always did when things didn't go to plan. I lit a fire and thought of all the other people I had expected to join me on my trip. To begin with, I never thought I would do the journey alone— I had imagined Sam and our friends Nat and Dan being there. When that had fallen through, I'd hoped other friends would join me for segments of the trip, but Covid-19 and my sheer remoteness had put a stop to that. It was as if I was meant to do this trip on my own. I stared as if hypnotised into the flames, deep in thought. When I reflected back, it seemed that my journey had in fact gone the best way it could. I had met all the right people at the right times, as if they'd been waiting in the wings to support me just enough to continue on alone. I was alone again on my final night, just as I had been alone on my first. It seemed fitting.

The following morning as I was saddling the camels for our final day's walk to Mount Clarence Station, I looked at them all sitting in a straight line, with their loads on, waiting for the day to begin. Even Jude, who perpetually had ants in his pants, was sitting still. They had come so far in so many ways. I remembered my frustration about how long it had taken me to train these wild animals to simply sit in a straight line. I knew them intimately now; I could pick who was who purely from the sound of them chewing their cud in the night, or how they moved in the dark. I could read their moods by the way they turned their ears, or the look in their eyes, or the tension of their lips. I had spent three months straight with them, twenty-four hours a day. It was going to be incredibly tough to leave them for the summer.

But as I studied their outlines beneath the saddles and gear, I knew I had made the right call to break the trip in half. Their loads were all light now, as I was barely carrying any water or food, and I had culled most of the unnecessary equipment before entering the desert. They were fit and strong, but the crossing had taken its toll. Most of their hip joints and ribs were showing, their humps were reduced and their coats were dull. I could tell in their eyes that they were tired.

'Only one more day's walk to go,' I said to them gently in the quiet of the morning. I took out my camera and tripod, set it up and sat in front of my team. The grin on my face in the photo revealed the extent of my pride.

As we walked, the mulga gave way to the bare open gibber plains surrounding Coober Pedy. Normally the red stones would have made the ground appear bare, but after the rain it was a blanket of green. I felt a pull back on the rope and turned to see Charlie sitting down in the string. It wasn't like him to sit while walking. I got him up, but he was limping badly. I checked his feet but could see nothing. I guessed his soft pads must have been bruised on the sudden stony ground.

'Come on, chicken. Only one more day of walking, darling.' Thank god it had happened on the final day and not halfway through the desert. Besides the empathy I felt for Charlie's miserable state, I was excited. We had done it; the desert was behind us.

Five kilometres from Mount Clarence Station I saw two vehicles approaching on the horizon. They pulled up in front of me and the camels, and I halted the string. Dad practically leapt out of the passenger seat: he had made it! Smiling from ear to ear, he strode over with such gusto that he looked like he might levitate. Tears streamed down my face as he embraced me in his arms. We had made it—and he had made it to see me arrive.

'Well done, well done!' he kept saying, unable to wipe the smile from his face. Finally, he tore himself away and turned to my camels. 'You've come a long way, you camels,' he grinned.

Dad stayed with me and the camels to walk the final five kilometres to Mount Clarence homestead. Neither of us could contain our joy.

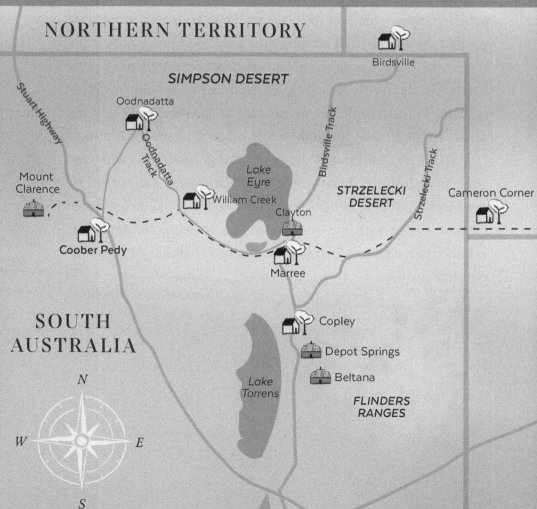

PART 2

renewal

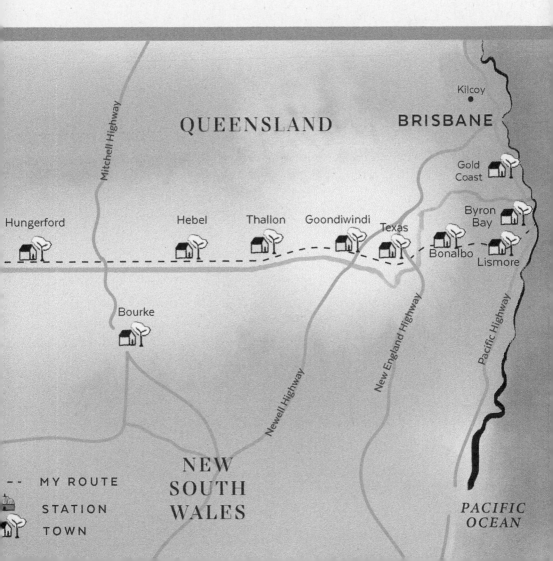

Kilcoy

QUEENSLAND BRISBANE

Mitchell Highway

Gold
Coast

Byron
Bay

Hungerford   Hebel   Thallon Goondiwindi   Texas

Bonalbo
Lismore

New England Highway

Pacific Highway

Bourke

Newell Highway

NEW
SOUTH
WALES

-- MY ROUTE
STATION
TOWN

PACIFIC
OCEAN

9

Summer

I was sitting with my morning cup of coffee on the soft sand in the yards at Beltana Station in the Flinders Ranges. It was time to release my camels for the summer. Not back into the wild, but the closest I could get for them.

Karen and Paul, whom I'd worked for at Camel Treks Australia, had arrived in mid-October to pick up my camels and drive us from Mount Clarence to Beltana Station. Karen had taken one look at Charlie's ribs and withered hump and made it her personal mission to nurse my camels back to health.

Paul and Karen's tours had finished for the winter and every summer they agisted their camels at Beltana Station. Their camels were allowed to roam across 900 square kilometres of the station, and when I'd called them from the desert, they

167

had kindly agreed that my five could run with theirs. Their thirty-two camels were some of the biggest I'd ever seen, with humps that looked like mountains on their backs—so if there was ever going to be somewhere for my camels to put on weight, it was Beltana. Nevertheless I was concerned; if Charlie's condition didn't improve over the summer, I would have to leave him behind.

I had arrived early at the Beltana yards to have a final moment alone with my five mates. Karen's camels surrounded us in separate yards, impatient to be let out for their summer vacation.

Tears suddenly started streaming down my face. *God, I would miss them!* They had been my lifeline, both physically and emotionally, and it would be strange not being with them every day. What would our relationship be like after their six months roaming practically wild across the station? Would they remember me? Would they forget all their training? I took Jude's head in my arms and rested my cheek on his crown. I then gently kissed him on the side of his face. 'Thank you,' I whispered to each of them in turn.

Karen, Paul and a troop of volunteers arrived and I wiped the tears from my face. It was time for my camels to simply be camels again. The other camels were pressed against the gates. They knew the summertime routine and were eager to leave the yards. My camels stood back a little way, unsure of the proceedings. I said my final goodbyes and we unlatched the gate.

Thirty-seven camels streamed out of the yards. Some at the front had a playful buck, while others at the back walked in a stately line. It was beautiful to see Jude, Delilah, Charlie,

Clayton and Mac striding out into the low sand dunes, un-encumbered by halters, ropes or hobbles, with the Flinders Ranges in the distance. My five stuck together but kept up with Karen and Paul's camels, their innate herd mentality running deep. They paused to nibble on a bush, and I thought I detected their heads turning back to look for me—but then they were off, following the herd up and over dunes, looking as they had when they first came out of the wild.

As sad as it was to leave my camels, a certain relief came with unburdening myself from the constant responsibility for their welfare. I was now free for the summer too. I would have a couple of weeks at the station to get my equipment in order and decompress before I flew back to Brisbane. To celebrate my new-found freedom, I decided to take myself out for coffee. In the remote northern Flinders Ranges, there weren't many options for such outings, but I knew of a bakery cafe in the little town of Copley, thirty minutes' drive north of the station.

I found myself a little self-conscious as I ordered a flat white from the young guy who served me. He was quite good-looking. After six months virtually alone in the Outback I wasn't used to meeting guys my own age, let alone good-looking ones. Besides my incessant longing for Sam, boys had been far from my mind. Jimmy, as he introduced himself, seemed keen to chat. In the small town of fifty people a new face did not go unnoticed.

'So, what brings you to town—are you just travelling through?'

'Um, no not exactly. I've been doing a walk with camels.'

'Oh yeah, are you working for Paul and Karen on Beltana Station?'

'I used to work for them, but now I have my own camels. They're agisted at Beltana Station for the summer. I've just finished a big walk with them,' I replied.

'Oh yeah, where did you walk?'

'Well, I've just walked from Shark Bay in Western Australia to Coober Pedy, then next winter I'll walk from Coober Pedy to Byron Bay—so, the whole way across the country,' I added self-consciously.

I was surprised by how unimpressed he seemed. He took this information completely in his stride, recounting some of the big hikes he had done in the area himself, keen to share the commonality of adventure with me. As I paid for my coffee he said, 'Say hi to Paul and Karen for me.'

I sat on a bench at the front of the bakery, enjoying the notion of going 'out' to a cafe. I phoned my best friend Ness, who had just had a baby—Valerie—who was born the night of the first storm I had experienced in the desert. I couldn't imagine returning home and seeing her with a baby in her arms. I had missed Ness's entire pregnancy while I was living at Uluru and on my trip. We had known each other since our first day of primary school, when we were six. When I discovered she was pregnant, I was happy for her, but also sad at the loss of our youthful friendship. It would no longer be the two of us. It was normal, natural, it was growing up, but the void between my lifestyle and that of my friends who were settling down and having families had never felt so great. My Instagram feed was now full of schoolfriends announcing their engagements, pregnancies and newborn babies. The house-less, career-less, partner-less and baby-less path I had chosen was a world apart, and there was always a niggling feeling that the destruction of my relationship with Sam had taken these things away from me.

As I sipped my coffee, I lowered my voice so that I could not be overheard and told Ness that I'd just met a hot guy. Ness's enthusiastic curiosity over the phone made me draw back, and think that, maybe, I was getting carried away. After a six-month stint of celibacy in the Outback, almost anyone would have seemed attractive to me.

Several days later, Jimmy turned up unannounced at the Beltana homestead, I assumed, to visit Paul and Karen. I found myself a little disconcerted by his sudden appearance.

'Sorry, they're away,' I told him when he got out of his car.

He seemed completely unperturbed and lingered out the front of the homestead, chatting happily. Paul and Karen were caretakers of Beltana Station, and Paul had asked if I could keep one of the old stone tanks on the property filled while he was away. Since Jimmy didn't seem to be in any hurry to leave, I invited him down to check the water level and have a beer. We ran the pump and sat around the circular stone ledge of the tank watching the water level rise as the sun set over the brown ranges.

Jimmy had grown up in Launceston and Melbourne and moved to the Outback in his early twenties. Most people did it the other way around, leaving the bush for the city. He was easy company, and had a detachment from this place that allowed him to see the idiosyncrasies of the people of the bush. It was refreshing to laugh and joke about them. We were not true 'bushies'; neither of us had grown up in the Outback, although Jimmy had now lived here for seven years. Still, I had never met anyone who had moved from the city and fallen as equally in love with the Outback as I had.

I didn't see Jimmy again before I flew home to see my parents in Brisbane. The city felt like an onslaught on the senses: too many people, too much advertising, too many lights. The supermarket felt like an alien place filled with too many options. Taking a shower every day seemed excessive and wasteful of water, and even toilets felt unnatural and unhygienic compared to squatting in nature. My body seized up, achy and sore from the sudden lack of movement, yet simultaneously I was itching with pent-up energy that I wasn't burning off, and felt compelled to run morning and night.

Eventually, feeling like I was languishing uselessly and needing to give myself something to do, I drove down to Byron Bay to plan the final and trickiest stretch of my journey into the busy beach town later that year.

It was the January school holidays and Byron was heaving with people. As I stood in The Farm, a local cafe, I could barely imagine walking back through here with ripped old jeans and tattered equipment with my five nervous and easily spooked wild camels. I was having heart palpitations just trying to order a coffee while hundreds of beautifully clad, wealthy, boho-loving visitors milled around. I felt suffocated. After the tough realities of survival in the desert, life here, with everyone enjoying their holidays and summer vibes, felt fake and hedonistic. I left without a coffee before I had a nervous breakdown.

I spent the following week driving every back road in the region, looking for the quietest streets to lead my string of camels to the beach. But there were none. With houses in Byron almost completely unaffordable, many people had moved out into the surrounding hills and hinterland. Small, winding, one-lane roads that I had known to be quiet country backstreets when I had lived here were now being driven by Porsches, BMWs and Mercedes at 100 km/hr. How the hell would I be able to walk my camels through here and stay alive? And before all this, I still had the problem of how to get over the Great Dividing Range. I pored over maps and drove and drove. A tentative route for the final, and probably hardest, leg of my journey took form— but staying safe in the traffic was a problem I would have to solve upon arrival.

Sam still lingered in my thoughts. I hadn't seen him in the two years since we'd broken up and was keen to spend time reconnecting with him over the summer. He was still living at our old apartment on the Gold Coast and our first meeting there was slightly glitchy and awkward, bringing up painful memories of our break-up. Afterwards he became distant, and the time that I had hoped and imagined that we might spend together didn't eventuate.

It wasn't until the end of the summer that I saw him again. I had called Sam when I was having major issues sighting my rifle for the second half of my trip. I was trying to find any way to keep Sam close. He agreed to drive to my dad's farm at Kilcoy to help me out. *Maybe this meant something, maybe he did still like me, and all of the unanswered messages and distant behaviour had meant nothing . . .* The two of us in the paddock at Kilcoy felt like we were back in the park in Adelaide, with Sam training me for the Heysen Trail. Finally, we were able to relax in each other's presence. I listened intently as he explained the process of sighting a rifle, as Murdoch had done, and which I'd promptly forgotten.

That night, I lay on the floor of my room and Sam lounged on the couch next to me, chatting about times past, as if none of the pain, heartache and deception of the last three years had ever happened. He told me of his plans to move to Canberra, and we spoke about the experiences we'd shared in the past, the moments of joy and adventure etched into our psyches forever. Nothing could obliterate those precious memories or the friendship that had begun when we were eighteen and still at school. Here we were, back at Kilcoy, where we'd been teenagers swimming in the dam naked at midnight and lying in the dewy grass staring up at the sky. I loved him as much now as I first had so youthfully back then. But I ached for him in the present tense, and not just the past. My heart was pounding. I badly wanted to make a move, but fear and uncertainty held me hostage. I didn't, I couldn't. Sam left to sleep in another room. I lay on my bed, wide awake, staring up at the ceiling. I desperately wanted to sneak into his room; I got up and paced about, stopping to press my ear against my door for any sounds of movement in the house. Should I, shouldn't I? Could he be lying awake thinking the same thing? I stayed standing, not knowing what to do, frozen in the darkness.

My mind raced. I had my trek to finish. I had both lost and gained so much from deciding to set off on my journey. I had hurt Sam and thrown away all that we had together, and now it seemed an injustice to him not to see it through. And an injustice to myself not to finish what I started. The thought of stopping now, only halfway through, was intolerable. I got back into bed and stared at the ceiling, unable to sleep.

The next day I said goodbye to Sam, thanked him for his help, and watched him drive away, wishing things could have been different.

Back in Brisbane, I became restless. I was itching to get back to the trip, yet dreading it at the same time. The first half of the journey had been so gruelling that I feared returning to Coober Pedy and resuming such hardship. I felt I had started to grow soft, accustomed again to sleeping in a real bed, under a roof, with fresh and delicious meals, Netflix and hot showers. I no longer knew what the cycle of the moon was doing, or where the constellations were in the sky. With too much time on my hands, a recurring anxiety made its way into my thoughts: what would I do with my life once the camel trek was over?

During my trek, my old high school had contacted me to say that the Year 9 students had written me letters, so I visited the school to pick these up. As I read them, I was amazed by the admiration the girls expressed and touched by their comments. Their own anxieties about the future were woven through the letters and mirrored my own. One girl wrote, *Being able to follow your passion is an incredible strength. I want to be able to just find my passion, let alone follow it. How did you do it? When did you know this was what you wanted to do?*

Another girl wrote that her parents really wanted her to do something in the medical field, a *safe job that will set me a secure future, but I am torn between doing something that I enjoy and something that I know is the right thing to do.*

I had no idea that my decision to choose an alternative path would be so inspirational. I felt like hugging each and every one of them and saying, *It doesn't matter, you are only in Year 9! You're not meant to know exactly what to do with the rest of your life. I still don't have a clue!*

The letters reminded me it was time to put my own worries aside. I had already walked 2351 kilometres with my five camels, and now it was time for the second leg of the journey— some 2600 kilometres more.

I left Brisbane, and in March, I took to the air with Paul and Karen in two light planes over the vast expanse of Beltana Station to find our camels. I spotted their forms in miniature below, and we marked a GPS coordinate of their location. Back on the ground, Paul and Karen rode out on motorbikes to muster the camels, while I stayed at the station yards to open the gates and wait for the mob to be herded in. They eventually appeared on the horizon, a spectacular sight, striding together with the mountain ranges in the background. As they drew closer, I recognised the familiar faces of my five friends. They all looked different with their sleek short summer coats, but I could not forget those faces. Jude turned his head to look at me, recognition dawning.

'Hey buddy!' I called out as he strolled sedately into the yards, tears welling in my eyes. As the bikes pushed the final camels in, I shut the gates.

I looked for my camels again among the mob and cautiously approached each of them in turn. They had just spent six months reassimilating to a wild setting, and I didn't want to overwhelm them with too much affection. Now that I stood before them, I could not believe my eyes. They were huge! They had all grown and put on a heap of weight since I'd released them five months ago. They looked spectacular.

I approached Charlie, my little teenage boy whom I had left with tired eyes, barely a hump, and hip bones protruding. He now stood tall, with a hump that looked like it had been magically conjured up with a wand. I left my hands down by my sides and let Charlie bring his face down to mine, sniffing my face deeply as I breathed out into his nostrils. It was a long, deep smelling of my face, a reading of my soul, as I relaxed and felt the connection between us. As I greeted the others I remembered why I loved these big, beautiful animals. I felt calm and sure in their presence. Even Clayton, who stood away from the mob in his own independent fashion, seemed to openly enjoy this human interaction.

Camels are amazing creatures. After roaming the vast expanse of Beltana Station for five months with nothing but other camels for company, I thought they may have reverted back to their wild ways, and I would be starting afresh with their training. But much to my surprise, it was as if no time had passed at all. They were perfectly happy to be saddled up again and get back to work.

While I waited for the weather to cool, I passed the rest of March and April on the station, exercising the camels, joining in on Paul and Karen's first trek for the season, tinkering with my equipment and making phone calls for the road ahead. During this time, Sam was like a movie on repeat in my brain. I couldn't let him go, but I was angry at myself for allowing the past to continually dominate my thoughts. I knew I couldn't spend the next six months of my walk fantasising about what may or may not be real. I had to know if I could keep burning this candle of hope. My unfaithfulness had pushed Sam away once, and now I knew it was up to me to lay my heart on the line and ask for him back.

I called him one night from my room on the station. I cut open my chest and dissected every hope and longing that had ever pulsed through my arteries. I had never got over him, never stopped regretting my actions, never stopped loving him through it all. I wanted us to be together, for us to get married and have children. But—and there always was a but with us—I still needed to finish this trip. I needed to see it through.

'What would you do afterwards, Soph? Move to Canberra with me? Find a paddock for the camels?' Sam said incredulously.

'Yes, I don't know . . . I guess so,' I stammered.

In that moment I would have done anything, even boxed up my own dreams, to be with him after the walk. But Sam sensed my hesitation. Fundamentally, he knew I wouldn't be happy to give it all up: the camels, the Outback, the wandering, the desire I felt to chase 'more', see 'more' and learn 'more'. Slowly and gently, he crushed all hope of us being together in the future. He had moved on. He was done. He was proud of me for following my dreams, but in that time he had been through another relationship. He simply wanted to remember our time with fondness rather than dredge up past wounds.

That was it—he didn't love me anymore. I had to accept it. I couldn't force love from him any more than I could force blood from a stone.

As much as it hurt, our conversation opened up a space within me. In no uncertain terms, and in more ways than one, I had to move on.

In the final weeks at Beltana before I left to return to Coober Pedy to resume my journey, Jimmy turned up at the station homestead again. News of my return must have spread through the bush telegraph. Again, he caught me unawares, wearing a daggy pair of shorts and an old work shirt, with the tray of my ute filled high with the station's rubbish.

'Do you want to come and burn the rubbish with me?' I asked, thinking what a peculiar invitation this was. I had never asked a guy out on a rubbish-burning date! Jimmy leapt into my ute with glee.

'I LOVE burning rubbish!' he said with abundant enthusiasm.

With the smell of burning diesel in the air and black smoke billowing around us, Jimmy and I chatted about life over the top of a wheelie bin, resting against the tray of my ute. It didn't seem there was much Jimmy didn't LOVE. His positivity was boundless.

His visits, under the guise of 'catching up with Paul and Karen', became more regular. One evening, the two of us went for a drive to a waterhole. We stopped on the way, as Jimmy had noticed a windmill leaking water. He climbed the steel ladder and adjusted the pump without hesitation. His confidence and ability impressed me; I wouldn't have had a clue what to do. He wasn't from the bush originally, but he certainly appeared comfortable here.

When we arrived at Puttapa Springs, the sun was setting. We lit a fire and spoke for hours until the trickle of water flowing off a rocky ledge into a small but deep waterhole beckoned us into the dark pool. I stripped down to my underwear and plunged in, with Jimmy close behind. The water was freezing and both of us were instantly covered in goose bumps. We huddled together as an excuse to keep warm, running our hands over one another's skin. I kissed him in the darkness, and when we drew apart he looked a little stunned.

'Well, what were you expecting when I suggested a swim in the waterhole at night?' I asked.

Jimmy grinned broadly, then leant in and kissed me again.

Jimmy still hadn't met the camels. When I had spoken of them, he seemed fairly uninterested. He'd told me he had no experience with horses, cattle or other large animals. His lack of enthusiasm over this one crucial component made me hesitate: I had no time for anyone who could not appreciate the camels.

Jimmy arrived one evening as the camels were out grazing in their hobbles around the homestead. The sun had just set and he walked out with me to gather them and bring them back to the yards.

I bent down next to Mac's front legs, undid his hobbles and linked him with the rope to Charlie. Without hesitation, Jimmy strode straight up to Jude. I barely let anyone else undo my camels' hobbles. They knew me and would quietly let me bend down in front of their legs, but I didn't know how they would react to a stranger.

Jimmy bent down in front of Jude's tall, thick front legs, apparently ignorant of the danger. I saw Jude freeze, his muscles tense, while this stranger entered his space. I held my breath, worried that if Jude didn't like him, Jimmy might be kicked or trampled in an instant. But Jude stayed very still as Jimmy fumbled with the hobbles, then rose back up with a winning smile on this face.

'That went well,' I said.

'I was shitting myself,' Jimmy admitted, handing me the hobbles.

Back at the yards, Jude lingered with the two of us. He was normally affectionate to me but reserved with strangers—yet here he was sinking into Jimmy's hand as Jimmy rubbed his neck. It seemed Jude had made his decision on Jimmy's character, but I reluctantly held myself aloof.

After a pause, I said awkwardly, 'Don't go getting too attached. I'm about to walk away.'

10

Back on New Tracks

**COOBER PEDY TO
MARREE—480 KM**

The day I left on the second half of my journey could not have been more different to the first. It was 2 May 2021, and a cold wind coated the sky in a thin veil of grey clouds that swept high across the open gibber-stone plains. Unlike my departure in April the previous year, this time I was not alone. Dad had flown from Brisbane to Adelaide, where I had picked him up and driven him six hours north to Beltana Station to meet with the convoy of vehicles heading a further eight hours north-west to Coober Pedy to see me off. Karen had carted my camels in her truck accompanied by some of her trekking volunteers and Jimmy had followed in his own car.

I said goodbye to Karen the day before I set off, hugging her tightly and thanking her for looking after my camels and giving them the best opportunity to put on weight over the summer.

Dad and Jimmy, and the station managers, Pat and Jose, stood waiting to see me off from the familiar surrounds of Mount Clarence Station. I was ready to leave. I said a brief goodbye to Jimmy for the day, as he planned to drive out and camp with me for a night before he headed back to the Flinders Ranges. Dad wouldn't be seeing me for some time, and I stifled tears as I said goodbye to him, touched that he'd been so keen to come to Coober Pedy to see me off. He gripped me tightly in a stiff hug that hid the emotion he felt behind it.

'Good luck, kiddo! Keep messaging me on the sat phone. See you when you get closer to the coast.'

We were back on the road, me and my gang of five humps. I had changed the order of the string slightly. Jude remained at the front, my best bud and leader, with his goofy camel smile. Clayton was now behind Jude, ears pinned back with a look of concerned concentration, as if he was silently and obsessively counting the number of kilometres in his head. Delilah was next, with the usual 'resting bitch face' she assumed while walking that read, 'What we're doing is the worst thing in the world'. Then there was Charlie, who looked around innocently, like a small child off on a big adventure. And finally, Mac at the back, looking stoic and handsome, pulling back on his rope and plodding slowly and sedately at the rear.

It felt good to be walking again. The act of movement dissipated the apprehension that I had felt in the lead-up to leaving. Questions had been whirring in my head: *Could I do it again? Did I have what it took, after getting 'soft' over the summer?* Now, with the lead rope in my hand and my string behind me, I was swamped with familiarity. *I know how to do this. I can do this.*

I thought about Jimmy as I walked. Our time together had happened so quickly and unexpectedly. After the night at the waterhole, I thought it would be a summer fling. I was the most geographically unobtainable person imaginable. I was also quite used to taking off, leaving a relationship, or ruining one to go travelling. I had invited Jimmy to see me off at Coober Pedy and never expected to see him beyond that. But now he had agreed to visit me at William Creek—223 kilometres and two weeks walk away—to bring hay for my camels. As I progressed east, my walk would be taking me closer and closer to him in the Flinders Ranges, without actually dipping that far south. Then there would be a turning point, where I stopped walking towards Jimmy and started walking away. I figured I may as well make the most of this summer fling, because there would come a point where I would simply walk too far away.

On day three, we crossed the Stuart Highway—the black vein of tarmac splitting the country in half from Port Augusta to Darwin. We were now about to tackle the eastern portion of the country. The landscape on the other side of the highway was something out of a *Mad Max* film, and very typically synonymous with the strangeness of Coober Pedy. The ground was pockmarked with opal diggings, like a mountain range of miniature hills dotted with old trucks and mining equipment. It looked like a staged movie set rather than a site of modern mineral exploration. We took a track that wove through the diggings, heading for the Kanku–Breakaways Conservation Park. Once on the main road that cuts through the park, I had my first taste of what it was like to be a spectacle.

A car approached and slowed, all five occupants hanging out the windows to goggle at us, iPhones in hand, filming as they drove past. It felt strange to be so 'on show'. Up until then I had taken private station tracks and the deserted Anne Beadell Highway through the centre of the desert. The pandemic restrictions had lifted somewhat, and it seemed that most of the Australian population, in a desperate attempt to flee the cities and take a holiday, had escaped into the Outback. I kept on moving with the camels, knowing that we had a big day's walk ahead of us if we were to reach the other side of the Breakaways.

'Where are you heading?' the person in the next car that passed me yelled.

'Do you mind if I take a photo?' asked a lady from the car after that.

I answered the questions politely but kept on walking with the camels. I had been glancing behind me, continually checking the camels' loads as I walked. Jude's saddle seemed to be creeping forward on a progressively vertical lean towards his neck, while Clayton's load hung substantially towards the left. I would have to stop. I sat Jude down and strapped his front legs by the side of the road, hoping that a car wouldn't stop and disturb me as I fixed the load. One by one I lifted each item off his saddle, loosened the girth and heaved the saddle backward so that it was sitting evenly on his hump. I then made a feeble attempt to pull Clayton's load back towards the right. I was puffing by the end; I had lost much of my fitness over the summer. The camels' summer vacation contributed to this problem, too. Their humps had grown so large from the extra feed that their saddles weren't fitting well.

I wouldn't make it to the eastern side of the Breakaways today. I wasn't entirely sad about this—the landscape was stunning, like being on Mars. We were crossing a huge open gibber-stone plain, out of which rose the worn-down remnants of mountains. Some were flat-topped, others were cone shaped, but all varied in colour from deep rust red through to orange, pink and pure white, like mountains of chalk standing out against the brilliant blue sky.

I followed the camels as they grazed, affection swelling within me as I recognised the arid plants they were eating: dead finish and bush plum. I may have even said, 'Hello my old friends!' I was only three days back on the trek and already I was talking to no one.

I could feel my world shrinking again: just me and the camels. There were no more of the to-do lists that plague everyday life. No more of the angst I had felt over summer, questioning what the trip meant and what I would do once it finished. I was back to the calming presence that daily walking and camping brings. Life was now focused around feeding my animals and feeding myself in order that we might every day put one foot in front of the other and keep moving forward to our next camp. Ironically, I felt that whatever the 'more' was that I seemed to be searching for in life, I was actually satisfied with less.

The next morning I adjusted the saddle pads on the metal frames so that the camels' saddles were fitting marginally better. The Breakaways fell away behind us as we skirted Coober Pedy, making our way towards the Oodnadatta Track along a portion of the Dingo Barrier Fence, or the Dog Fence as it is commonly known. I looked up at its tall wire mesh, thinking what a huge number of hours must have gone into constructing and maintaining this 5614-kilometre fence that stretched from the Great Australian Bight all the way into Queensland. As I passed through a gate that allowed access to the northern side of the fence, a signboard said it was the longest man-made structure in the world. It originally had been built in 1884 as a rabbit-proof fence, until graziers to the south lobbied for it to be extended in height and length to keep dingoes out. As I knew from the Western Australian pastoralists, dingoes and sheep do not mix well, so this was a gate I definitely didn't want to forget to shut.

Besides the fence's imposing structure, there was nothing: not a tree or shrub in sight, just barren rocky ground as far as the eye could see. It was as if I had walked from the Martian landscape of the Breakaways to the moon. I had seen vistas with endless horizons during my time in the desert, but this was completely different. The treeless expanse made it feel impossible to judge distance, and I felt as though I could almost see the curvature of the Earth. There would be no trouble losing the camels in this kind of landscape—but where to tie them up at night? My topographical maps showed I was passing through creek lines, but in reality, most were eroded washouts, as bare and stark as the plains that surrounded them.

The Oodnadatta Track is one of three main outback roads in central Australia on the bucket-list itinerary for caravanners and four-wheel drivers. I had decided to take the Oodnadatta Track simply because it was the most direct route to take me to the south end of Kati Thanda–Lake Eyre. By the end of my first day on the Oodnadatta, I had passed more cars than during my entire six months walking across Western Australia the previous year!

Slowly I grew used to being a spectacle to be gawked at. In the mornings, when the day stretched out before us and I felt fresh, it was nice to have the added energy boost of a human interaction. Sometimes an entire row of caravans would pull off the track to talk to me. People were enthused and curious, wanting to know all about where I'd come from, why I was doing what I was doing, whether I was doing it for a cause, what had been some of the difficulties, what camels were like to work with, and what I ate on the road. My passion for both camels and adventure shone through, and after months of inconspicuous walking through the Great Victoria Desert, I was humbled that people were interested in what I was doing.

As I made my way towards the small township of William Creek, another lady stopped to ask where I was going. I told her that I'd reach the town in several days.

'But there are no campsites between here and William Creek,' she replied with great concern. 'How will you do it?'

'I'll camp where I stop.'

'But there will be no amenities!' She looked as if she was going to start hyperventilating—how could I possibly survive somewhere other than a designated campsite?

'It's okay,' I tried to reassure her. 'We've walked from Western Australia.'

The woman seemed to be in a state of complete shock and drove away before I gave any more distressing answers.

Eventually I got sick of people and decided to go cross-country for a time. The gibber plains had turned into small low sand dunes. I arrived at a cattle grid on the road, and traced the line of the fence around to the gate. As I unhitched the latch, I noticed a white Copley Bush Bakery sticker and a zip-lock bag containing a note from Jimmy: *Sophie, I hope everything is going well! Can't wait to see you in William Creek! Jimmy xoxo.*

It was the first of a trail of stickers and notes always placed at a gate that Jimmy knew only I would be crossing through. They were short and sweet, written on the back of a torn bit of a Coopers Pale Ale beer carton. Jimmy had stopped again and again on the road home, not only to leave notes, but also to check for me that there was a gate for the camels to pass by a grid, a concern he knew was ever-present in my mind.

I headed up and over a dune, leading the camels cross-country into a swale parallel to the road in order to avoid the traffic. Only one sand dune across from the busy track, I felt again as if I was in a world of my own. The country was experiencing what bush folk refer to as 'a good year'. The dead acacia bushes that revealed the severe drought of the previous years now formed shelters for healthy clumps of lush green ruby-red saltbush, bursting with little berries of all different colours, red, purple, orange and yellow. I picked and ate them, enjoying their salty sweetness as I crisscrossed the dunes, navigating my way up and down the sand hills and across the claypans between. The natural world around me made me feel alive and curious again. I was enjoying observing all the new plants that had come about as a result of the rain, and the change of topography. The camels were more settled, the country was green and open, and there was no constant worry over feed or losing my camels in thick bush.

As the Oodnadatta Track turned a corner, I found myself back walking on the road. After one night of rain along the

Dog Fence, it had been nothing but glorious sunny autumn days. This day was no different, and I was revelling in the enjoyment of the walk. A caravan slowed and a lady got out to take some photos and comment on how wonderful it was to see the camels.

'Are they always this well behaved?' she said.

'Yes, most of the time,' I called back happily. The lady got back in her car, and waved as she passed by. Shortly after, a four-wheel drive came up behind us but didn't stop, then another. By the time a third car had sped past us, Jude was getting agitated, and the camels had jogged up behind me. I looked back, telling them to steady, and noticed that both Jude and Clayton's back girths had come undone.

No problem, I thought. Camels have three girths on the saddle, and the back one is only ever done loosely. *When I get to the bottom of this slope, I'll tie them to a tree and do their girths back up.* In the split second that this thought crossed my mind, the joy of the day came crashing down around me.

Suddenly, Jude's saddle slipped forward off his hump. Feeling the load fall onto his neck, he took fright and started bucking. Saddle bags were flying, and Jude's saddle was now careering around his neck in wild circles. He bucked and bucked and somehow managed to completely rid himself of his saddle while I dropped the safety control of the precious nose line. All I had was the lead rope, and in a situation that was all too familiar, I was being pulled off my feet by Jude's strength and dragged along the ground. My head was bouncing along gibber stones, my body trailing along limply behind my bucking and cavorting camels. From my position, head scraping along the dirt, I could see Jude's powerful back legs and thundering feet only inches away from crushing my skull. Flashbacks of losing control of my camels came streaming through my consciousness and I gripped the end of the lead rope with fierce determination. There was no way I was going to be the girl whose camels ran off on her twice. I was NOT LETTING GO! Even the threat of being trampled to death did not loosen my grip on the lead rope as my body was dragged horizontally on the rough ground by all five camels roped together.

Miraculously, Jude must have felt my determination. The anchor that my body created caused him to slow down enough for me to find my feet. Puffing and panting, I grabbed his loose nose line and regained control of the string. But the disaster wasn't over yet. Clayton's saddle was also on a precarious lean towards his neck. I sat Jude down, followed by Clayton—but as Clayton dropped to his knees to sit, the saddle slipped forward and the whole scene with Jude repeated itself. Clayton's neck whirled around in circles as he tried to free himself of the terrifying saddle that now dangled from his neck. Pack bags were being torn and girths snapped, and finally he was rid of it all as well. I stood in a state of shock and disbelief, looking at two completely naked camels at the front of my string who were foaming at the mouth and wide-eyed with terror. I looked down at the lead rope and nose line still grasped in my white-knuckled hand. Blood was pouring from a fingernail that had been wrenched off and was dangling by a thread of skin. I felt my head; no blood. Amazingly, besides my finger, I was seemingly unhurt, although there would be bruises that appeared later. The torn remnant of a nail was by far a better loss than my five precious camels.

Shaking, I walked to the nearest tree and tied up the camels. This time I wasn't furious. It hadn't been their fault, but mine— my own badly fitted saddles, which I should have addressed sooner. I had to remain calm. I wanted to stop right where I was, lie down on the ground and cry, but I had learnt from months past that this was a futile act. I had to pick myself up and keep on going. My calmness surprised me. I didn't call Sam this time; I could deal with this on my own. I spoke softly and calmly to the camels as I sat them down. I found my first aid kit and roughly taped my finger. I then went about the slow and painful process of retrieving the saddles and gear and hauling them back to the camels.

Two hours later, I had made temporary fixes on what I could, tightened the girths to almost breaking point, then stood the camels up and a little nervously and shakily continued to walk. The Oodnadatta Track was now crossing Anna Creek Station—the world's largest working cattle station. It would not have been a good place to lose my camels.

The two extra hours I'd spent resaddling Jude and Clayton meant it was late in the afternoon when I found myself looking for a camp at Anna Creek. I was exhausted, the adrenaline of the day having sapped my energy in its lowest ebb. In the middle of the wide, heavily vegetated creek line, I could feel the camels on edge, never comfortable in an area they couldn't see out of. I heard a convoy of cars approaching and made a large arc with the camels so that they could see the vehicles coming from behind. All six four-wheel drives stopped, and people piled out. *Damn!* I didn't want to talk to anyone. My camels were feeling spooked, it was getting near sunset and we still hadn't found a camp.

'We heard from some other travellers that we might meet you on the track! We have a lady in our group who is desperate to meet some camels!' a man exclaimed. The usual bombardment of questions followed from other members of the group.

One bloke piped up, 'We thought you'd have boyfriends hiding in the bushes with guns.' His strange comment rubbed me up the wrong way.

'You're so pretty to be doing something like this,' said a woman who was blithely patting Charlie, oblivious to the fact that she was standing in a dangerous position, easily knocked over or kicked if the camels were to spook. I was irrationally irritated that they couldn't read the camels' mood.

I was over it. I was tired and battered and did not want to answer stupid questions. The assumption that I couldn't possibly be doing this trip without the aid of a boyfriend annoyed me, as did the idea that a girl would have to be big and bloke-ish to do this trip alone.

'Sorry, I have to get going and make camp,' I told them firmly, containing my anger and pushing past them to carry on walking. They seemed disappointed and got back into their cars, accelerating behind me and spooking the camels further as they drove out of the creek.

It was a relief to reach William Creek the following afternoon. I could hear a Cessna above us, coming in to land from a scenic tourist flight over Lake Eyre, as I skirted around the busy airstrip of the little one-pub outpost. The Cessna gently touched down on the tarmac as I located the steel-railed cattle yards at the far side of the runway. At the same time, Jimmy appeared, grinning ear to ear, driving a Hilux ute with a huge bale of hay hanging out the back of the open canopy.

I hugged and kissed him and exploded with the news of the previous day's ordeal and showed him my torn fingernail. He sympathised, but I could tell by his expression that he didn't fully comprehend the severity of the situation—how bad it might have been if I had let the camels go, or been trampled. How could he? How could anyone really understand what I went through on a daily basis?

My disappointment was short-lived. Jimmy went about unloading the hay and cleaning the water trough, filling it for the camels. This practicality reminded me of watching him fix the windmill. He was focused and confident with his hands, and I liked that he clearly knew to put the camels first. He quietly helped me unload the gear from their backs and listened for my instructions as to the order and position that each saddle was to be placed. I could tell he was making mental notes so that he knew my routine for next time. I removed the camels' halters and showed him how I wound their ropes. He studied me, then neatly replicated my movements, hanging the rolled ropes in an orderly fashion along the railing next to each camel's halter. I could tell he appreciated things being done carefully and methodically.

With the camels looked after, Jimmy pulled out a few beers from an esky that I could see was packed full of food that he had brought for my rest days. It felt nice to be in his presence, to know that he would cook and help me do the often tedious jobs that came with stopping for a break, like repairing saddlery, doing my washing and filling the jerries with water.

We climbed the rail of the yards with our beers.

'Cheers,' we said to one another as we clinked cans. The camels knew by now that yards meant rest days. After a couple of mouthfuls of hay, they were frisky. The temperature was dropping, dust hung in the air and the golden light of the setting sun illuminated their antics. Mac nipped Jude on the bum and Jude started running. Before long they were all running in circles around the yards, playing chasey with one another. They bucked and farted and ran with their necks outstretched and lips flopping while Jimmy and I cheered and laughed from the railing.

'Get him, Delilah! Go, Maccie boy!'

I was inching closer and closer to the Flinders Ranges, heading in the direction of Marree. Still, I had never anticipated just how willing Jimmy would be to drive hundreds of kilometres back and forth to see me every time I took a break. A 300-kilometre round trip on rough dirt roads seemed to mean nothing to him in order to drop hay for the camels and see me for a couple of nights. At William Creek I had recognised, almost begrudgingly, that it was actually nice to have a companion when I stopped. Jimmy had done a lot of outback travel. He knew the area, and many of the station owners and locals, and through his connections he was able to organise hay and yards for the camels, and places to stay. I made the most of it, knowing that there'd be a point where I would walk too far away from his radius. Our time together felt like an odd kind of travel romance.

After William Creek, Jimmy arrived to meet me at Coward Springs, another tourist hub on the Oodnadatta Track, with date palms and artesian pools. He appeared as suddenly as he always did, this time from the back of a random tourist's car, having hitched a ride two kilometres up the track from where he had parked, to walk the short distance to the Coward Springs yards with me. After saying hello to me, he approached the camels. They bent their long necks down to greet him, smelling his face deeply and gently. I could sense their ease in his presence.

Their affection didn't just come from the boxes of fresh vegetable treats he brought them every time we stopped. It was more than that. They liked him. And their approval made me like him all the more.

Leaving Coward Springs, we made our way towards the south end of Kati Thanda–Lake Eyre. Soon the shimmering shoreline of the salt lake came into view. From ground level, it was hard to imagine the sheer size of the lake—one of the largest salt lakes in the world. In the distance, I could see where the salty crust merged with a shallow inch of water that disappeared into the mirage of the horizon.

We crossed yellow sand dunes covered in poached egg daisies, wildflowers that literally looked like a cartoon poached egg on a stalk. I found a line of decaying sleepers marking the old Ghan railway line, and felt like I was following in the footsteps of the early cameleers—men from India, Pakistan and Afghanistan, who worked strings of camels to haul the huge railway sleepers that I was now walking across. The Ghan Railway, named after the 'Afghan' cameleers, now takes a different route that mirrors the Stuart Highway, connecting Adelaide to Darwin. The remnants of the line I was following were from the time when locomotives needed access to underground water for the steam engines.

I camped that night next to its old sleepers, a reminder that much of the country here would not have been settled if it were not for the camels and cameleers. As the sun grew low on the horizon and the camels grazed peacefully, two utes pulled up. Out jumped four people dressed in khaki uniforms. One of them introduced himself as Sam from the Arabana Rangers team. I had been in contact with him about crossing Finniss Springs, which was Aboriginal land.

'We'll come back tomorrow night and do a barbecue for you, if you'd like?' he said as he passed me a beer and they stayed to talk for a while.

The next night, chops, sausages and chicken wings were sizzling on a hot plate on the fire. Sam was teaching me some words in the Arabana language as we all huddled around the flames, smelling the delicious cooking meat. They were a newly formed ranger team, and Sam spoke with passion about the importance of the water table in this area. Although it is one of the driest parts of the country, underneath lies the Great Artesian Basin, from the depths of which fresh water bubbles up, forming mound springs surrounded by crowns of reeds in the middle of the gibber plains. But the springs that had once bubbled vigorously in the days of Sam's father had dropped significantly.

'Mining activity in northern Queensland can affect our water supply down here, thousands of kilometres away,' Sam explained earnestly. It was horrible to imagine that without the springs this landscape could become a new man-made desert. Not the sort I would ever want to encounter with my camels.

The next day I turned off the Oodnadatta Track and wove my way through a series of these life-giving mound springs. Sam's point became very real to me when I connected with a pipeline that pumped artesian water for BHP.

Whether it was my conversation with the rangers the previous night, or the energy in the area itself, I felt the familiar prickling feeling that strong spirits resided in the area. I felt there was a power to Finniss Springs, a power in the landscape I was walking through.

As further confirmation of my feelings, the next morning I was visited by an old Aboriginal man, who turned up at my camp just as I was about to retrieve the camels for saddling. He gave me a one-toothed smile and introduced himself as Reg, a local Elder in the Marree area.

'I've come to warn you that I've seen a big bull camel in the area. You got a rifle?' he asked.

I reassured Reg that I had one and was prepared.

'Which way you going?'

I told him and Reg bent over with a stick and drew a mud map of the area in the dirt.

'You see this mountain? This is known as the Pregnant Lady. At her base is where her waters broke and formed the springs. This mountain behind you here is the Crested Pigeon, where men's business took place.'

I delayed my departure until late morning, lingering to talk to Reg, fascinated by his knowledge of the area. His keen eyes pointed out circles of stones where Aboriginal camps had been, perhaps hundreds of years ago. His roguish appearance belied his intelligence, and I discovered that he had authored a book and received a Medal of the Order of Australia.

That night I camped next to the pipeline, and the spirits visited me once more. I dreamed that I was pregnant, to whom I did not know. I didn't realise until my belly was well and truly swollen. In my dream, Jimmy was there; he was accepting and supportive that I was pregnant to a stranger. When I woke, I felt disconcerted by the wanderings of my sleeping mind. I couldn't stop thinking about it all day as I walked with the camels. This year I would be turning thirty-three. I could feel the beginnings of a ticking biological clock.

I had hoped I would have children with Sam one day, but I wasn't ready to relinquish the call of adventure. What did this time with Jimmy mean? Was there a future in it? Or was it just a romance born of the lonely life I was leading on the road?

I was walking towards Clayton Station, where I had first fallen in love with camel trekking and these wide open spaces. The station where my life had made an abrupt turn, and had decided I wasn't ready to be settled, that I wanted more, and this is what I wanted to be doing, walking Australia with camels. The rocky treeless plains made the sky feel huge and endless, and my thoughts of past, present and future danced about in the infinite space.

11

The Strzelecki Desert

MARREE TO CAMERON CORNER—371 KM

A loud crack of thunder made me jump. I stopped the camels, reached up on tiptoe and opened one of Jude's pack bags to retrieve my Driza-Bone. I pulled the oilskin coat tightly around me and trudged forward into the wind and rain. The storm had been circling for some time. I'd hoped it might miss us, but no such luck. Our path had met up with the Dog Fence again and we were traversing a high, bare, rocky plateau. I could see lightning dancing on the horizon to our north across Kati Thanda–Lake Eyre. The last crack of thunder sounded right above us and had me worried. There was nothing out here except the fence, me and the camels. The metal saddles on the camels' backs were by far the tallest point around. I prayed for the lightning to stay where it was, in the distance to the north.

Please, please don't hit me or the camels. There was nowhere to take shelter. All I could do was walk on.

Luckily it did remain in the distance, dancing over the lake, and by afternoon the sun had returned once more. We had crossed from Muloorina Station onto Clayton Station and were making our way on station tracks towards the Clayton and then Murnpeowie homesteads. These were all vast cattle stations in the north-east of South Australia. It was a reprieve from the busy Oodnadatta Track and I was relieved to be alone in nature once more.

The camels seemed to be a point of curiosity with the local wildlife everywhere they went. Dingoes stopped and stared, bearded dragons cocked their heads sideways to look up at the enormity of the camels, and the day that the storm rolled through, a papa emu and his two young emus followed us along the fence for over ten kilometres. They swaggered along comically, checking us out, darting right and left with their rear-end plumage bobbing.

I took several days off at Clayton. Jimmy arrived to visit and I enjoyed showing him parts of the station I knew; he, in turn, enjoyed introducing me to the locals of Marree. The township was only 120 kilometres from where he lived— basically his backyard, by outback standards.

The wind was increasing in cold ferocity when I left Clayton Station's familiar yards. Jimmy had stayed to help me saddle the camels, which I was thankful for, as a strong gust had just lifted off all my carefully placed blankets and strewn them across the dirt. We started again, Jimmy holding down blankets while I carted saddles across to pin them down. I was envious watching him pull away in the comfort of a heated car, protected from the biting wind.

The camels and I set off, following a mud map of the station that Shane, the owner, had drawn for me, showing a back track that would lead us directly to Murnpeowie homestead.

'Halfway along, you'll reach Clayton Mumpie bore. There's an old camp there, so you'll be able to have a night inside. The hot water might even be turned on and there should be power connected,' Shane had told me.

I held this warming thought in my head, picturing an idyllic little cottage as I set out across the station, buffeted by the cold wind.

After a big twenty-seven-kilometre day, visualising this cosy, warm cottage that I seemed to have conjured in my imagination out of nowhere, we reached a desolate scene. Clayton Mumpie bore looked like a post-apocalyptic trailer park in an American zombie movie. A seedy old train carriage and two grubby demountable buildings made up a U-shape with a radio tower to the side, on a bleak expanse of dirt. Inside the train carriage was a kitchen in which everything was covered in ten centimetres of dust. I couldn't get any of the lights to work, nor did the hot water seem to be on when I checked the shower block. I opened the creaky door to the demountable that contained bedrooms with dusty upturned mattresses. It felt as if some kind of disaster had struck and the inhabitants had left in a hurry. It gave me the creeps and I got out of there immediately. I would definitely be sleeping outside again tonight.

I put the camels in the holding paddock nearby and returned to the buildings, which did at least offer some protection from the wind. I lit a fire and unrolled my swag. It still felt spooky and lonely without the camels for company. I wondered why I had been so excited about reaching these buildings. I was much happier when I camped on my tarp in the bush with my animals. I didn't miss electricity—I had my head torch—and I was perfectly comfy and cosy in my swag. I rarely even missed a hot shower, being quite happy to wash with my 'shammy' every night. I drifted off to sleep, unsettled by the creaks from the buildings, and missing the sound of the camels chewing their cud around me.

Murnpeowie Station had been part of the Sir Thomas Elder lease, which had included Beltana, where my camels had been agisted for the summer. In the 1800s, the Scottish-born Elder's land holdings in Australia exceeded the size of his entire country of birth. It was for these far-flung sheep runs like Mumpie, as it was fondly known, that he imported and bred camels. Long strings of camels would cart wool for export from Murnpeowie and return from the terminus of the Ghan railway line with supplies for the station. Again I felt like I was exploring the pages of outback history firsthand.

Mumpie's driveway led to another of the famous outback tracks, the Strzelecki. Over the next five days, the cold winter wind continued to whip across the landscape, unabated by any form of tree. The blue sky felt immense and was met by a blanket of green below. It had rained here, and every form of spiky but succulent burr and prickle was growing between the ochre gibber stones. While the camels devoured the plants with their soft lips, unperturbed by the huge thorns, I wondered at this landscape of boom and bust. I was incredibly thankful that I was traversing this country in a 'good year' after rain. I passed the turn-off for an old, abandoned outstation called Mount Hopeless, named after a nearby rocky rise where Edward Eyre had exclaimed 'cheerless and hopeless indeed was the prospect before us'. I could imagine it must have felt that way to early settlers trying to sustain flocks of sheep in this country during a drought.

For twenty kilometres I barely passed a shrub, and in the afternoon, I was forced to detour several kilometres off the track to find some bushes to tie the camels to. Firewood was also scarce. I made a meagre smoky fire from twigs and dried cow poo to cook my dinner. It was better than nothing: camping without a fire was a sad and lonely affair.

Several days later the ferocious winter wind suddenly dropped, timed perfectly with an abrupt change in the landscape. I was entering an area known as The Cobbler. It was a desert landscape like no other. The rocks were replaced by a maze of small sand mounds, roughly three metres high, with several metres in between. On top of the mounds grew nitre bush, a shrub that seemed to be only found in the poorest of soils.

Visible in the sides of these sand hills were snake and lizard holes. It felt like a jungle of sand. Later, the station owner of nearby Lindon Station told me that the entire Cobbler portion of his property was unusable for running stock, as it was simply too difficult to muster here.

At the cattle grid on the Lindon boundary, I hadn't been able to find the gate in the fence line, so I pulled a loose star picket out of the sand to peel a section of the fence back to pass through with the camels. I was fiddling with the post and wire, trying to replace what I had undone, when I heard a car approach. I looked around uncertainly. Jimmy got out of the car, his customary grin stretched from ear to ear.

On his last visit, we had arranged that he would hitch a ride up the Strzelecki Track and walk with me and the camels for five days. I was both nervous and excited. No one had managed to join me for a section of my trek, and I was looking forward to being able to share a little of what my adventure was actually like.

Star picket and fencing pliers in hand, I shook my head in disbelief and laughed as the car drove off. Jimmy was standing by the side of a remote outback track, clad in a hoodie and jeans, carrying nothing but a small plastic bag containing a pair of socks, jocks, a change of shirt, a toothbrush—and some fresh fruit for me. It was a stark contrast to the tourists I saw charging up and down these outback tracks with everything, literally including a kitchen sink. Clearly, Jimmy was not a high-maintenance guy. Clearly, he was also expecting to be sleeping in my swag.

I was also excited because we would be deviating from the Strzelecki Track and following the Strzelecki Creek on its parallel journey northward, before I then headed east along the road to Cameron Corner, where Queensland and New South Wales meet South Australia. It would involve several days of navigating cross-country, away from the road, and charting relatively untouched and remote wilderness.

With his small plastic bag of possessions stashed easily in one of Jude's saddle bags, Jimmy slipped into the routine of camel trekking with me. He was a natural explorer and had an equal love and excitement for discovering new landscapes. Two days after his arrival, we had wound our way through the maze of sand hills of The Cobbler and were standing on the embankment of Strzelecki Creek, staring down at the remnants of a chimney and several crumbling stone walls from an old homestead. Carraweena Ruins was marked on my maps, but I doubted many people had ever visited this place. There had been no sign of tracks leading through the creek, and the terrain was too rough for a vehicle.

'It's remote out here even now,' I marvelled. 'Imagine living here in this small stone hut in the 1800s.'

'There's none of the stone used to build the buildings here in the creek,' Jimmy observed. 'They would have had to cart materials a long way.'

'Andrew from Lindon Station told me there used to be a Cobb & Co. route through here.'

It had seemed a constant theme in my travels that in the 1800s and early 1900s, the Outback had been a much busier place and more people called these arid interior regions home. Aside from the tourists who hurtled through towing monstrous rigs, covering huge kilometres in an attempt to squeeze in all of the Outback's highlights, these places off the few well-worn tracks were all but empty—lonely and forgotten. Carving out an existence in these remote locations was a life that few on Australia's coastal fringes understood. My trip had given me a new insight and admiration for this way of life. Jimmy, like me, had grown up in a city, yet understood and appreciated the history of the bush. As we walked, we spoke more about all the different outback characters we had met, their quirks, colourful natures and steadfast grit. Who would replace these icons of the bush in years to come, when everyone wanted a softer and easier life?

The Strzelecki creek bed was wide—perhaps a kilometre or so in places. In its centre was a strip of pure white sand, like a natural highway leading us north along its bed. In the afternoon it started to drizzle, and soon the drizzle turned to rain. I pulled on my Driza-Bone, but Jimmy was getting wet. Even the rain could not dampen Jimmy's positive attitude. He pushed on in front of us and we chatted away excitedly. Soon we were all soaking wet. The felt on my Akubra was sodden, my jeans clung to me, and the camels looked sad as rain dripped down their long eyelashes. I called a halt for the day and Jimmy and I went about unsaddling. He knew the routine now and we barely spoke a word to one another, working together as a team to do it at record speed in the wet.

We sat huddled under the shelter, laughing and watching the rain fall. I thought of all the times I had sat huddled under this same tarp on my own, looking out at the rain. I wouldn't have wanted to swap those occasionally lonely times; they had been tough but empowering. But now with company—human company—and the joy and laughter that Jimmy brought, I had to admit that I was far less miserable on this rainy afternoon.

By the time we had saddled the next morning, the mist that had formed in the early hours had cleared, revealing a glorious sunny winter's day. As we made our way up the creek, our conversation was light and easy. We were like two eager kids exploring the beauty of the natural world. We paused so I could take photos of wild budgerigars nesting in the hollows of gum trees. Deep down I'd wondered whether this was more than a temporary romance, but the tranquillity of Strzelecki Creek completely vanquished thoughts of the future, just as the rain from the previous evening had been swept away. All that mattered was that we were experiencing this untouched corner of the country together, right now. I admitted to Jimmy that this had probably been the most scenic stretch of my entire journey.

That night we sipped port by the fire and admired the broad full moon rising golden over the creek. It was like being in our own little world, hidden and secluded in the creek's meandering midst.

The next day we left its sanctuary to be greeted by an even more spectacular scene. As we had walked along the creek line, we had no idea that the red sand dunes that now surrounded it on either side were completely blanketed in a sea of wildflowers. This was an Outback I could never have imagined I would get to see. In the Great Victoria Desert, I had seen the landscape beginning to creep back to life—but never like this, in full bloom. The rolling dunes were coated by a sea of yellow, white and green, the camels almost tripping over themselves to take huge mouthfuls as they walked. If Jimmy hadn't been here, it would have been a sight that I would have held in my solitary memory, but his presence meant we had shared this special portion of the trip.

'I can come and visit you at Cameron Corner,' he told me before we parted ways on the Strzelecki Track.

'Really? That's a long drive . . .' Still, I had imagined he might say this. Yes, it was a long way, but it was most likely the last destination he could feasibly see me before I entered Queensland and slipped even further away.

'It's not that far. I can even bring up your food supplies if you tell me what you want.'

On the Strzelecki Track Jimmy stuck out his thumb and hitched a ride home with his local town mechanic, who was, coincidentally, recovering a broken-down vehicle. The silence of the bush descended once more, and I was left alone to digest my feelings, standing on top of a dune with my camels. I thought of the times in Western Australia when I had left stations, or when Greg, Murdoch and the Oak Valley Rangers had driven away from me. I had felt like the silence of the desert might drown me. I didn't feel that way any longer. In fact, I felt like I had a busy social life out here with Jimmy's regular visits.

So, I'd get to see him one last time. I was looking forward to it. The week had been enjoyable, but above all else, his company had been easy. We had stepped into a rhythm with one another, functioning as a team. He hadn't felt like a visitor but rather a participant, one of the herd.

I took out my diary and sat in the shade of an acacia bush. Delilah lay next to me. We were having a day off from walking, and after eating her fill of juicy succulents, she lay on her side like a giant awkward dog, belly bulging, legs outstretched, farting in a very unladylike fashion. I looked out at the wildflowers that surrounded us and then opened my journal. A postcard fell out.

> Dear Sophie,
> Thank you and your five camels for letting me come
> walking and talking for the last five days! Strez Creek
> was wicked and a trip I'll remember forever!
> Jimmy xx
> Address: (About) 300 km north of Lyndhurst up the
> Strez, 5732 SA

His words touched me. Early in my trip, I felt like I had been the only one who was inspired to explore the country by camels. No matter how much I had hoped that Sam would be part of my dream, I had failed to persuade him of its plausibility or romance. Others had valued the concept of the trip, and even Sam, I knew, appreciated what the trip meant to me, but no one had shared it with me.

Jimmy understood it now, firsthand, like no one else ever would.

I was travelling through desert again, but it had little comparison to my crossing of the Great Victoria. This month on the road was proving to be very social indeed. From several messages from sat phone to sat phone, I had organised to cross paths with fellow camel trekker John Elliott, who was attempting to be the first to take his camels to every state in Australia. By the looks of his social media posts, he was also attempting a camel pub crawl of Australia! He was heading westward with his string of camels, while I was heading east. When we had spoken, it seemed astounding that we would both be crossing the country on separate expeditions in the same year. We simply had to make our routes cross so that we could meet.

I first met John as he leapt out of a car. He had known we would cross paths today and, having found a good place to camp, he had left his camels and travelling partner Cam, and hitched a ride to meet me. John leapt out of the car and lifted me off the ground in a huge hug. Leading me back to his camp, he strode along next to me, towering above me, wearing the same brown Akubra as mine, but adorned with a large eagle feather on the side.

After a quiet day of walking on my own, his camp was like arriving at a party. His dog Brusky was barking, music was playing from a boom box, camels were dotted about everywhere tied to separate bushes, and his baby camel—also named Charlie—was calling out loudly. I met Cam, the French girl who was travelling with John, and also Naz, a girl who was travelling in her van and would be camping with us for the night. The sudden increase in humans and animals made the quiet of the sand dunes feel like chaos.

Respectively, we both began to unsaddle our camel strings. I noticed John and Cam hauling huge heavy-looking saddle bags with surprising efficiency. While his bags were strewn in no particular order, mine were all neatly arranged along the back of my tarp. As I was placing hobbles on my camels, John and Cam took out an electric fence reel and began assembling a pen for John's camels. This was a totally different means of securing camels, one I had never considered or been taught by my mentors. It was always considered traditional to graze camels in hobbles, as they often needed a large area to wander and select a range of plants for their own nutrition. With the unusual abundance of good feed, John was able to set up a fifty-square-metre holding pen. Still, I watched on dubiously.

With his camels secure, a camp table was erected and camp chairs produced. He had carried enough chairs for everyone, and beckoned me to sit down. John unzipped a saddle bag and reached into its depths, handing cold beers around. When he assembled a platter with camembert, crackers and smoked prawns, I was shaking my head in disbelief. And when he pulled out an electric chainsaw and started it up, chopping wood for a fire, my eyes almost fell out of my head. I knew from his posts on social media that he was somehow managing to travel with a fridge, but the electric chainsaw doubly confirmed the extravagance of the way in which John travelled with camels. Noticing my disbelief, John turned to me.

'You're now realising it's all true right? All these rumours that you've heard about all the gear I'm travelling with? And wait, I'll show you more stuff to start more rumours!' John proudly proceeded to give me a tour of his equipment—the fridge, table, chairs and more. He had a generator, an antenna with a Telstra signal booster mounted to one of his camel's saddles and an inflatable couch. Unzipping his swag, he said with great pleasure, 'I even carry three different kinds of pillows, just in case I want one that's softer or firmer.' If my eyes weren't already popping out of my head, I then had to pick them up from the ground and dust them off when he assembled a set of five large household speakers around camp and connected them to his full-size boom box: 'surround sound music!'

I looked at the beer in my hand, the camembert on the table, the chairs and music system, then across to my small tarp with its line of smallish saddle bags, no table, no chairs, no generator, chainsaw or fridge. It was like comparing a playboy mansion with a hermit's hut. Was this really camel trekking? The electric fence, putting your feet up and having a beer? I thought of the extra kilometres I had walked, shepherding my camels in hobbles, my paranoia over finding them enough feed, my struggles with water and drought. Would John face these challenges as he headed west, into a land with no pubs? Or had I made it hard on myself? Whose way was the right way? On the one hand, I was envious of how relaxed the electric fence had allowed him to be, and on the other I felt a little superior, as though I had done it the 'real' way.

My thoughts were broken by burbling, followed by a violent clanging of bells. I looked up to see Mac, acting like a bucking bronco, head and neck flying up and down as he bolted across the flat, entangled in John's electric fence, pulling out poles and dragging the entire paddock with him. I rushed over with John, my little pocketknife in hand ready to cut him free. I was in a panic. Mac was foaming at the mouth, and I could see blood. I realised he'd been zapped by the fence and taken fright.

'Can I cut the fence?' I yelled, my pocketknife at the ready. John grabbed Mac's rope.

'It's okay, mate. He's pulled out the earth stake, so it won't be zapping him anymore.' I was impressed by John's calm and confident air, compared with my complete 'worried mother' frenzy. We untangled Mac and I checked him over. He must have bitten his tongue when he was wildly bucking and that's where the blood had come from. John's camels were looking on completely unfazed by the commotion. John resurrected the fence and demonstrated its power.

'It's barely enough to make a kid cry,' he said. After summoning up enough courage to touch it myself, I had to agree. It was a bit of an overreaction on Mac's part! Although Mac wasn't wearing rubber-soled boots like I was.

My camels, like me, were not used to this kind of camp. Once they were tied to bushes that evening, they stood, unsettled by the loud music from John's speaker system. My camp sat cold and untouched. I couldn't contribute anything to the party that night, not a chair or a cold beer. About the most I could offer was a can of tuna.

Before the party was over, while the music still blared, I called it a night, tired and overwhelmed by the onslaught of socialisation. I was awake hours before the rest of the camp had stirred. As usual, I had let the camels off at first light, and sat on the sand dune among the wildflowers, drinking coffee. I couldn't help feeling that John had somehow ruined the sanctity of camel trekking. What he was doing felt little different to those beer-slugging four-wheel drivers tackling the desert in their $200,000 set-ups. The precious feeling of peace and tranquillity that I felt alone with my animals in these wild places had been shattered.

Later that day, as we watched our camels interact, John and I spoke about our respective trips. He had taken his camels onto the lawns of Parliament House in Canberra and to the Victorian High Country, where he had had a scary incident when he and two of his camels had tumbled down a steep hillside and had to be rescued.

He seemed like a strange candidate for camel trekking. He had made money in the insurance industry, but the constant drive to obtain more had eventually led to a hollow sense of dissatisfaction, so he had retired young and decided to live differently, exploring Australia by camel. He had known absolutely nothing about camels before he obtained his own, and he had never worked for camel companies taking tours. He completely winged it. In his words, 'No one told me I couldn't take a fridge on a camel trip!'

I had to respect him; he had been bold and pushed the boundaries. I recognised we did things in very different ways, and I couldn't—and wouldn't have wanted to—travel with the amount of equipment he carried. But I could see it worked for him and that, despite what anyone thought, he was having a good time. I couldn't begrudge him that. Adventures were not meant to be all about pain and suffering.

On our second evening together, I shared with John my experiences in the desert and he gave me some advice about navigating traffic in towns.

'I always have someone walking at the back of my string to slow cars down. Having an extra person will really help you manage the traffic with the camels,' John said.

I admitted to John that I was hesitant to have anyone join me. I was almost reluctant to tell anybody Jimmy had walked with me for five days. If I had someone else with me, did that make the trip my own? Could I claim it as a solo endeavour?

'Of course you can! No one's going to question you on the details. It's your trip. You can do what you want,' John said, but I wasn't convinced. Still, my second night with John had completely changed my opinion of him. I respected his brazen attitude and the fact that he did what he wanted. Despite the difference in our trips, we would remain united as friends in our support for one another's separate adventures. There was no right or wrong way to do a camel trek.

The next day we said our goodbyes, and our two strings of camels crossing the country set off in opposite directions, one west and the other east.

12

The Cherished Empty

Jimmy and I stood on either side of Mac with our brows deeply furrowed. Each of my camels was getting what Jimmy had termed 'the full measure and quote' for their saddles. Since I'd left on the second half of my journey, I'd had nothing but problems with the saddles not fitting properly. Finally, with Jimmy's help, I was confronting the problem and fixing them for good. Jimmy was a baker by day, but a mechanic by trade, and his practical ingenuity meant he took to saddle-fixing with the attention to detail and performance that he had used working on race cars.

We were camped in the swale between two dunes at Cameron Corner. Without a proper toolshed, Jimmy was using his car jack combined with two ratchet straps to bend the metal of the saddle frames to accommodate the camels' larger humps.

'I hope this white mark goes away,' I said, looking at where Mac's saddle had created a pressure point and turned his hair white. These white patches that had developed on all of my camels felt like symbols that proved my ineptitude. Jimmy was so focused on the saddles that he didn't answer—I was touched that he cared so much about the camels' comfort. He had developed the understanding that, as he put it, 'Happy camels equals happy Sophie.'

The night we arrived at Cameron Corner there had been a bit of a party. The Corner Store, as it was named, was rather more a pub in a demountable. The store part consisted of three small shelves at the front bar with a small array of miscellaneous camping items for sale, including an out of place sex toy that had jokingly been deemed a 'necessary' camping item.

When I walked into the pub I saw many familiar faces—station owners and locals I had met along the way in the days prior to arriving at the Corner. 'Mouse', the local grader driver, called out with his sharp Aussie twang and beamed a gap-toothed smile at me. When I asked him later how he'd got this nickname, he roared with raucous laughter and said it was because he was as quiet as a mouse! I could see Grant, the owner of Bollards Lagoon Station, with his small stature and exceptionally tall-crowned Akubra. I had developed a theory: the taller the hat, the longer a person had been on the land. In Australia, the larger hats seemed to go with the most understated landowners, whose modesty hid their wealth of knowledge and the great swathes of country they maintained.

'Ozzie', the owner of both The Corner Store and Omicron Station, was helping himself to a XXXX beer from the fridge. Tall and angular, with a weathered face and piercing blue eyes, he was gentle and soft spoken. I'd never seen him without a tinnie in one hand and a cigarette in the other, and often wearing Ugg boots. I felt instant warmth seeing all these motley colourful characters gathered together. I introduced Jimmy to Grant and Gina, whom I'd met the previous night when I'd stayed at Bollards, then leant in eagerly to listen to Ken, the elderly owner of Lindon Station, above the din of the bar. I was fascinated by all these legends of the bush and wanted to hear their stories of the changes that had taken place at this wild frontier.

After the party we drove back to our camp between the dunes in Jimmy's old Nissan Patrol. We trundled along in the dark, singing 'Trembling Hands' by The Temper Trap. I loved how Jimmy could switch between 'station talk'—stock and weather—to listening to contemporary indie music. Like me, he was a bit of a chameleon who could inhabit two worlds, the city and the bush.

'I hope the camels are okay,' I said as the song came to an end. 'I'm sorry everything revolves around them,' I added as we drove around bushes in the dark looking for them. It had been nagging at me that my obsession with camels had been a factor in my break-up with Sam.

'It's okay, Soph, the camels are part of you. You guys are a package deal,' Jimmy replied. We caught their shapes in the car headlights and pulled up. They sat huddled together as usual, and we said goodnight to each of them.

Between saddle fitting, repacking food boxes and other jobs, we camped together at Cameron Corner for a week. The old Nissan had been kitted out with a double-bed mattress in the back, and Jimmy always arrived with the bed neatly made and the car fridge filled with beer, meat and fresh vegetables. It felt like luxury, a hotel on wheels, complete with catering service. In the mornings I'd sit with a sweet slice he'd brought from the bakery, sipping coffee and reading the newspaper, reconnecting with the events of the outside world.

Three days into our time at the Corner, piles of food surrounded us as Jimmy and I sat on my tarp sorting out a month's worth of stores he had brought for me.

'So, will it be the same shopping list for Hungerford and Hebel?' Jimmy asked.

'Hungerford . . . Hebel? Jimmy, that's way too far for you to drive!' Hungerford was a 2000-kilometre return trip from where he lived and Hebel was 3000 kilometres return.

'It's not that far. It's worth it,' he said. Then added, imitating Laurie, the Lyndhurst publican he stopped to see every time he drove the Strzelecki Track to visit me, 'Just keep trying young fella, eventually they give in.' The 77-year-old's resounding advice on women always made me laugh, but I could tell that Jimmy was not about to let me walk away.

Once the saddle fitting was complete, we headed back to The Corner Store for a beer—this time, with the camels in tow. John Elliott had suggested tying my camels out the front of pubs to expose them to the sights and sounds of a busy environment.

As I drew closer to the east coast, I knew they would have to get used to the crowds.

I hitched the camels to a rail right at the front of the pub and we ordered a beer. At first they were all wide eyes and taut lips, but then they began to relax. By the time I had finished my beer they were chewing their cud and allowing strangers to pat them.

At sunset we left the pub and walked to the post marking the juncture of three states: South Australia, New South Wales and Queensland. In the fading light, Jude bent his neck down and touched it with his lips. The Queensland leg of our journey was about to begin.

I said goodbye to Jimmy at the Dog Fence. I would be following the fence for an entire month in a straight line east along the Queensland and New South Wales border. I was almost crying as I walked away, not because I would miss Jimmy—I'd see him soon in Hungerford—but because I couldn't believe how generous he had been with his time. He had gone above and beyond for the camels and me.

The track running next to the Dog Fence made for easy walking; there was no public traffic, it was a straight line east and Omicron Station was beautiful. We were travelling through the last of the fiery-red sand dunes of the Strzelecki Desert, between which were shallow pools of fresh water, a surprise to see in this arid country. I took photos in disbelief of the rich green clover that had appeared in these low-lying swales. Along the fence I could make out the shorter posts that must have been the original Rabbit-Proof Fence, before it was extended for dingoes. I remembered Grant from Bollards Lagoon Station telling me that his father had seen rabbits piled knee-high and a metre thick against the mesh, desperately trying to continue their march north having eaten out all the country in their wake.

At intermittent gates along the fence, I passed imposing government warning signs with the message: 'Coronavirus Quarantine. Police Border Control. Restricted access. Penalties apply. Border pass required.' They seemed oddly out of place in this wild landscape, where I had been roaming free. I had chosen to walk the Queensland side of the fence so that I could spend my birthday with my family from Brisbane. The border between Queensland and South Australia was open but between New South Wales and Queensland the border remained shut. I could enter New South Wales from Queensland but once I had crossed the border, I wouldn't be able to return. But here, in the far west of the state, no one was patrolling the border and the whole notion of hard borders seemed arbitrary—part of a restricted world I could not imagine.

That evening I picked one of the prettiest places I had ever camped—a shallow pool with a perfect lawn of short green clover, rimmed by yellow-flowering acacia and surrounded by red dunes dotted with mulga in seed. I stood atop a dune and looked at the mirror image of the scene in the glassy pool, breathing in the quiet serenity. Experiencing these vast landscapes every day, it was easy to take this feeling for granted.

I realised with a tinge of sadness that this might be my final camp in the sand dunes. The same maze of parallel lines on the map, marking the dunes that I had once dreaded, but now loved, ended beyond this point. But, as always, forward was the direction I must go. I bottled that feeling of freedom, knowing I would always want to open the lid and feel it again.

The following day the dunes petered out and I arrived at Toona House on the Dog Fence. Phyllis was expecting me. She had just returned from Tibooburra, the nearest town, 120 kilometres to the south on a rough dirt track. Phyllis was a boundary rider, in charge of maintaining a 100-kilometre stretch of the fence, and lived a solitary life. Toona House had none of the grandeur of some station homesteads, which looked like small townships with their many outbuildings. Toona was one simple solitary house in the middle of nowhere, and I figured you'd have to be tough and resourceful to live out here alone. Nonetheless, I immediately got a warm vibe from the place.

Phyllis handed me a beer. 'One of my rules for staying here is you have to have a bloody drink with me,' she said.

That I could do, but I felt a little dubious about my ability to keep up with Phyllis. She struck me as the kind of woman who could drink most men under the table.

We settled into an afternoon of beers around the fire while the camels grazed nearby. Phyllis wielded her chainsaw with gusto, cutting logs for the evening.

'They're just like goats with what they eat,' Phyllis said, looking at the camels as she switched off the saw. 'I had goats here at one point. I loved my goats. But they used to get

Walking through the Mars-like environment of Kanku–Breakaways Conservation Park as we begin the second half of the journey.

Meeting the Arabana rangers near Kati Thanda–Lake Eyre.

Walking a stretch of the very straight 5614-kilometre Dog Fence, on Muloorina Station, South Australia.

Jimmy and I fix saddlery together on Murnpeowie Station while I take a day's rest from walking. Jimmy's practicality was often invaluable.

John Elliott and I say goodbye after crossing paths in the Strzelecki Desert. John, a fellow camel trekker, was attempting to visit every state in Australia with his camels.

The feed was mainly lush and bountiful on the second half of my journey, after ample rains. On the Queensland border, the camels graze close to camp allowing me a moment's peace to journal and relax on my swag.

After some erratic behaviour from Jude, Delilah stepped up to become lead camel as we followed the Dog Fence through the Bullagree.

Outside the Hebel hotel. A police checkpoint was positioned in the little outback Queensland town to enforce Queensland's hard border with New South Wales during the Covid-19 pandemic.

Measuring our combined weight—4.06 tonnes—on a weighbridge usually used for grain near the town of Thallon in Queensland.

Leaving Texas and ascending into the foothills of the Great Dividing Range.

Jimmy and I hang out with Charlie as he rests in the grass on a day off from walking through the mountains. Camels have a strong preference for flat ground.

My final days walking alone through the forests of the Great Dividing Range, after crossing my last state border for the trip into New South Wales.

Playgroup with the camels—my big furry children with my friends and their children. Ness and her daughter Valerie, and Dan and Nat with their twin boys River and Jarrah at Bonalbo Showground.

Our final trek to the beach—following an abandoned railway line to the coast and avoiding the perils of the Pacific Highway above.

An ecstatic Keirin as we arrive at The Farm, Byron Bay. She had safely escorted us as we navigated dangerously busy roads during our final two weeks of walking.

Filled with joy and pride, Delilah, Jude, Clayton, Charlie, Mac and I finish our thirteen-month trek on Tyagarah Beach, just north of the lighthouse at Byron Bay.

out into the national park and then they'd come back with boyfriends. I told the girls, "If you're going to come back here with boyfriends, I'll shoot them" . . . and I did!'

I didn't doubt her. Chainsaw in hand, she looked formidable, and by her own admission, didn't take bullshit.

Further into the afternoon, I discovered another side of Phyllis. I told her my camels had spooked at the huge athel pine in the garden at Toona House.

'That's because the fairies live in my tree,' she said with complete seriousness. 'A lot of my friends think I'm a witch.' On a table inside her front door were various assortments of New Age oracle cards, and her shelves were lined with crystals and witch and wizard figurines.

The next morning I sat at her kitchen table drinking tea. I had decided to stay an extra day and was sifting through the oracle cards. This type of fortune-telling wasn't new to me: I had grown up with an aunty who interpreted astrological birth charts and a grandmother who did past-life readings.

'Sometimes I give my friends tarot readings,' Phyllis told me.

A tarot reading, in the middle of the Outback? It was as odd as watching Pink Floyd Live on the edge of the desert and I couldn't resist. Phyllis made me shuffle a deck of cards before laying three out before her: Moderation, Love and Synchronicity. She gave me a deeply considered reading for over an hour. Her words encapsulated the essence of my trip, highlighting the reasons I had done it and many of the lessons I was learning from it. I knew that many of the themes, like 'trust in the universe', were common in New Age spirituality, but it felt encouraging and positive to hear it.

I picked several more cards from different decks, including the Eight of Raphael, a card she made me examine closely.

'What stands out for you?' Phyllis asked. It was a scene with a princess standing on one side of a bridge that crossed a flowing stream, and a dark prince in the distance on the far side. I wasn't drawn to any of the obvious elements, but I did notice there was a dog by her side. It was only days later that I came up with my own interpretation. I wasn't interested in the prince. Jimmy's boundless enthusiasm had always reminded me of a puppy; I had even worried that his eagerness made him immature. But dogs were a symbol of loyalty, and Jimmy had certainly proved himself in that regard.

The final feel-good affirmation card I had picked up from Phyllis's table said it all.

> Trust
> Trust in the process
> You've got this
> You'll get there
> p.s. you look so cute today!

And with those words in my head, I walked away from Toona House the following day, smiling to myself and singing.

From Phyllis's place, I headed into no-man's-land. There would be no more houses along the fence until I reached

Hungerford—only the long, straight stretch of wire mesh reaching into the distance to keep me company. I was back into the gibber plains and heading for a swampy region Phyllis had told me was known as the Bullagree. For some reason the name sounded ominous as I repeated it over and over to myself. *The Bullagree, the Bullagree.*

The knowledge that I'd see no one for weeks settled in around me and I found I was looking forward to this precious time alone. Alone was different from lonely, I had come to realise. It was in this space that I did my best thinking. I could recharge and withdraw to the quiet of my own presence and the rhythm of the natural world around me. Humans are social creatures and I couldn't exist in this state forever, but I'd come to appreciate the feeling of being just a tiny speck in a vast landscape. Knowing that this might be the final stretch that would be truly remote made this feeling even more poignant. I thought of the impending populated east coast. The maze of dunes on the maps would soon be replaced by a maze of roads, and I had been thinking more about John Elliott's suggestion that I needed an extra person to help me with the camels in the traffic. But, for now, the desolate beauty of the treeless gibber plains pulled me back into its midst, and I gazed ahead at where the earth met the sky.

I got to know the fence well. It was my constant companion. This straight stretch was the most direct way to make ground towards my destination, but Jude did not consider it so. He was a camel that could turn the simplest of tasks into a big deal. He walked along a dead-straight road like a drunken sailor, weaving right then left.

229

'We're not going through the gate, Jude,' I told him, shaking my head with exasperation as he turned his body sideways, pre-empting a change in direction when he saw a gate in the fence. When we didn't turn, his pace suddenly slowed, and I was back to feeling like I was not only walking close to 5000 kilometres across the country, but doing so dragging the weight of five slow-coach camels.

Jude's behaviour was totally irrational, and I had begun to doubt whether he was the best camel to lead the string into busy Byron Bay. I loved him, but he was unpredictable and lost his cool quickly. A few days earlier, my jacket had fallen from his saddle and landed near his feet. While the rest of us looked on placidly, Jude's world imploded. On the spot he began wildly bucking and bucking, until I finally broke his mindless terror by yelling, 'JUDE! It's okay, buddy, it's just my jacket. Calm down, mate!'

Behind me, mid-walk, Jude took the liberty of sitting down for the second time that day. He had sat yesterday as well. I'd checked him out the previous night, running my hands down his muscles to check if he flinched and was sore. He seemed to be perfectly fine.

'Hup, Jude!'

Jude roared back at me like a dinosaur, but stood up. He was then back to the same swerving routine. Right, left, fast, slow. I was over it.

'That's it, Jude! If you don't want to do it, then you're being demoted.'

Jude roared at me again as I tied his rope to the fence and untied Delilah from behind him.

'Missy Moo, you're going to get a go at lead camel.'

We set off again with Delilah in lead position, looking a little hesitant and unsure why this change in placement had occurred. Behind her, Jude looked slightly crestfallen. Demoting Jude was like choosing not to hang out with that friend you love so much, the one who is a bit of a trainwreck and always gets you into trouble by making poor life choices. We were best mates, and I had always felt that it was me and him leading the others across Australia. But if I was going to use Delilah as lead, I had better train her up now before we arrived at the busy roads. Delilah was older and more autonomous, less inclined towards affection, with a more even nature and perhaps a better temperament for a lead camel.

Like Delilah, I was a little uncertain. I gripped the lead rope slightly tighter, not knowing what her reactions might be at the front of the string. We had travelled all day through bare gibber country, and I was searching for camp with a clump of shrubs to tie the camels to. At this time of day, tired from walking, my decision-making skills were always at their lowest. I ummed and ahhed, walking forward several paces then stopping, then walking some more, wondering whether to stop or push on. I was a bit like Jude, swerving all over the place. Delilah was trying to guess at my irrational behaviour. As I wavered on the spot, there was a miscommunication about what was going on. She let a front leg fly and walloped me in the back of the calf. I was shocked by this seemingly inexplicable act of violence. Jude would never have done that.

'What the fuck, Delilah, what was that for?' I turned and whacked her with the end of the lead rope. She pulled back,

231

her neck arched up in defiance, as we both stared angrily at one another. 'You are getting a one-week trial at this. If it doesn't work out, Jude is back in lead!'

I could feel my anger bubbling inside. I was always ashamed when I retaliated at the camels like this, but fatigue from days of walking was rendering me irrational.

I let the camels off to graze and sat on my tarp feeling shattered. The same familiar cold wind blew as I huddled behind the largest of my pack bags. I heard a familiar chirping and looked up to see a huge flock of budgerigars soar into a nearby tree. Hundreds of them sat braced against the wind, bobbing around on the swaying branches like little fighter pilots ready for launch. They took off, soaring upward, then changed direction in unison as if they had been given an order by their commander. They arced out right, then left, in a blaze of yellow and green, dancing with the wind. Another separate formation of budgies flew over, holding rank. They twisted and turned about with one another, like two schools of fish. Not a single member of their dancing group put a wing out of line; it was as if they were one single moving organism.

This is what I needed my camels and I to be, a team—especially as things got hairier as we neared the coast. The budgies were beautiful to watch. Mesmerising, they held my attention for hours until the sun set, and my anger had completely dissipated.

Delilah and I came to an understanding. We were not so much friends, but working colleagues. The type who would chat politely in the office, but probably wouldn't go out for a drink after work. I hated to admit it, but she was doing incredibly well as a lead camel. Secretly I had hoped she would put a foot wrong, to justify returning Jude to the lead, but she was quiet and solid, and the others followed her well. Even Jude looked relieved at the realisation that he could now shirk all responsibility and follow behind her mindlessly.

The rocky ground was replaced by a grey dried swamp as we left the gibber plains and entered the run-off of the Bulloo River, the Bullagree. In her new role, I nicknamed Delilah 'Queen of the Bullagree'. I hadn't seen another soul in a week, and was regularly talking out loud to the camels again.

The Bullagree, I said to myself again. It felt like a mythical name that conjured up a sense of foreboding—a feeling that was confirmed as I walked further into the bleak grey swamp. My thoughts turned dark. It seemed a place to be survived rather than enjoyed. It was flat, monotone, hard-packed ground, devoid of all vegetation as far as the eye could see, without even the warming presence of the ochre gibber stones. The camels found it bleak as well; there was not a single bit of feed to eat all day.

Just as I began to worry that I might have to tie them to the fence that night and have them go hungry, I saw a rise in the landscape in the distance. We climbed the hill, and when we reached the crest, I saw we were surrounded by waves of unexpected golden sand dunes. They weren't parallel or rich red like those around Cameron Corner, but a mess of hollows and rises. It was beautiful and endless, and I felt that joyful expansiveness that comes from unspoilt nature and pure isolation.

I rolled out my swag in the sand on the crest of a dune that night. The camels were tied close to a cluster of sand-hill acacia, surrounding me. I slept deeply, with an all-encompassing peace that I have only felt in the most powerful of landscapes. It was as if this dune was cradling me in its embrace. As if I was sleeping with my head on Mother Earth herself.

My watch alarm sounded before daybreak. I woke with ease and crawled out of the swag to look at the multitude of stars above me. Orion's Belt—the Saucepan—was rising and I named all the stars around it with familiarity. As I went about lighting my morning fire, a revelation swept over me. Yes, I still set an alarm each morning, but somewhere along this walking year I had relinquished my obsession with time and timings. Throughout my first year's walk, I had obsessed over it. In the middle of the Great Victoria Desert, I'd clutched hold of numbers as if clinging to a life raft. Numbers played over and over in my head—how many kilometres I was walking, what time I had set off, how many hours I would walk, how many kilometres that would be, how many hours grazing the camels would have, and how many hours' sleep I would get. I realised with sudden clarity that I had stopped doing that. I was finally going with the flow, letting the rhythms of nature and the landscape itself take care of it for me. It didn't matter how far or how fast we walked; nature dictated that. Could I dare to say that I was actually living in the moment?

I looked up from my fire and on the far distant horizon I could make out a speck of light. A car headlight. Immediately I felt on edge. I didn't want this prism of pristine solitude to be shattered. I didn't want the deep connection that I was feeling with the natural world to be burst by another human. The quiet of a week's walking on my own had heightened my senses and I felt like a nervous animal, alert and ready to take flight. For an hour the car's headlights lingered on the flat horizon, and I couldn't make out if it was coming or going. Eventually the lights disappeared out of sight. I felt my muscles relax as I settled back down, staring into the flames.

I had never expected the Bullagree to be so spectacular. I lingered, relishing these last unexpected dunes and the openness of the landscape. Between the dunes the swamp was present again, but now it was filled with wiry tufts of cane grass that created homes for tiny birds. I could see flashes of blue where a splendid fairy wren darted, or a streak of red that was a crimson chat escaping into the reeds. What I liked most was the beeping song of the ever-present zebra finches, which sounded as if they were happily talking to one another in Morse code.

For the first time I wasn't pushing forward to the next location, the next rest stop. I took my time, not covering many kilometres each day, enjoying this last stretch of truly remote country.

235

It wasn't far past midday when I made camp, pulling up on an island of sand protruding from the swampy terrain below. There was feed for the camels on our island and it was an easy place to contain them for a day's rest, the land clearly visible for kilometres around. I peeled off my boots and socks, airing out my sweaty feet, and rolled up my jeans to reveal my hairy legs. I stuffed a piece of fruit cake into my mouth, then looked down the fence line the way we had come.

What was that in the distance? It looked like a car driving up the dog fence. I clutched my cup of tea, feeling my body tense again. As the car came closer, rocking about like a giant boat as it navigated the dips and rises in the sand, I could see it wasn't the generic white ute driven by government boundary riders. It was an old Nissan Patrol. Jimmy's old Nissan Patrol! *What the hell? What was he doing here, in the middle of the Bullagree?*

'Hi, how are you?' Jimmy said, leaping from the car to hug me. I wiped the crumbs from my mouth and stared at him, speechless. Seeing my confusion, Jimmy added, 'South Australia's just gone into lockdown for a week and we've shut the bakery. I packed up the car yesterday and got the hell out of there. I crossed into Queensland first thing this morning. I wasn't going to miss meeting up with you at Hungerford.'

'What?' I stammered. 'How did you know where I was?'

'Pretty easy, really. I calculated how many days' walk you were from Cameron Corner. I knew you were going to stop a day with Phyllis, and I know roughly how many kays you walk a day, so I cut down to the Dog Fence and followed the track along. I stopped about ten kays back to look for your tracks, but you're almost exactly where I thought you'd be.'

'Oh my god, only you would track me down out here!'

Jimmy grinned broadly and my mind flashed back to the puppy on Phyllis's tarot card. I hugged him again and pushed the thought away.

The next day had a lazy Sunday vibe about it, although I had no idea what day of the week it was. I sat on the sand reading the paper while Jimmy cooked up breakfast from the Nissan Patrol hotel on wheels. His plan was to drive on to Hungerford while I carried on walking, and help out with some of the logistics that lay ahead.

In the evening we walked the camels back to our sand island for the night, each of us leading several camels separately. I was confident in letting Jimmy handle them now. He rested his face on Delilah's neck and patted her affectionately, and her ear gave a little wiggle of pleasure. I was surprised; she seemed much more tolerant of Jimmy than me. Jimmy had started referring to the two of us as 'his girls', and I wasn't sure at times which of us was his favourite. He truly seemed just as enamoured of the camels as he was of me.

That night the wind whipped up, bringing a couple of drops of rain. We sheltered inside the Hotel Patrol with dinner resting on our laps.

'I've been thinking about the end of the trip,' I told him, putting my fork down.

'Me too. I'll be there at Byron Bay,' Jimmy said. This didn't come as much of a surprise. If he was willing to drive back and forth thousands of kilometres to see me in Hungerford and Hebel, there was no way he wouldn't see me finish.

I hesitated. 'It's my birthday in October. I think I'll be in Texas for it.'

'I know. Would you like me to come to that too?' Jimmy asked a little shyly.

'Yeah, I'd love you to be there—but you can't drive all the way to Texas, then back to South Australia and then back again to Byron. All this driving's crazy!'

'It's not that far,' said Jimmy with a shrug.

'I think I really need help on the final leg. I'm so worried about the busy roads and the camels in the traffic. And I've barely organised any logistics beyond Hungerford. What am I going to do when I get close to the coast? Knock on someone's door with the camels in hand and ask if I can stay the night? I feel completely unorganised,' I said, all my anxieties suddenly bubbling to the surface.

Jimmy didn't miss a beat. 'Well, why don't I just stay with you from Texas to Byron, and I can organise logistics and help with the roads?'

He was watching me calmly, without a skerrick of hesitation in his eyes. A weight lifted off my shoulders. I remembered distinctly the terror I had felt driving the backstreets of Byron, wondering how I was going to navigate fences, highways and high-speed roads with guard rails and not cause a hazard with five large and laden camels. I also silently wondered whether I would lose my claim to self-sufficiency if Jimmy joined me for the final stretch. But I had no choice, and I realised that I didn't want him to leave.

It felt right, so I smiled back at him and agreed.

A week later I said goodbye to the empty expanse of the Bullagree and walked into the mulga. It was thick and suffocating on each side of the track, and horrendously monotonous. The camels weren't happy either—much of the mulga seemed to be a variety that was sour, and they were on edge in the confined space of the track. My emotions mirrored theirs. After the high of the Bullagree I found myself slipping into tired irritability.

The boredom and monotony of the scenery, however, was abated by Jimmy's return. He arrived with a notepad filled with ten handwritten pages of notes listing property names, owners' names, phone numbers, directions and shortcuts, where gates were located to cross over cattle grids, and yards and holding paddocks that I might be able to keep the camels in overnight. While I had been walking, he'd had countless cups of tea with station owners, and had organised my entire journey between Hungerford and Hebel. In typical Jimmy fashion, he now knew everyone in the south-west corner of the state. He excelled in the role of logistics coordinator. He also knew me, and he knew the camels, and could pick what we would need.

'So, all the way to Hebel is sorted?' I said in disbelief. 'Jimmy, I don't know how to thank you!'

He nodded and grinned. 'That's okay, you can just pay me in kisses. I charge a kiss per kilometre of travel time.'

13

The Last of the Bush

HUNGERFORD TO HEBEL—415 KM

When Jimmy and I arrived at Hungerford with the camels, we increased the tiny town's population at the time from five to seven. It was a backwater, in an endearing way, situated by a gate on the Dog Fence leading to New South Wales, which was padlocked shut due to the Queensland border closure. No caravans and four-wheel drives could pass through, so the town was particularly quiet. Jimmy had befriended the elderly couple who ran the Royal Mail Hotel, Graham and Carol, and they had kindly offered us their vacant house across the road for the week. It felt strange to be in a house with Jimmy, as we had only ever camped together. It seemed like a test for what might lie ahead.

As we filled the old Patrol with fuel, Carol came to ask us, in a kind grandmotherly way, 'Now, are you kids okay for money? Let me know if you need us to lend you some.' My heart broke with her kindness. We assured her that we were okay. She had taken to calling us 'the kids', which I loved. The night before we'd arrived in Hungerford, there had been dark clouds and a spot of rain. Carol told me that she had rolled over and said to Graham in the night, 'What about the kids out in this weather!' I'd endured far wilder storms on the journey, but I was touched, nonetheless.

I left Hungerford a week later, in early August, and Jimmy drove back to South Australia. My walk to Hebel was along private station tracks, and was marked by yet more examples of outback hospitality and meetings with memorable people of the bush. The first of these was Kerry from Ningaling Station.

She trundled up alongside me and the camels as I was passing through a gate on her property. She was rugged up in a fashion that, at first, made it impossible to discern her gender. She looked tough and imposing, with a rifle on the dash— until she gently lifted a small lamb in a knitted jumper out of the ute and tenderly placed it on the ground. She then pulled out a flask of coffee and a tin of home-made Anzac biscuits, and beckoned me over to have morning tea on the back of the ute. Kerry told me how she would drive down to the paddock and spend time with 'the girls', as she called her cattle, talking to them and sitting with them. I liked her relationship with her animals; I could relate.

'I think I'll call the lamb Sophie,' she said.

As I leant against the ute, chatting to Kerry, I thought how meeting all the landowners had been an unexpected highlight. They were a diverse mix of characters, the one similarity being their contagious passion for the land. Their presence lent a deeper understanding of the country I was travelling through, weaving a rich tapestry that gave the journey colour and meaning.

On Tinnenburra Station I met another memorably strong lady of the land, Carol. Her husband Lindsay had been the mayor of nearby Cunnamulla, but it was Carol who mostly ran the property. She drove the grader, could fly a light plane, and had a chopper pilot's licence to do her own cattle mustering. It seemed there wasn't much that this powerhouse of a woman couldn't do. 'Sometimes I find it hard to be able to talk to other women on stations,' Carol admitted. 'I don't want to talk about bringing up the kids.'

We were in Carol's ute, driving around Tinnenburra and delivering mineral licks to her cattle. I liked spending time with station owners when I took a break on their properties, keen to learn all I could about how they managed their land. It helped me make sense of the landscapes I was walking through day to day. I quizzed Carol about the thick mulga on each side of the track, knowing it was illegal in Queensland to clear it.

'It never used to be this thick,' Carol explained. 'And I'm not afraid to go to jail for pushing it down!' she said in her tenacious way.

At nearby Amenda Station the following day, the topic of mulga came up again. I was sharing a roast dinner with Dusty and Christie, who managed the property, and their three children. We were discussing aspects of regenerative agriculture, which they were both passionate about, reminding me of my time with David and Frances on Wooleen Station more than a year earlier. It was a catch-22 situation, Dusty explained. When mulga is pushed down, it creates a bed for new seedlings. But the tannins from those new mulga trees are too bitter for stock to eat for the first several years, so it grows back twice as thick, until nothing can reach the upper branches and nothing grows underneath its canopy. Now I could understand why this country had made me feel so claustrophobic.

After dinner, I sat with Christie in her living room while she folded huge piles of washing. She spoke about how she'd just seen the movie *Wild*, based on the book by Cheryl Strayed—the story of a woman who found healing and self-discovery by hiking 1100 miles along the Pacific Crest Trail in North America. Christie had been inspired, and hoped she could take off walking when the kids grew up. Her comment sparked in me a wave of gratitude to be doing what I was doing—that I had given myself this time and space before the responsibilities of children and family crept into my life. I recognised that familiar longing in Christie for freedom and adventure, and hoped that one day she would go on her own walk.

High mesh fencing, similar to that of the Dog Fence, surrounded the boundary of Yankalilla Station. As I passed through the gate next to the cattle grid, I set off a loud high-pitched siren that was designed to deter dingoes from crossing the grid. *Wee-ooo-wee-ooo* it wailed loudly. I gripped the rope, thinking the camels would take fright, but when I turned around to see their faces, they remained completely unperturbed. I will never fully understand what goes through a camel's head.

I unsaddled my camels at Yankalilla Station and left them in a small paddock eating juicy weeds. Will, the owner, drove me to the homestead, balancing one-year-old Ned on his knee while Ned's pudgy fingers gripped the steering wheel of the Landcruiser. The homestead was modern and grand, complete with tennis court and swimming pool, with an east and west wing of bedrooms on each side of the central living room and kitchen. Despite its grand appearance, Will and his wife Hollie were down-to-earth. They had friends staying, and their homestead felt at ease with hosting visitors, relaxed and communal.

Hollie and I were both from Brisbane and we spent time talking about the city–country divide, and how our friends in the city had little comprehension of what life in the Outback was really like. Why was it that so many Australians hugged the coast?

That evening, Will and Hollie took me to 'Noorama Night'—a monthly social event at a sports ground with a racecourse, tennis courts and a tin-shed bar that sold beers for not much more than a gold coin donation. Everyone from the stations around Yankalilla and as far as Cunnamulla had gathered for a barbecue. To my complete amazement, many of them were young. The vast majority of station owners I had encountered were older couples, in their fifties, sixties and seventies. It was lovely to see so much dynamic energy, with babies and pregnant women everywhere.

I had often wondered about the future of the Outback as I walked. Stations were unaffordable to buy, and a lot of land was taken up by companies who employed a single caretaker. Other properties were passed down through the generations, but the kids knew how hard the work was and many did not care to inherit the family farm. Outback life was tough and isolated, without the conveniences and connection that cities offered. Who would reside in these far-flung places in days to come? Who would replace the colourful characters I had met along the way? But here at Noorama and south-west Queensland, a different story was playing out—one in which a younger generation was finding a new-found appreciation for life on the land. I wondered whether I would be drawn back to the Outback, now that I had found someone who loved its space and uniqueness as much as I did.

In the weeks that I had spent passing through these stations, the country had changed dramatically. The mulga made way for the Brigalow Belt, the soil had turned from red to black, and I no longer recognised many of the plants.

I pulled up to camp for the night and opened my *Plants of Inland Australia* guide to identify some ground-covering greenery that the camels were consuming with glee. I thumbed through the pages, and found the plant with the closest resemblance. The words jumped out and hit me square in the stomach: . . . *release cyanide in the gut when consumed by ruminant animals such as sheep. Death may follow soon after consumption.* DEATH!

I ran around in a frenzy, shooing the camels away from the plant. Worries about poisoning had never been far from my mind. In *Spinifex and Sand,* David Carnegie had written that several of his favourite camels had died suddenly from eating the poisonous wallflower plant in north-west Western Australia.

I took Clayton's hobbles off and walked him away from the suspicious plant. In an outright panic, I thought I detected a slight wobble in one of his back legs. I moved Jude to assess his gait. *Was he wobbly in the back legs too? Or was I just imagining it?* Clouds were gathering quickly this afternoon, and lightning was coming closer. I left the camels for a moment, convinced that I was becoming paranoid. None of the station owners had warned me about potentially poisonous plants in the area.

I rushed about camp, stringing up my tarp and covering all the gear, battening down the hatches for the storm. A tell-tale gust of wind announced the storm's imminent arrival, and I collected the camels to tie them at camp. Delilah tripped and my heart caught in my throat. Was she sick, or did she just lose her footing? I looked back to see Mac's back legs momentarily collapse underneath him. Terror was rising inside me. Something wasn't right. I tied the camels to trees, pulled out the satellite phone and messaged both Dad and Jimmy: *Can you*

be on stand-by? I think the camels have eaten something bad.
Can't talk, big storm.

I stashed away the sat phone so it wouldn't get wet. The
sky had quickly grown dark and the camels were sitting down.
Next to my shelter, Clayton dropped to his front knees, and
as his back legs lowered to follow suit, I noticed them trembling. He threatened to topple over on his side as he lowered
himself to the ground. At that point, I began to pray, begging
the universe, or God, or whoever was listening, to help me.

'Please, please, please let my camels be okay!' I pleaded
desperately. Images of them all lying dead by morning haunted
my thoughts as I stared out into the rain. What could I do?
The nearest vet was most likely in Cunnamulla or Saint George,
five or six hours away by car—and if more rain fell, nobody
would reach me on this dirt road anyway. I spent a sleepless
night, getting up hour by hour to check on the camels. I shone
a torch on each of their faces to check their eyes were alert and
they were still sitting upright and chewing their cud.

The endless night finally broke with a blue-sky dawn. The
camels were all still with me. I stood them up. Jude, Charlie
and Delilah seemed fine, but I still detected a stumble in
Mac's and Clayton's back legs, as if they were drunk. I phoned
Dad and Jimmy, who had also had sleepless nights, both
researching potential causes and dreading receiving a phone
call with bad news.

'They're okay . . . I think,' I reported. 'Can you get me the
number of a local vet, just in case?'

The vet I phoned was equally perplexed. It wasn't a case of
ryegrass staggers, as the camels hadn't eaten any ryegrass. She

had never heard of the plant I described, but said it would take about eight hours for them to show signs of poisoning—so it would have been something they ate well before we'd arrived at camp yesterday afternoon. She advised me to fill their guts with something bland that I knew to be okay, or to confine them to hay if possible. It wasn't. Tentatively, I saddled them up and walked slowly and gently away from that mysterious camp, stopping continually to let them browse on wattle and fill their bellies.

By the afternoon, grazing at our new camp, they all seemed perfectly fine, and I wondered whether I had imagined the whole episode. *Had the storm made them shaky? Had I simply seen them trip when they walked? Or had they in fact eaten something they shouldn't?* I realised just how frightened I was to lose them. Always, the weight of responsibility I felt for the welfare of my camels rested heavy on my shoulders. They were the most important thing in my world.

Everything around us was changing as we got closer to Hebel. I had gone from taking a week to cross a station to walking through several properties in a day.

I was crossing through the Culgoa Floodplain, a pretty national park that few Australians seemed to know about. The tracks were empty, but suddenly I felt the presence of a vehicle behind us. To my complete shock, it was Jimmy in the old

Patrol. I was still a week's walk from Hebel and wasn't expecting to see him until we got there. He'd left South Australia early to surprise me.

'I thought I'd sort out the hay for the camels at Hebel, then hitch a ride back and walk with you,' he said, adding a little bashfully, 'Sorry I didn't tell you I was coming.'

Jimmy left to drive ahead and find a camp for the night. When he left, I realised I was hanging on to a niggle of resentment. At Yankalilla Station, I had read an article about my trip in the local paper. It wasn't a bad write-up, but it had concluded that one of my highlights had been 'meeting a new love, Jimmy, in the Flinders Ranges'. It made me question whether I could still claim my adventure as a solo journey. Was it still my own? Was I coming to rely on Jimmy's help too much? Could I still claim self-sufficiency and independence— the very qualities that had made my trip so empowering? I was annoyed that this was the second time Jimmy had encroached on my time alone.

That afternoon we reached the camp that Jimmy had picked. It was a pretty and peaceful spot and the camels were happy immediately. My irritation faded away.

We spent the afternoon joking about the camels' unique personalities and explaining their behaviours in anthropomorphic terms. Mac would be the footy player and Delilah would be his cougar girlfriend, wearing leopard print and sipping caramel lattes. Clayton was like Rain Man, exceptionally gifted but socially awkward, and Charlie would be the dorky kid at school who drives his parents' Volvo. Jude, we both agreed, either had a million thoughts going through his head or nothing at all.

We looked at him, smiling his camel smile and gazing off into space absent-mindedly, and laughed.

'You'd never know he can be such a lunatic. What do you think is going through his head?' I asked.

'I think it's white noise, or just a soundtrack of the wind, *Shhhhhhhh . . .*'

I laughed and stroked Jude's neck fondly. Jimmy knew them all so well now. It reminded me of just how much time he'd spent with us, and again I felt the irksome push–pull of pride in my independence, and the need to accept that Jimmy could no longer be disentangled from my trip.

The following day, Jimmy drove on to Hebel to sort out hay and yards and leave the car in town, and I spent most of the day walking with mixed feelings raging in my head. Jimmy hitched a ride back, and we carried on walking together.

I had bought an electric fence like John Elliott's, knowing that soon I'd have to use it near busy roads. Jimmy had brought it with him and we spent an evening on our way to Hebel giving it a trial run.

On our last night before we reached Hebel, we made camp in a patch of clover burr in a dip in the road surrounded by thick, dry swamp vegetation. I went about unsaddling as usual. Charlie was nervous, apparently certain there was something dark and unsettling hiding in the bushes beside us. I had put leg straps on both of his front legs, but Charlie was now crawling on his knees, intent on getting out of there. As he kneed his way along, his leg hooked around Delilah's nose line, which was resting on the ground where she sat. Delilah let out an almighty roar: the string of the nose line was pulling at the piercing in her nose. I rushed forward with my pocketknife. The string was at breaking point. Charlie was doubly scared now, with his leg caught in the nose line coupled with the commotion from Delilah. As I reached to cut the strained nose line with my knife, it snapped from the force. Now the camels were all up, hopping around, trying to make a mass exodus from camp on three legs or crawling with both knees bound. My patience was in tatters.

'*HOOSH* DOWN, JUDE!' I bellowed. 'CHARLIE, YOU DICKHEAD, GET BACK HERE! SIT DOWN, MAC!'

It was chaos. The camels were in full flight mode, and I was yelling at Jimmy to grab them and bring them back to camp. Delilah's nose was bleeding, and my hands were shaking as I tried to remove the torn twine from her nose peg. 'It's okay, Missy Moo.' Delilah roared, her nose clearly still in pain. I couldn't get the string off, and my fiddling only served to piss her off further. She gurgled and before I could move, thick hot oozing cud travelled up her throat and hit me square in the face. I stopped my fiddling and Jimmy turned to me and said calmly, 'Sit down, Soph. I'll put the billy on and make a cup of tea.'

It was the second time a cup of tea saved my sanity in a camel crisis, but I also couldn't deny the soothing effect of Jimmy's calm collectedness. He assembled the electric fence while I took deep breaths in the shade. The blood in Delilah's nose was superficial and it would be okay. The camels, now contained within the confines of the fence, slowly chilled out. I felt ashamed that I had lost it. But I was also glad that Jimmy had been here to experience it. This kind of mayhem had happened so often in the early days but no one had witnessed it. Now that the camels were better behaved, it was hard for anyone to understand just how far they had come. All I wanted was for someone to understand, and I felt that now Jimmy could. And that meant a lot.

The rickety old single-storey Hebel pub, with its peeling rust-red roof, looked like a facade, a purpose-made outback gimmick. But when Jimmy entered to order us a beer, he realised from the prominent slope of the bar that the pub's age was genuine. I stood outside with the camels, watching semi-trailers pass, carting cattle across Queensland. It didn't take long for the camels to calm down and start chewing their cud.

As satisfying as it was to see them relax and become the object of attraction at the pub, I couldn't help my thoughts reverting to Jimmy's role in my trek. I wasn't comfortable with the fact that people might construe that I wasn't doing this adventure alone. *Maybe I needed to stop worrying?* I thought of John Elliott's style. He didn't give a shit what people thought; he did it to have a good time. Maybe adventures didn't have to be all about hard work and proving oneself. Sometimes they were about meeting new people—or, in my case, 'a new love'. As cheesy as I felt that sounded.

But then a backpacker who worked at the pub came out to pat my camels.

'It's amazing, what you've done,' he said to me, patting Delilah. Then he turned to Jimmy. 'And you're like the photographer from the movie.'

I knew he was alluding to *Tracks*, and suddenly I felt unsure again.

14

A Different Road

HEBEL TO TEXAS—392 KM

With the quirky Hebel pub at my back, I strode through a police checkpoint on the Queensland side of the border, sipping a latte. During our stay in Hebel the police had met the camels and knew we weren't travelling from another state, so they took photos and waved me through with friendly smiles hidden behind facemasks. It was like stepping between two worlds. Hebel felt like the edge of the Outback, and before us lay the bitumen road.

Mike, a former Air Force fighter pilot who had heard about my adventure, arrived to walk with me and the camels for several days. Mike was an impressive adventurer in his own right, a bit like an Aussie version of Bear Grylls. He had begun a trek with camels when he was stationed in Saudi Arabia, and wanted to film everything for a short YouTube series and learn some more about camels so he could do his own trek in Australia one day.

It was the final stretch of walking in which my routine remained the same: I cooked on the fire, hobbled the camels so they could graze—not yet needing the electric fence—and brought them into camp in the evening. I had felt self-conscious when Mike first arrived that my adventure paled in comparison to his survival feats. But as I confidently went about my routine while he turned the camera upon me, I realised how capable I had become at living alone, outdoors in the bush with my animals.

Mike had set his camera up to film a time-lapse of the camels and the stars one evening as we sat around the fire scoffing chocolate and sipping port. We talked about the questions we were commonly asked about our trips. It seemed that all adventurers, no matter what they were doing, were asked 'Why?' Any adventure often contained within it a multitude of reasons. And why did we have to give a reason at all? Couldn't it simply be for the love of adventure itself? Mike had never asked me why I was walking my camels across Australia. Nor had I asked him why he carved a boat with his bare hands and sailed it through croc-infested waters for forty-two days. If I had questioned the sanity and practicality of my trip, I wouldn't be sitting here, enjoying a fire, having a thought-provoking conversation with a new friend whom I had only happened to meet through my trip, sharing chocolate, listening to the contented grunts of camels and looking up at the blanket of stars above us.

After Mike left, we walked into grain country. Fields of ripening wheat billowed on either side of the road, and a constant stream of trucks passed us, clearing ground for grain bunkers for the impending harvest. It was a totally foreign landscape and I was suddenly aware that the camels looked completely out of place. Every night when we made camp, I felt as if we were hiding. We were being squeezed into a tighter and busier world. We could no longer camp on private land; fences had put a stop to that. I was forced to find nooks and easements on the side of the road where I could string up our electric fence.

At the edge of the town of Thallon, near some grain silos, I discovered a weighbridge for the grain trucks. It was too tempting; I had to walk the camels over it. The digital figures flickered as we plodded our way onto its surface, taking up most of its length: *4.06 tonne*, it read. I mulled this over as we walked the final stretch into town. I made up less than the .06, weighing in at about fifty kilograms. I estimated the gear to be about 500 kilograms, making each of my camels an average of roughly 700 kilograms. It dawned on me that four tonnes was a hefty amount to control on a daily basis, particularly in these tighter places.

'The camel lady has arrived!' I heard as I pulled up at the Thallon pub. After having had several beers thrust into my hand, I left the pub feeling a little tipsy, leading my four tonnes of camels through the main street, on the way to James and Jenna's house. They had kindly offered to put the camels in their one-acre paddock attached to the house.

As I unsaddled the camels I heard children laughing. 'We've got camels staying in our backyard!' I heard them yell, as

James and Jenna's three children, Hartley, Milly and Madison, appeared with their schoolfriends in tow.

'Make sure you wait for Sophie to tell you what to do,' James instructed.

I took the kids from camel to camel, introducing them to each in turn and telling them a little about their personalities. More kids from the primary school arrived, and I could hear Hartley reiterating every detail about the camels to his class-mates: 'This is Delilah. Delilah is Mac's girlfriend. Mac is the boss. And this is Clayton. Clayton doesn't really like to be patted much.'

I smiled and ushered the kids over. 'Come and say hello to Jude.'

All nine children gathered around, reaching their hands up to Jude's face. While camels do not like to be touched around the face by strangers, I've come to realise that they can react differently to children. Jude lowered his big head only inches from the ground, and let nine soft hands gently stroke his face. His eyelids softened; his lips hung loose with the corners of his mouth turned upward in a camel smile. He appeared to be in a state of bliss under their soft caress. In that moment, it was hard to imagine that just over two years ago he was a totally wild creature and had never been touched by a human.

The morning I left Thallon, I woke to the sound of a grain train screeching into town. I pulled aside the curtain of my bedroom window on the second floor of the pub and peered down. In the pre-dawn light, the train loomed like a big ugly creature, its empty graffiti-covered tubs stretching down the track. It would surely seem like a monster to the camels. But by the time I had saddled the camels and walked through town—meeting other terrifying creatures, such as a cute miniature pony that the camels swore was up to no good—the train had left.

I had decided to follow the service road that ran along the railway line to Goondiwindi. It was the most direct route and avoided the stream of trucks on the highway. I had hoped the railway line would be unused, so I wouldn't have to deal with a train spooking the camels. Unfortunately, with the grain harvest beginning, the train had commenced running, but no one seemed to know what time it came or went.

I found a fairly secluded place on the side of the train tracks to make camp, feeling like a vagabond trying to hide my five large out-of-place camels. I tied them to a gate while I checked the spot I'd selected. A strip of bush was partially fenced on the easement, and I could use the electric fence to complete the square as an overnight holding pen for the camels. Satisfied that it would do for the night, I went back to collect the camels. I gazed down the railway line, wondering idly what the light in the distance was, thinking it was just the sun glinting off the shiny rails. But the light seemed to be getting bigger. *What WAS that? Fuck, it's a fucking train!!!* I'd thought there would be no more trains that day. Mac's back end was right across the tracks. I rushed to untie Delilah and move them all forward. The train was screeching towards us now, sounding its horn. We only just made it out of the way. I retied the camels but they still danced around, crashing into one another with their pack bags, trying to escape this new terror. It had come upon us so quickly, catching all of us unawares.

I set off the next morning feeling hemmed in and nervous. I had no idea when the trains were coming and going, and was terrified I might not be able to hold the camels if one snuck up on us again. The easement had narrowed and there was only a car's width between the train tracks and a tall, solid fence on each side. But it was this or battle it out on the road, with fifty trucks passing us a day. I chose to deal with the lesser of two evils—one or possibly two trains a day. Before we left camp that morning, the train had passed us again on its way to Thallon, so I knew it was bound to come back down the line at some point. I checked over my shoulder for the hundredth time for any sight or sound of the train. Again, nothing. My neck was starting to hurt from incessantly looking behind my back.

Further down the line I came upon some men working for Queensland Rail, doing repairs for the line. I ran through an apologetic sob story in my head. I hadn't asked permission to walk on the train line. It would have meant dealing with a large corporation and there would be no clause or legislation regarding 'Girl seeks permission to take camels down active railway line.' But to my surprise, the guys couldn't care less. They switched off their angle grinders and stared at me, before asking for a selfie with the camels.

After several rounds of selfies, I walked away having discovered an approximate time the train would be heading back down the line.

Roughly on time, two hours later, I turned to see the train accelerating towards us. I quickly tied Delilah to the fence; I doubted I had the strength to hold the camels if they were to pull away in earnest. The train barrelled towards us as I held my breath. The camels danced and bucked around, slamming saddle bags into one another and trying to run, but were held between the fence and the moving, squealing carriages.

And then, with a whoosh of wind, the train was gone.

The walk from Thallon to Goondiwindi was like a game of snakes and ladders. We would make good progress, climbing rows of the board upward, before sliding back down a snake in the form of some obstacle or another. There were parts where the service road along the railway line had been recently mowed and the going was good, and other parts that no one had driven in years, where I scrambled through mustard weed as tall as the camels' heads. Sometimes I walked on the track itself to escape the overgrown road, but then the track would cross a river, and the gaps between the sleepers would make it impassable, forcing me back onto the highway to battle with fence lines and passing trucks.

I secretly relished the challenge this stretch was presenting, and it was amazing to watch the camels' progress. By the fourth day, the camels simply stood and watched the train go by—but the constant vigilance required was making me weary.

On my final night on the train line before I reached Goon-diwindi, I found a holding paddock for the camels. The line ran through a property and we were far away from the road. The paddock was perfect, about two acres, with secure fencing and good feed. I let the camels off without hobbles and watched them enjoy loping about with ease. I felt instantly peaceful. I'd been so focused on navigating the railway line and highway that when I saw the huge orange dome of a full moon rising above the horizon it took me by surprise. It was beautiful. I thought how lucky I had been to see it rise in so many memorable locations across Australia.

Then I realised with a shock that this might be my final night alone. At Goondiwindi I would be joined by my friend Kathy, who would walk with me to Texas, where Jimmy would take over from her.

I didn't feel happy or sad about this final moment alone; it just felt like a poignant moment of change. The part that I had wanted to experience the most—trekking through wild and remote country alone with my animals—was over. Everything had changed almost as soon as we left Hebel. I had never looked forward to navigating the roads, but it was also part of the challenge I had set myself in walking from west to east.

As I stared at the moon growing paler and smaller, rising in the twilight, I said goodbye to the trip as I knew it. Change was upon us.

Our journey down the railway line came to an end on the outskirts of Goondiwindi, where Kevin, a truck driver I'd met at the Thallon pub, had offered to let us stay at his house, which had an accompanying paddock for the camels.

Down a back road on our way to one of the highways that surrounded Goondiwindi, we managed to set off every horse in the area. Now, it is well known that horses hate camels. Camels, on the other hand, are indifferent to horses (except for miniature ponies, which are of course terrifying). But Delilah, Jude, Clayton, Charlie and Mac eyed these galloping equines with alarm, unable to discern why the horses were having such an extreme reaction to them. I held the rope and nose line short and tight.

'We've got this, Missy Moo,' I told Delilah. 'Let's get these boys across town.'

I pulled out onto the highway and a huge truck roared up behind, pushing us against a barbed-wire fence, where we set another horse galloping off. In front of us, I could see a harvester on the back of a truck, coming down the road with a wide-vehicle escort and flashing lights. I could feel the camels' strength pushing me forward, hard up against the barbed wire. I could barely hold them.

'Steady, guys, steady.'

Horses were whinnying around us, dogs were barking, and the traffic was thunderous. I shoved the camels even further into the fence to keep them in a line and stop them running me over. At last we reached the turn-off for Kevin's place and waited to cross the highway. Car, truck, car, truck, tractor, car, truck. Eventually there was a break in the traffic and I walked the camels across with a calm bravado. This was ridiculous; we needed help badly.

I had stubbornly wanted to cling to my independence, but I realised now that this was crazy. I could not do this on my own. It was just too dangerous.

When I arrived at Kevin's house, no one was there. I unsaddled the camels and let them go in the small paddock. Charlie had diarrhoea caused by the ordeal on the road.

On dusk, Kevin's son Matt arrived home with his wife Chantelle. Kevin wouldn't finish his week working away until the following evening, but Matt and Chantelle kindly prepared dinner for me. A builder and an accountant, they had lived in Goondiwindi most of their lives, and planned to stay in Goondiwindi forever. They had married young, and were the very image of settled, saving to build a house in the town.

'When Dad called to say there was a girl walking with camels coming to stay, I thought he'd had too much to drink at the pub,' Matt told me.

'But this is the sort of stuff Kevin always does. He's always meeting people on big adventures,' Chantelle said. She hesitated, looking down at the salad she was preparing, before looking up at me. 'So, why are you doing this?' she asked, looking bewildered.

I went through my usual spiel: how I'd fallen in love with camels at the camel dairy, how I wanted a big adventure, how I had loved exploring the deserts here in Australia on foot.

'But why wouldn't you just drive?' Matt asked. 'I hate even walking from the house to the car in the driveway.'

They didn't get it. I had come to realise that lots of people didn't—and I could understand that. There were times when things went wrong, and when it had been dangerous, as it had been today, and I wondered what the hell I was doing. There were times when I moved from place to place, never feeling settled, constantly yearning for the next exciting thing, when my feet were itchy, when I wondered whether some of this normality would be good for me. Would I have been happier if I hadn't been bitten by the travel bug, and was instead satisfied with a 'normal' life, doing the things society deemed normal? I could have been settled, in a stable relationship, with a house, maybe kids. I wondered, as we sat watching *The Block* on television and eating dinner together, what *that* Sophie would have been like.

The next day, as if to pull me out of my thoughts about that parallel universe, my lovable, vibrant, anything-but-conventional camel friend turned up. Kathy was an independent single mum who worked for herself. She owned camels, bred dogs and owned an Airbnb in Hervey Bay, where she loved stand-up paddle-boarding among the whales with her free-spirited daughter.

Shortly after Kathy arrived, Kevin returned home for the weekend. The three of us sat on the deck of his house, watching the camels in the paddock, and talking about Kevin's many and varied adventurous jobs—including running alligator tours in the Northern Territory. He seemed a natural with animals and my camels warmed to him immediately. He understood without having to ask why I was doing the trip.

'You've got a car coming up behind you,' Kathy said. We had set off for Texas and it had become instantly clear how great it was to have help on the road. Kathy had donned a hi-vis jacket and was striding out into the centre of the road, flagging a car to slow down as she walked at the end of the string next to Mac. Kathy was not new to working with camels in public environments. Her camels did beach rides, fairs and nativities, and she had even walked them down the aisle of a church. By standing out on the road, Kathy was creating a safe zone around the camels, meaning no one could drive up behind Mac and get too close. She was like a lollipop lady directing traffic around my precious children. I had also mounted a hi-vis flag on the back of Mac's saddle, another idea I had borrowed from John Elliott. Jimmy's dad had made the bracket for it, which Jimmy had fitted when we were in Hebel. I didn't want to have a dorky flag flying on my romantic-looking string of camels, but from here on, I knew we needed it.

Although the road was bitumen and busy, we were in fact following an old stock route. There were fenced reserves dotted along the Macintyre River that now marked the border between Queensland and New South Wales. We found a pretty billabong hidden away in one of these reserves. The water was brown and murky, but Kathy and I wasted no time stripping off and wading into its cool mirrored surface in our undies.

'I'm so glad you love doing crazy stuff like this, Kathy. I'm so glad you *get it!*' I stopped. 'Do you think we both would have been happier if we had decided to live more normal lives?' I asked.

I had often wondered this. Would I be forever plagued by my restless wandering spirit, never satisfied until I had lived my life bigger and bolder? Kathy was quick to put an end to my questioning.

'Nah,' she said and flung off her bra, diving under the water. She broke the surface, whooping and screaming with her arms thrown in the air. I followed, diving into the billabong and emerged screaming with Kathy, twirling joyfully in the brown waters.

Jimmy messaged that evening to say he'd be arriving tomorrow. He was early again, and my independent nature arced up. Kathy and I discussed the push-and-pull I was feeling. I loved Jimmy, and we had begun to plan a future together, but I didn't want to give up my free spirit. I was still struggling to let go of controlling how the trip *should* look. I was longing for what had been, rather than appreciating what it had become. At the start of my trip, I had longed so much for Sam's presence, and now that I had finally relinquished that yearning and moved on, I longed once again for the autonomy that had accompanied those early days.

'I know how you feel,' Kathy said as we leant against the swag, listening to the crickets and watching the camels dust-bathing. 'You're like me, the idea of being caged in by a relationship freaks you out. But you've got to give him a chance. Look at what this guy is willing to do for you!' She had a point. By now, Jimmy had driven over 11,000 kilometres back and forth to see me.

The next day, as we emerged from the creek, having navigated a tricky shortcut, Jimmy arrived in a Nissan Pulsar sedan he'd bought for $400, so he could leave it behind when he picked up my ute to use as a support vehicle. It was covered in dust, with no hub caps and no numberplates (the plates hadn't arrived on time), after having tackled a 3000-kilometre journey, one-third of which had been on dirt, crawling along at a snail's pace over the rough corrugations of the remote Strzelecki Track. Most people would not have attempted such a trip without a four-wheel drive and every bit of off-road paraphernalia. But this was Jimmy: a glass was always half full and nothing was impossible. How could I not love his adventurous spirit? He was hardly the sort of guy to cage me in. He *got it*, the way Kathy and I did.

That night, the three of us sat on my tarp playing our favourite game of comparing my camels to people. Jimmy's accurate portrayal of each of my camel's idiosyncrasies had Kathy in stitches. Maybe we were all crazy? Maybe crazy wasn't such a bad thing.

Jimmy drove the dusty little car to Brisbane to collect my ute. A few days later he met us on our arrival into Texas. I laughed and rolled my eyes as I saw my ute driving towards us with a flashing utility light, courtesy of Dad, mounted on the roof.

So here we were, a long way from the romantic image of a string of camels crossing the desert that Robyn Davidson had inspired. Kathy and I were both wearing hi-vis vests, Mac was flying his hi-vis flag and Jimmy was driving a white ute with a flashing light. We were no longer desert wanderers; we looked like we were about to construct the next major highway.

And with lights flashing and flag flying, we strode into Texas for my 33rd birthday, where I would be surrounded by my family in a beautiful Airbnb with good food, good wine and cake—a stark contrast to my previous birthday in the desert.

15

The Great Dividing Range

TEXAS TO BONALBO—252 KM

I left Texas with the warmth of my birthday still buzzing around me. Mum had given a heartwarming toast that kept playing through my mind. She had acknowledged how brave I had been, alone in the desert, fending off wild camels and dealing with water issues. She had also praised Dad for his concern and involvement in my trip, speaking of how he had now passed the baton to Jimmy, who would help us reach the coast. I felt so lucky to have my family supporting me. They had not once questioned the value of the trip—in fact they were all, at times, embarrassingly proud of it.

The sun was shining, the weather was warm, the paddocks were a sea of rich green burr clover and flowers, and Jimmy was walking with me and the camels, who were well behaved as we navigated down the main street and out of town. I could see the hills rising in the distance, leading towards the Great Dividing Range; the undulating landscape reminded me of Dad's farm at Kilcoy.

How far away the desert felt now. I thought back to those heart-rending moments when there had been no feed for the camels and they looked thin and tired, and when I slept with the barrel of the rifle against me for fear of a wild bull in the night. I thought about the friends who had planned to visit me along the Anne Beadell, and how devastated I'd been when they had told me they couldn't make it, the loneliness that I thought might crush me. But I had survived all that, and I would carry that feeling of empowerment within me. That was part of the trip no one could share. But over the next few weeks I would be joined by more friends as I made my way closer to the east coast.

A day out of Texas my friend Bronson joined me. I had known him since I was a child and he was the closest thing to a brother I had. Over the next few days he was followed, in succession, by my friend Elliot, then my friend Nikki and her partner Sam, as well as an impromptu visit from Uncle Steve, my friend from Uluru. Each visitor became a small part of the trip, and the slow pace of walking provided a quiet, and sometimes hilarious, space to open up.

As well as the visits from friends, I also met many more people along the way. Strangers opened their homes and properties to us and others stopped on the road for a chat. Two lovely old ladies from the Texas op shop, who reminded Kathy and me of Thelma and Louise, drove out to meet us in their convertible BMW, their white hair blowing in the breeze around their fashionable sunglasses.

Bruce and Deb, a couple touring Australia, served me hot coffee with cream on the side of the road, and Deb took a photo of Delilah from which she would later sketch a beautiful portrait, one that I will treasure forever.

Georgia and her dad delivered us free lucerne hay from their property for the camels.

Matt allowed us to camp for four nights in his hay shed while we waited out bad weather. His cute daughter Quinny rode everywhere in the tractor with him, opening and shutting gates.

There were other more fleeting encounters, like Rambo (as we later called him, as nobody could recall his name) who strode out to meet me, Jimmy, Elliot and the camels as we walked past his property. He was a huge man, wearing quick-dry outdoor adventure clothing, and when he shook our hands in his vice-like grip, we noticed each of his fingers was the size of a banana, and he had a big hunting knife in a sheath on his belt. With his hands on his hips he towered over us and exclaimed, 'This is fantastic! This is the most incredible thing I've ever seen! How absolutely wonderful that you're doing something like this! This has made my day!'

Elliot replied with a stifled laugh, 'And you've made ours too!' Rambo's enthusiasm was contagious.

Over the week that followed, my enthusiasm began to wane with the ceaseless questions about my trip. The constant *why, why, why* started to wear me down. *Don't camels spit? What's that thing in their nose? Do they have personalities?* This last question Jimmy particularly hated, and once the person had driven off he would turn to me and scoff, 'Does your dog have a personality? Do your children have personalities? Nah, they're just robots that follow us along mindlessly. Of *course* they have personalities!'

Day in, day out, repeating the same answers a zillion times was becoming exhausting, and I longed to speak about something other than my trip. My adventure had consumed me for so long now, but I was tired of being 'the camel lady'. At times I just wanted to be Sophie, with other passions and interests, and a future beyond the trek.

At the same time, I was sad and terrified to leave my trip behind. Who was I without it? Would this be the biggest and best thing I did in my life, and would it be all downhill from here? I felt I was in an emotional limbo, wanting to prolong it, yet also knowing that the trip in its original form was done and I was ready for it to end. The camels were no longer tied around me at night, and I no longer wandered with them as they grazed. They were often in a paddock at someone's house, and I was off socialising with the kind people who were hosting me.

On one such evening, I snuck away from our hosts for the night, leaving Jimmy to do the talking and entertaining. I walked out to the paddock where the camels were peacefully grazing. It was sunset and the sky grew orange. I missed being part of this tranquil scene. I scratched Jude behind the ear, then he lowered his head and I held its weight in my arms. I breathed out a long slow breath, and so did he. I drank in the moment for as long as I could before I summoned the energy to go back inside and play the role of the chatty guest.

At some point I was going to break, and Stanthorpe was that place. It was becoming a social overload for me; my inner introvert was in turmoil.

We were on our way to stay with Keresi, a lady who had reached out to me on Facebook, kindly offering us her place to stay. My phone pinged from Keresi as we were walking.

'Can you let me know what roads you will be taking Sophie, lots of people on Facebook are asking?'

My phone pinged again.

'I've contacted a lady from the local paper—she's on her way out to meet you.'

Keresi had taken it upon herself to organise my social calendar while in Stanthorpe. She had posted on the Stanthorpe Facebook page that I would be coming to town, and I was now being flooded with messages from strangers.

'Hi Sophie, I was wondering what days you are going to be in Stanthorpe. I have an eleven-year-old daughter who would really love to meet your camels.'

'Hi Sophie, when will you be arriving in town? I see you have a camel called Jude. That's my husband's name! We would love to come meet you.'

It was thrilling that so many people were interested in meeting the camels, but I just didn't know how I was going to give everyone my time. After living out of range for months I felt under pressure to reply to everyone. I was juggling my phone in one hand and trying to manage the camels with the other while keeping an eye out for cars.

When the journalist from the local paper arrived, I was fidgety. I couldn't do an interview while standing with the camels on a blind corner in the middle of the road. My natural instinct was always to prioritise the camels' time grazing in the afternoon. I hated them standing around not eating, with a load on their backs. Every person who stopped to talk to us was cutting into their time off. I agreed to meet the journalist at Keresi's instead.

As we walked up the driveway, after politely pausing to talk to a neighbour, followed by another passer-by, Keresi came bowling over to us, brimming with excitement, her phone in her hand as she filmed our arrival. She was commentating as she approached. 'They've arrived! This is Sophie and Jimmy. Wave hello! And what are the camels' names? This is Delilah, Jude, Clayton, Charlie . . . hello, Charlie! And Mac . . . hello, Mac. Welcome everyone!'

The lady from the paper returned, with her husband and son in tow, and began asking questions as Jimmy and I unsaddled. What she saw were calm, well-behaved camels, being unsaddled with ease by two people, in a semi-rural environment. I wished I could teleport her to the desert so she could grasp the full picture—the harsh and rugged beauty, the tough and empowering months I'd spent alone in the solitude of the Outback. I answered her questions with a smiling face but beneath it I was irritable.

My frustration at her questioning was in fact frustration about the trip. The challenge was gone. I felt I had lost it along with my autonomy. All the decisions had now been taken away from me. I couldn't camp where I wanted to any longer; I was forced to rely on the kindness of strangers for a paddock and a place off the road. Every camp was organised, so nothing was a surprise. It wasn't organic anymore; I didn't stop when I wanted and when the feed was good. The kind intentions of the people around me, offering places to stay and cooking me food, were unwittingly eroding my self-sufficiency. But there was no way around it—we were camel trekking in a place that wasn't appropriate for such acts of nomadic living. We had even bought hay for the camels now, as the short grass didn't provide enough of the variety of feed and roughage they were used to.

Meanwhile, Keresi had her arm around Delilah's neck and was attempting to take selfies. I could see Delilah tensing; she didn't like such blatant disregard for her personal space from a stranger. The journalist's son crawled under the fence and began to clamber onto Mac's back before I noticed and pulled him away.

'I want to ride the camels!' he said insistently.

More cars arrived; Keresi had invited members from her church group and was in her element playing hostess. She was flitting to and fro, introducing everyone to me and Jimmy, then introducing the camels to all her guests. 'This is Mac . . . go stand near Mac, darling, and I'll take a photo of you. Everybody say *Camels*!'

My camels now felt like a carnival show rather than noble ships of the desert. The quiet romance of what I was doing was gone. I felt swamped and tired, and just wanted to turn around and walk hundreds of kilometres back into the quiet of the bush.

I mumbled something to Jimmy about wanting to check the fence line of the paddock and walked off. I couldn't handle it anymore.

The Facebook and Instagram messages kept coming. They were nice gestures, friendly hellos and questions from strangers taking an interest in my trip, but my inbox was becoming unmanageable.

'The problem is,' I complained to Jimmy, after Keresi's guests had finally departed, 'that I spend so much time on Facebook and Instagram replying to these messages that it's taking away from my trip. The ironic thing is that people want to live vicariously through my adventure, but it takes me hours to reply to them all, and by engaging with them, I spend less time *on* my adventure.'

'Then don't do it, Soph,' Jimmy said. 'You don't have to reply to all these people.'

Still, it seemed a shame to bring the camels so far and not share them with people, so I organised for us to be at the Stanthorpe Information Centre at lunchtime on the Saturday.

Mum and my grandmother, who was soon to turn ninety, had driven to Stanthorpe the evening before. Mum walked with me, while Jimmy drove my grandmother to the information centre to see the camels arrive. It was nice to walk with

Mum, but I wished it could have been back on the quiet and calm red-dirt roads.

We were walking through suburbia and all the obstacles that came with it. There were houses, driveways, dogs, cars and people, and drains that I was worried the camels might put a foot through—everything that only a month ago the camels would have spooked at. I was exceptionally proud of how far they had come. On the opposite side of an intersection was the information centre, next to a park. It was packed. I had no idea this many people would turn up. I felt humbled and glad, but the camels had never been surrounded by such a large crowd and I was worried how they would go. I gripped the lead rope tightly, trying to exude calm and confident leadership. As we approached the intersection, a lady called out from a balcony of a motel apartment, 'Do you need any water?'

If I hadn't been so tense, I would have laughed. My troubles with water in the desert were a long time gone and it seemed such a funny thing to be asking in the middle of suburbia.

Keresi, who had insisted on driving behind Mum and me, had pulled over and was getting out of her car. As I crossed the intersection she raised her hands. 'Let's give Sophie a big round of applause!' she yelled, conducting the crowd with glowing importance. I turned red with embarrassment and gripped the rope tighter, praying for the camels not to lose it. I spotted Jimmy's face in the crowd and breathed a sigh of relief. There he was standing calmly, making space for me to move the camels off the road and into the park.

Carried on the excitement of such a large crowd, I spoke for over an hour, answering questions about the camels and my journey. It could not have gone more smoothly. The camels didn't miss a beat, standing relaxed and patient the entire time, allowing strangers and children to pat them. One child seemed insistent on trying to cuddle Mac's back leg, but Jimmy was keeping a close eye and quickly rescued him from harm's way. When he wandered back for the fourth time, a no-nonsense farmer we had been talking to yelled out, 'All right, whose kid is this!', and the mother sheepishly ducked down to pick the boy up.

Once the crowd dispersed, I said goodbye to Mum and my grandma. We still had several hours of walking along a busy road to reach tonight's paddock, where another lovely local had offered up their house for us to stay.

When we arrived, my energy levels came crashing down. It had been a hugely social day following an increasingly social couple of weeks. I sat on my tarp feeling so shattered I wanted to cry. The family's kids would be arriving home soon, and would want to meet the camels. And the family had kindly asked us to have dinner with them.

'I can't do it,' I told Jimmy. 'I can't speak to anyone anymore. I need a night off. I miss being able to relax after walking with a cup of tea, and watch the camels graze. I need that. Do you think we have to go to dinner with them? They seem really nice, and I don't want to be rude, but I'm just so tired.'

A huge crack of thunder sounded. Lightning flashed in the distance and a dark mushroom cloud was quickly growing in size. It was spring storm season, and rain had become more frequent since leaving the Outback. I sighed. Maybe a nice dinner inside, out of the storm, wouldn't be so bad after all.

Ian pushed the gate open to let us pass through into New South Wales. This was our final state border crossing. It was a forested area on Ian and Sue's property that connected with a back road in Queensland. In a normal year, this would simply be a back gate on their property. But in this age of Covid-19, it felt like we were illegal immigrants, Mexicans clambering across the border into the United States or stowaways hiding in trucks at Calais. It wasn't that it was illegal to cross from Queensland into New South Wales at the time (the only restricted border was returning to Queensland) but 'technically' we should have been crossing through a busy official border checkpoint. Something that would have been a little more difficult with camels in tow.

Ian and Sue's secluded property lay between the plateau of Stanthorpe and the hills of the Great Dividing Range, with no visible neighbours or roads. It felt like a different world, and I could feel my body relaxing. Their land was a beautiful mix of rolling hills, open grazing country with wild patches of eucalypt forests and crystalline creeks, home to platypus, spotted quolls and native orchids.

After unsaddling the camels and releasing them into a paddock, Jimmy and I sat on Ian and Sue's verandah, where they served up a delicious lunch of home-made quiche and salad picked from the garden. We ate watching their two horses graze, fairy wrens hopping from bush to flowered bush, and listening to bamboo wind chimes overhead. I felt as if I had arrived at a yoga retreat, complete with prayer flags above.

The La Niña predicted by the weather bureau was in full swing, so we waited out the rain on Ian and Sue's property, reluctant to leave this oasis of calm. There was no reception here, no social media, and I could take one tiny moment to forget the fear of what lay ahead. On our final night in Queensland, the family we'd stayed with had mentioned that on a clear night, from their neighbours' property, you could see the light from the Byron Bay lighthouse. I'd been shocked, the words sending shivers up my spine. *Surely we weren't that close?* Byron had always seemed like a mythical destination that I dared not think about—partly because I never actually imagined arriving at the end of my journey, and also because I had avoided thinking about the terrifying problems it posed. I was taking the camels to one of the busiest places on the east coast. Anything could happen with the camels in the crowds and traffic—and anything often did. I was just as scared of this challenge as I'd been to cross the Great Victoria Desert.

I sat cosied up with a book in Ian and Sue's warm house, gazing out the window, watching the rain come down in sheets, as my poor camels stood with their backs to the weather, stoically resigned to their fate.

Once the rain had cleared, I went out to check on them. Mac had a wound on his hump, from when I'd packed the shovel incorrectly one day. The load had caused a tiny pressure point, which in turn had created a sore—and, to my disgust, I had found maggots in the fat of Mac's hump. Luckily, Ian happened to be a vet, and gave me advice on treating the wound.

I was washing it and applying ointment daily, but this wet, humid weather wasn't helping. I ran my hand down Mac's hump, stroking his fur. He was sitting unrestrained, uncomplaining while I dressed the wound, like the good patient that he was. Wet hair stuck to my hands; the camels were starting to lose their winter coats. Pulling out some loose clumps of wool on Mac's shoulder, I noticed a strange circular scab that looked suspiciously like ringworm. We'd never had problems like this in the desert. But we had left the camels' natural environment long ago and this wet climate was no good for them.

Mountains were also completely unfamiliar to camels, and we were now confronting Australia's largest mountain range, the Great Dividing Range—our final geographical obstacle before the coast. I had asked Jimmy to go on ahead and recce the route to Byron in my ute. I planned on taking private roads and fire trails through the range, so this would be my last stretch without needing support, and I wanted to do it alone.

Bellbirds were calling as we climbed up out of farmland into the forest that covered the steep mountains. We were walking through tall, straight eucalypts with smatterings of rainforest, palms and staghorn ferns, and thick clumps of lantana. It smelt and sounded familiar. This was the type of Australian bush I had grown up with, scratching my legs crawling through thickets of lantana, picking the flowers to make home-made dye. Whenever I drove up the range behind the house I grew up in, I would wind down the window to hear the bellbirds chiming. I felt like I was taking the camels on holiday to show them where I had grown up. They had shown me the desert, and now I was showing them the mountains.

However, judging by their expressions, this was a holiday the camels were not thoroughly enjoying, especially Delilah. I felt like an over-enthusiastic boot camp instructor: 'Come on, Delilah, you got this. Work it, baby! Get those thighs moving.'

We inched our way up the steep incline, stopping continually for the camels to take a breather. Camels are by nature lazy, always inclined to opt for flat ground, where their languid energy-conserving gait makes sense. It was entirely against their nature to drag themselves up and over mountains. But we took it steadily, and again I marvelled at the adaptability and compliance of my friends.

A clearing in the lantana on the crest of a ridgeline provided a good place to camp. I almost felt I could smell the sea across the mountains. It seemed strange now to think of the end of the trip. When my journey had changed from one year to two, thinking of the trip in its entirety always felt too daunting, too immeasurable for my mind, and I had forced myself to only consider it in chapters. But Byron Bay suddenly felt real and reachable. I would soon be across the range and on the other side.

Memories of Byron came into my head as I prodded my fire, searching for coals to cook on. Sam meandered into my thoughts; my first time in Byron had been with him. Spontaneously, I decided to call him. It had been a while since we had spoken.

'Hey, Soph, it's good to hear from you. Where are you at the moment?' His words were like honey, sweet and familiar. It was nice to hear his deep calm voice, drawing me back into memories of the past, times and places we had enjoyed together, and personal jokes that only come from knowing someone intimately for a long time. 'Wow, I can't believe how close you are now! Seriously Soph, it's so awesome what you've achieved.' We spoke of friends and family, of work and adventure. I told him about Jimmy, and he told me about the girl he was seeing. We were genuinely happy for one another. For the first time I felt we could speak openly of new partners without daggers of jealously stabbing me. In the past, Sam's voice had caused me to bubble over with bittersweet regret; I had never been able to let go of what could have been between us. A deep love would always remain for him, but the past was the past. My adventure had led me down a different pathway, into a different life with a different person. I finally could accept that I hadn't completely fucked up and thrown it all away with my restless wanderings. Sam and I were still friends and I valued that deeply.

After that phone call I sat staring into the flames, enjoying the natural symphony of the bush. The fire crackled, the drone of cicadas was dying down and the frogs were starting their evening chorus while the camels chewed their cud.

I had taken one step at a time, always moving forward, and this is where it had led me—all the way to the Great Dividing Range, looking out onto the mountains, with Byron Bay within reach. I had to trust that this was exactly where I should be, and that my innate wisdom would lead me to where I needed to go next.

But right now, all I could think of was the present moment. The peaceful chorus of nature on my final night, in my own company, alone with the camels.

Downhill was hard; harder than uphill. The camels' long stiff limbs seemed incapable of bending under themselves. On the steeper sections it felt as if four tonnes of animal was towering over my head, threatening to topple down the slope on top of me.

Delilah stopped halfway down a hill, hovering her left front foot in the air. It was hurting her. I had noticed that this ankle caused her trouble from time to time, and every now and then I would spot a little bit of lameness. It might have been arthritis in the joint. Now, with the added pressure the ankle tendon was taking on the hills, it was really affecting her.

'Come on, Missy Moo, slowly, slowly,' I cajoled.

We shuffled down the steep fire trail all morning, inching our way painfully down to the valley below. At the bottom, the trees opened out to reveal a meadow with the Clarence River cutting through the centre. I let them rest for a while in the sun. They had done well in this foreign terrain.

A while later I interrupted their midday nap to ask them to stand. I was worried that I might not be able to get them through the Clarence River, and didn't want to make camp until we had tackled this obstacle.

I tied the camels to a tree by the water's edge, took off my boots and socks and waded to the other side. The water was flowing swiftly over the rocks below and rose to my thighs, wetting my shorts. I had never taken the camels through such deep water; in fact, I had never taken the camels through much water at all. We were used to dry creek beds, not flowing rivers. I placed my boots on the far bank and waded back to my animals. This was going to be interesting. It would be a long way back and around if we couldn't get through. I untied Delilah. To my complete surprise, all five camels strode into the water without the slightest hesitation, as if they had been born in this kind of country. We stopped in the middle so that Jude could raise his leg and splash the water on his chest. He was a water-loving camel, it seemed.

Jimmy joined me on the other side of the river, having planned every camp spot all the way to the coast. I unsaddled, and we lay on my tarp staring up at the clouds drifting overhead. I had picked my own camp for the final time, and the camels were wandering where they pleased with hobbles on. It felt like we were back in our own little world. The seclusion of the valley next to the Clarence River meant I didn't need to string up the electric fence.

'I miss this already,' Jimmy said, also pining for the lost freedom of the Outback. He knew the impending stress of the roads that lay ahead.

We walked down to the river, stripped off and waded in, letting the flow of water wash over our bodies. The evening was clear, but more rain was predicted. We would be lucky to make it to Bonalbo before it hit.

'What's wrong with this place!?' yelled Jimmy over the thunder of the rain on the tin roof. 'Every day is a weather event here!'

It was 1 a.m. We were camped at the Bonalbo Showground and the camels had been given the run of the pavilion, a huge shed with lovely comfortable sawdust on the floor.

The rain was bucketing down outside. The gutters had over-flowed, and water was streaming down from the roof, creating huge puddles. I pulled the saddles and pack bags further under the eaves, and made sure the tarps were tightly wrapped around them. Jimmy looked out at the downpour in disbelief, shaking his head. In the Flinders Ranges, they might get rain like this only once a year.

'Welcome to the Northern Rivers,' I said. At least I didn't have to worry about the camels tonight. Considering that when we began our trip at Shark Bay, the camels had spooked at even the sight of a beach shack, it was again to my complete astonishment that they walked straight into the showground pavilion and made it home. They stood under their new shelter all day, cosy and dry, with their heads in the doorways looking out at the rain falling outside.

While the camels were cosy in their shed, Jimmy and I were cosily shacked up in the chicken pavilion. Rows of empty cages for show birds lined the walls on either side of our swag. It was one of the more unusual places we had camped, but it was dry.

After days of rain at Bonalbo slowing our progress, the sun arrived, along with my friends Nat and Dan with their twin boys, and my friends Ness and James and their daughter.

The camels had finally been coaxed from their bedroom and were eating hay in the morning sun. James stood with one-year-old Valerie on his hip, offering her handfuls of hay, which she was tentatively feeding to Charlie; she had just been taught to say *camel*. The twins lay on a rug next to the camels, smearing their breakfast on themselves, and the rest of us sat around chatting in this odd playgroup scenario. It seemed like a distant memory to think that at one point, when I had first dreamed about my trek, I had hoped Nat and Dan might have been full-time participants in my adventure. Clearly life had other plans for them, as well as for me. Still, I was swelling with happiness, surrounded by my friends and their kids and the camels. Even though our lives now were seemingly very different, it did not mean that our friendships were any less close, and that our lives could not still intersect.

16

The Blue Horizon

BONALBO TO BYRON BAY—159 KM

We were through the Great Dividing Range, and only 100 kilometres from the coast. The roads had become busier, as if building towards a crescendo, timed with the arrival of my friend Keirin—my other gorgeous, loud, lovable and crazy camel friend. It was Keirin's crystals that I had carried in my swag and clutched every night when I doubted my strength.

We were about to commence the 'three-day burn', as Jimmy was calling it, warning that these would be the most intense three days of traffic for the entire trip.

Keirin had met us, with her dog Naru, just outside Casino. After the social overload of Stanthorpe, Jimmy had scouted out secluded corners of paddocks to maintain my sanity, and we were now sitting among Scotch thistles drinking wine together.

'I was as dry as a dingo's dick in the desert!' Keirin exclaimed after taking a sip.

Loud and vivacious, Keirin had a bawdy sense of humour, and had been a beauty therapist before camels took her in a different direction. With her blonde hair, pink lip gloss and a wine and smoke in hand, she could come across a little like Patsy from *Ab Fab*. Today Keirin was wearing a T-shirt that said 'Outback Princess', with a picture of Snow White holding a cigarette surrounded by Aussie animals. It was Keirin all over.

After several wines, we paused to watch Jimmy sharing a quiet moment with Charlie, standing with the sunset behind him.

'I'll stab you if you don't give this guy a chance,' Keirin said, her face melting with affection. 'I said you'd meet someone on your trip.'

The next day we set off with our final team assembled. Jimmy was at the front, followed by me leading the camels, and Keirin at the back walking Naru. We had a day of walking before the 'three-day burn' began.

As soon as we reached the main road, about ten kilometres north of Casino, it was clear this system was not going to work. Another muggy day, the intense humidity had brought huge numbers of horse flies and buffalo flies that agitated the camels every time we stopped. Keirin and Naru were also struggling with the heat. Keirin had developed blisters and had to change her shoes, and Naru constantly needed a bowl of water. As the day wore on, the school pick-up traffic grew heavier. Cars whizzed past us, getting far too close to the camels. I needed Keirin to stand out on the road like Kathy had done, but the bitumen was too hot for Naru's paws, and Keirin was in a state of anxiety trying to protect Naru from being attacked by other dogs while attempting to slow the traffic. None of us had worn hi-vis and we looked like an odd bunch of travelling drifters. One of us was going to get hit by a car.

When we reached camp in the evening, tired, stressed and sweaty, we reconvened. As much as Keirin wanted to walk, we all agreed it would be safer to have a vehicle behind me and the camels. Jimmy was useful on the ground, because he could run ahead to a corner and flag a fast-moving car to slow down. So, after some more logistics coordination, Keirin was appointed the support crew driver of my ute, with Naru riding shotgun in the front seat as her assistant.

The following morning—day one of the 'three-day burn'—we held a team meeting. I wolfed down two cans of tuna, ready to tackle the day's walk, knowing there'd be no other opportunity to stop. Jimmy tuned two UHF radios to the same frequency and handed one to Keirin.

'What's your radio name, Jimmy?' Keirin asked. Jimmy looked at her blankly. 'Like your porn star name,' she said.

'Like the name of your first pet and the first street you lived on?' he asked.

'Yeah, exactly.'

'I'm Jessie Bridgenorth.'

'Copy that, Jessie Bridgenorth. This is Heidi Penrose,' Keirin said, holding down the button and speaking into the UHF. It was the beginning of the radio banter that would be my soundtrack to the coast.

We paused again only a little way up the road. A fluoro-yellow temporary road sign had caught Jimmy's eye. A dip in the road had flooded recently and the sign lay face down, knocked over. In large black capitals it read 'Caution Traffic Hazard Ahead'. Jimmy was ecstatic as he pulled the sign off the fallen metal stand.

'This is perfect!' he said, zip-tying it to the back of my white ute with the flashing light. It sure looked official.

With all of us in our hi-vis vests and with Jimmy and Keirin on the UHF radios, we were ready.

We pulled out onto the main road and put the system into practice. A P-plater drove past and I could see her goggling at the camels. As she stared, she automatically turned towards us. Realising what she had done, she corrected herself, swerving back out and almost hitting Jimmy, whose presence she'd been completely unaware of. She was voted 'dickhead of the day'. But our new system worked well. If there was a blind corner, Jimmy would run ahead and check for cars, slowing them down, and if a car came up behind us, Keirin would block their path in the ute and radio Jimmy: 'I've got a car behind me here, Jessie, are you okay for me to let him through?' If the coast was clear in front, Jimmy would signal them to pull out and around the camels.

However, by the afternoon, a series of trucks combined with a very narrow verge put my nerves on edge. We rounded a bend and, unannounced, I crossed the road into a side street to escape the trucks.

'What are you doing?' Jimmy demanded. 'Why didn't you just stay on the left side of the road?' His tone surprised me; he never got angry. Before I could answer, he continued, 'Look, you have to trust Keirin and I to manage the traffic. You don't worry about any of it. Just keep walking with the camels.'

I realised his anger stemmed from how seriously he was taking his new role. He was right. I was trying to manage on my own again, ducking off the road if I felt it was too hairy. But I couldn't keep doing this. There was too much traffic now and I had to trust Keirin and Jimmy to keep me and the camels safe. So, I shut up and didn't argue, knowing that for once I had the easier job: keep hold of the lead rope and keep on walking with the camels.

Later that afternoon we reached Caniaber Road, in the outer suburbs of Lismore, where my trust in the system would be pushed to the max. There are few road names that I remember with so much dread. It was a steep, narrow, winding road with sporadic guard rails, a sharp drop-off on the left-hand side and a speed limit of 80 km/hr. As we reached the bottom of the hill, Keirin's UHF battery went flat; with no communication between Jimmy and Keirin, this stretch would be even more dangerous. A dairy farmer and his family had walked down their driveway to check us out as we walked by, so we enlisted their help, asking one of their farmhands to drive ahead of us and slow down traffic on the tight, winding road.

At the driveway to the dairy farm, I watched in terror as cars sped up and down the hill at top speed. Our helper drew out, and Jimmy gave me a look that said, 'it's now or never'. We pulled out onto the road, thanking the dairy farmer profusely for lending us his worker, and started plodding uphill. Cars were piling up behind my slow-moving camel train. Without communication from Jimmy at the front, Keirin had no idea when to let people through. Drivers were getting pissed off and started pulling out anyway, accelerating up the hill past the camels as a bus came down in the opposite direction.

Delilah in the lead held it together, but Jude was starting to lose it. In typical Jude lunacy, rather than pushing forward and moving the string to the left, he swung his bum to the right, into the middle of the road, pulling the tail end of the string into the passing traffic. The camels' legs looked only inches away from the cars. It's amazing how naively safe people feel in a little metal box. Still the cars accelerated past, totally ignorant of my animals' unpredictable behaviour. I could see the farm girl creeping up the hill in front, her arm waving out the car window for cars to slow down. Jimmy was running backward and forward too, the back of his shirt drenched in sweat as he tried to control the traffic around me.

I kept on moving, but Jude was swinging all over the place, pulling the other camels with him. A truck shifted through the gears, motoring up the hill to pass me. I pulled the camels further to the left, with the drop-off down the hill looming below.

'Almost there, Soph,' said Jimmy, reading the panic on Jude's face and mine.

'This is fucked!' I replied.

'Camp is just at the top of this hill.'

After an eternity, we reached the top, the sound of screeching brakes and revving engines still reverberating through my bones when we pulled into the driveway of the property we were staying at. The farm girl pulled up to turn around. If she hadn't been there to thank, I would have burst into tears.

'You said you felt the trip wasn't a challenge anymore,' Jimmy said with a weary grin. He was right; I had whinged about that. I should have known by now: lows always come with highs, and highs with lows.

It was day two of the 'three-day burn'. Despite being loaded with 120 kilograms of water, Jude sprang to his feet when I asked him to stand. It was completely unnecessary now for Jude to be carrying so much water, but I hoped the weight might tire him out and stop him panicking in the traffic. I was incredibly nervous and incredibly wrong.

We set off through a new suburban housing development on the outer suburbs of Lismore with cookie-cutter homes. Keirin and Jimmy were bantering on the two-way while I focused on Jude, trying to keep him calm. I called several stops along the road to allow Jude to 'panic eat'. This seemed to relieve some of his tension.

'Maybe when Jude was in the wild, he was almost hit by a semi,' joked Jimmy. It was true that Jude did seem to be unreasonably terrified of trucks—but Jude was a bit of an eccentric, so maybe that was just him.

With these short emotional eating breaks I managed to hold Jude's angst at bay. As we descended another windy road into the Lismore valley, things started to heat up.

'Some dickhead almost rear-ended me! What a fucking tosser!' I could hear Keirin through Jimmy's two-way clipped to the buttons on his shirt. He was trying to put a hand over the speaker while he politely spoke to a man who had pulled over in his car: 'If you don't mind going slow, we've just got some camels coming around the bend.'

About ten cars were now backed up behind Keirin, with a stream of cars coming at us from the front. A lady slowed down, holding up all the traffic behind her.

'Is it okay if my kids pat your camels?' I couldn't believe my ears. Some people really couldn't read a situation. I explained that we were on a main road holding up cars at each end and that the camels were very nervous. She looked disgruntled and sped off.

Jimmy held up his hand, signalling the next car to stop.

'All right, Heidi, send them through.' He stood in the centre of the road with his left hand creating a stop signal for the oncoming traffic while his right beckoned the cars behind through. He looked the complete professional. We were all getting the hang of this.

Besides Keirin copping the odd bit of abuse, the reaction from the public was amazing. Almost everyone waved, some beeped, others wound down their windows and gave a big thumbs up. As the cars drove past, I could hear voices from the open windows.

'Cool, camels!'

'Good work, keep it up!'

'That's amazing!'

We carried on into the centre of Lismore, passing a row of ramshackle houses with junk lying about in the front yard. Some tattooed, piercing-studded teens stumbled out in a daze, bleary-eyed, holding up their phones, filming us as we walked by.

'Those guys have definitely been punching some cones,' said Keirin jokingly on the two-way.

'Probably thought they were hallucinating,' came Jimmy's reply.

Even without being in a drug-induced state, most of the Lismore residents probably thought they were hallucinating when they saw the camels.

When we arrived at the final bridge out of town, Jimmy and Keirin held up the entire flow of traffic in and out of Lismore so the camels and I had the whole bridge to ourselves. I looked down at the river flowing below and the cars on either end, thinking how utterly foreign every element in this landscape was for the camels.

The rain rolled in overnight, and day three of the 'three-day burn' seemed grey and miserable. In record speed, as a team of three, we saddled up the soggy camels in the wet grass and hit the road.

The roads were empty on this drizzly Sunday morning, and the three of us could relax from the constant traffic vigilance. Jude was more relaxed, too. He loved puddles. Even though he had no need to drink, he insisted on stopping at every puddle, swirling the water around in his lips and splashing it with his foot, spraying the other camels with mud like a big kid.

Residents began to emerge from their Sunday sleep-ins. Calls were made on mobiles and word passed round that we were on the road. Before we knew it, every driveway down the street had people in gumboots waiting to meet the camels at their front gate. They all waved from under their umbrellas and wished us luck, and I introduced them to the camels as we walked on by. I laughed, remembering something John Elliott had told me: 'Let's get this straight, I'm not famous. No one would give a shit if it was just me walking around. It's only the camels who are famous. I'm simply their PA.'

Still, I felt touched by everyone's support and presence. A man shoved a $50 note into my hand. I tried to give it back, saying there was no need, that I wasn't raising money for anyone or anything, but he refused. 'We want to give you this; we think it's wonderful what you're doing,' he said. I guiltily pocketed the note and profusely thanked him, telling him I'd buy hay for the camels.

It wasn't the first note I had been handed. People had forced small donations on us since we had entered the built-up areas. I told people I wasn't raising money, but people gave it all the same. I think many of them recognised that adventure didn't need to have a cause attached to it. One could simply have a dream and pursue it.

We had one final challenging road before we reached the Eltham Hotel, the finale of our 'three-day burn'. At the top of the hill leading out onto Bangalow Road, Jimmy strode into oncoming traffic hurtling past at 100 km/hr with the confidence of a police officer. Nobody questioned his authority, and the traffic ground to a halt while I plodded out onto the road at 3 km/hr. It was the most heavily trafficked road so far. We needed to walk a two-kilometre stretch, with absolutely no verges, around blind bends. Even so, you can't rush camels—slow and steady wins the race! While Jimmy ran up and down directing traffic like a symphony orchestra conductor, I kept to the camels' snail-like pace. With well over fifty cars backed up behind Keirin, it felt like a city at peak hour as Jimmy let the approaching traffic through.

'Just keep walking, Soph,' Jimmy said, taking off at a run again to stop the next car so the rear traffic could pass. I was terrified, but compared with Jimmy sprinting back and forth, I had the easy job.

Once we turned off the main road, along the last stretch to the pub, I heard a truck approaching from behind. It didn't sound as if it was braking. I rushed the camels off the road just in time to see a double-decker stock crate carrying pigs swaying violently as it swerved around Keirin, overtaking her on a blind corner. Keirin swore into the radio again while I slammed up along a fence on the edge of the road. For once, Jude's truck paranoia had come in handy. He'd been quick to pull the other camels forward out of harm's way.

We reached the Eltham pub to find the place packed. The streets were lined with cars, live music was playing and people were milling around everywhere. This would be our biggest pub visit yet. Directly out the front, Luke the owner had placed two witches hats with a line of tape between them. On the tape was an A4 sheet of paper with a hand-drawn camel and the words 'Camel Parking' written below. It seemed the camels had been reserved prime VIP valet parking. The only problem was that Luke had drawn a camel with two humps.

'Excuse me, where's the parking for one-humped camels?' I teased as we approached.

'Oh no, we got it wrong! The staff had an argument while I was drawing it whether camels in Australia have one hump or two,' Luke laughed.

In my tattered shorts and battered Akubra, I felt daggy among this hipster Byron crowd, but I didn't care. We had just survived the 'three-day burn'. Jimmy, Keirin and I were ecstatic.

I squeezed the camels into their parking zone, hemmed in by cars, tables and people. For animals that are notoriously claustrophobic it was amazing to see them relax in such a setting, chewing their cud placidly amid the mayhem of a Sunday session. A photographer from *The Sydney Morning Herald* introduced herself, then snapped away as I sipped a beer holding my five camels in front of the pub. Jimmy hung back, keeping out of the photos, letting me have my moment with the camels. I couldn't imagine too many guys would support their partner to this extent, running into oncoming traffic, yet claiming none of the spotlight. After those busy roads, I no longer saw the puppy dog in him. I saw a man with the ability to command a situation, who kept his cool with a steely determination and focus that showed he was intent on keeping me safe. I took the full load of responsibility for my animals' safety on my shoulders, but I hadn't recognised until then how much Jimmy had taken the weight of my own safety upon his.

As the photographer knelt down to angle her camera upward at the pub with me and the camels in the foreground, I realised this wasn't my moment as much as it was the camels'. They were the stars. I remembered right back to the beginning, when they were fearfully huddled in the corner of a yard at Uluru and I knew nothing of them as individuals. I thought of my first weeks on the road, and the list I had compiled of everything they were afraid of. I thought of all the 'silent' noises in the bush that had spooked them and the black cow that had sent them bolting. It seemed completely unimaginable that they were here now, at a packed and lively pub, in the lush green surrounds of the Northern Rivers, thousands of kilometres away from the red dirt and endless horizon they were used to.

What amazingly clever, adaptable and compliant animals they were. How far they had come.

I woke late, looking out through the floor-to-ceiling glass windows, onto the camels' paddock below, grey clouds hovering over the Byron hills beyond. Friends of Keirin, Pete and Tori had a beautiful, bright and airy Balinese-inspired house that would become another cherished home away from home.

I lay in bed, staring up at the fan circling overhead, and thought of all the people who had opened up their homes to me and the camels. I had received countless gestures of kindness from so many strangers, many of whom I now considered close friends. I thought of the properties I had stayed at, the meals people had cooked for me, the equipment they had helped me fix, the knowledge they shared and the gifts I'd been given. But what touched me most was the time that people had taken out of their busy lives to simply be involved in my adventure. I felt strong and capable now, but I also understood that no man or woman is an island. If it hadn't been for the people I had met, I might not be in this beautiful house in the Byron hills, with only four days' walk ahead of me to the end.

My phone pinged, breaking my trance-like thoughts. There was a stream of messages. Delilah and I had made it onto the front page of *The Sydney Morning Herald* and now the *Today* show wanted me for a breakfast TV interview.

In the past, when I had pondered my arrival into Byron, I had wistfully thought how nice it would be to somehow sneak in quietly, through the back door, so to speak. I had secretly hoped I might have time alone on the beach at the end. But the sudden media attention was making this unlikely. At the beginning, it had just been me and the camels by the Indian Ocean, and I wanted an equal moment of solitude with the camels at the finish, on the shores of the Pacific Ocean.

After leaving Pete and Tori's house, we were forced to string our final four days of walking across a week, waiting out the rain again and again. We stayed at beautiful hinterland homes, taking lush, winding back roads lined with archways of camphor laurel trees, being passed by luxury cars that were dodging the maze of potholes in these once peaceful streets.

On day three, we passed yet another multi-million-dollar mansion with brand-new horse stables, tennis courts and views across the rolling hills. We crested a rise and I stopped dead in my tracks, the camels pulling up behind me.

I gasped, and instantly felt hot salty tears in my eyes. There it was. All of a sudden. The Pacific Ocean, staring back at us. A wide strip of sparkling blue water just beyond the green hills. *We could actually see the ocean.*

The hugeness of what I'd just done hit me square in the chest. I'd been so focused on the walk itself that I'd never really thought what it would be like to be staring at the Pacific, looking down to Byron Bay, the most easterly point of Australia. Even when people had commented on what a huge distance I had travelled, it didn't really seem as if I was doing anything special. Every day I just got up, conducted the same routine and went for a walk with my camels. But now this big strip of blue on the horizon suddenly put it in context. The camels and I had walked 4743 kilometres and had only ten more to go. But the kilometres didn't matter, they were just numbers. And as I stared at that mesmerising blue horizon, what I was struck by most was the fact that I had walked every step of the way, across an entire continent, me and my five camels. Step by step, we had seen the country together.

And then, as suddenly as the Pacific Ocean had appeared before us, I was wrenched back to the present. A truck had hurtled by the main road we were approaching and Jude was losing his cool. We were not at the beach yet.

After managing to calm Jude down and navigate the busy road, we descended from the Byron hills to the low swampy region that stretches out to the beach. The furthest east I was able to take the camels on the beach would be Tyagarah, about five kilometres north of the Byron Bay lighthouse, but there was still one last major obstacle to traverse—the Pacific Highway. But I had worked out a way to get past this thundering arterial thoroughfare.

We had left the road and had connected with an abandoned railway line that ran through the swamp towards the coast. I urged the camels on, past the graffiti-plastered concrete under the Pacific Highway overpass. It was a hidden jungle down here, beneath the highway, and none of the trucks and cars that belted along overhead would have had any idea that below their wheels, five camels and a girl were heading for the beach. *Maybe I would get my sneaky backdoor arrival?*

On the other side of the highway, we pulled off the train line and waded through some suspiciously snaky territory to the house we would be camping at for our final night.

I strung up the electric fence for the camels in a sandy area next to the guesthouse. Kathy had arrived for the final day. We would be setting off early the following morning to coordinate my arrival on the beach with the low tide.

The camels were all rolling in their paddock, scratching the mosquito and buffalo fly bites that had plagued them in the humid weather. I couldn't wait to get them back to the arid country where they belonged. Sand was flying everywhere, and they were becoming filthy rubbing themselves in the dirt. But they were happy, feeling the sand in their coats.

In the lead-up to the finish of the journey, everyone had been asking me how I was feeling. Again and again, it would come up in conversation. And the more everyone asked, the more I didn't know. How was one meant to feel at the end of a camel trek? What did finishing such a journey mean? I couldn't articulate it. I looked at the camels, happily making themselves completely grubby. They had no idea tonight would be the last night of the trek. To them this was just another camp.

In many ways, it didn't feel like the end of a journey, but a morphing into something new and different. For me, the beginning had started long before I took my first steps at Shark Bay. In fact, it was hard to even pinpoint its start. Was it when I first began training my camels at Uluru? Or when I started milking camels at QCamel on the Sunshine Coast? Or even when I first experienced the Outback, walking the Heysen Trail in the Flinders Ranges? I knew that the endpoint of this journey would be similarly ambiguous. Did it end when I reached the Pacific Ocean? Or did it end when the camels were back with me in the Flinders Ranges? I had by now decided to return there and live with Jimmy. I never intended to part with my camels; they would stay with me for life.

I thought about how I'd be returning to the Flinders, and how circular it felt. It wasn't a case of simply growing up, getting the restlessness out of your system and then settling down—at least not for me. Life wasn't linear in that way. There would be ups and downs that I couldn't control or foresee, and all I could do was what the camels had taught me: live for the moment, and every day get up and move forward with life to the next camp.

We woke at 3 a.m. to saddle the camels and walk the final three kilometres to the beach. A storm had loomed last night. It had mainly skirted around us, but I still couldn't see a single star in the sky. Jimmy walked a distance ahead of me, and Kathy and Keirin followed in the ute.

In the dark, I listened to the camels chew their cud as we walked—the sound that had been my constant companion for thirteen months. I spent the hour in silent contemplation, casting my mind back over all the places I had rolled out my swag, all the salt lakes we had seen, sand dunes we had stood atop, gibber plains we had crossed, rivers and highways too. In the darkness of the morning, I felt like I could visualise every small detail of every camp I had made. I could hear the sounds of the bush, smell the vegetation and touch the earth we had lain on. I had been part of the elements around me, felt the changes in the seasons and the coming and going of weather. I thanked the camels for this. With them I had been self-sufficient, able to survive in the landscape alone. There was a freedom in this that I would forever treasure. I also thought of the people, too. They had been the colours that painted a truly astonishing picture of Australia. I had experienced the best in humanity. I had been so lucky that the right people had arrived in my life at the right time. And when I thought all the way back to the Heysen Trail and the camel dairy, it seemed like fate that I should end up where I was now.

In the muted light of pre-dawn, we reached the Tyagarah Beach car park. I took off my boots and socks and tucked them away in my satchel; I wanted to feel the sand between my toes. I hugged Kathy and Keirin, and kissed and held Jimmy tight. 'Thank you for getting us here safely,' I said, knowing my words could never convey the immense love and gratitude I felt for everything he had done for us.

The camels and I stepped out onto the sand. At that moment a thin gap in the clouds on the horizon allowed the rays of the rising sun to light up the Byron lighthouse in the distance, emanating the most amazing purple glow. In that moment, time stood still for me.

I walked the camels to the water's edge. Waves surged forward and lapped at Delilah's toes. She pulled back on the rope, but stood feeling the unfamiliar sensation of water retreating from the sand, creating suction around her foot. Another wave surged forward, and Jude lifted his foot and let it splash in the water.

The sun rose higher, diminishing the glowing purple light, then disappearing back behind clouds. I waved to Keirin, Kathy and Jimmy atop the sand dune, signalling that I was going to take a walk down the beach. I turned my back to the lighthouse and walked northward along the wide strip of sand.

This stretch of beach felt wild and untouched, being a marine park and nature reserve, with no houses on the shoreline. To my surprise, the beach was also devoid of people. It was just me and the camels, in serene solitude.

The wind picked up as we walked, shuffling the clouds aside, and all of a sudden we were walking in dazzling perfect sunshine. Looking at the wild ocean horizon I felt that same familiar expansive feeling that I had experienced in the desert. It was a feeling that raw nature drew from deep within me— the sensation of being alive and free.

We walked and walked, as if after all these days, walking had never got old. I didn't want this long stretch of beach to end. Maybe I could keep going? Leaving my family and friends at the other end to say, 'She just walked off. I guess she must really like walking.'

It was tempting, but I stopped. It was time to close the chapter of this adventure.

My mum and dad, old friends who loved and supported me, as well as new friends whom we'd met along the road would all be gathering on the beach now. I stood with the camels, letting the sunshine radiate down on my face, with my toes in the cool water of the Pacific Ocean, soaking in the enormity of the moment. I raised my arms up, feeling the wind in my face, and laughed with joy. The camels looked at me with mild curiosity.

I looked at each of their faces in turn, thanking them for all they had done for me. We had made it. We had done it together, stuck it through, and had a roller-coaster of a journey on the way.

The boundless ocean horizon lay before us, beckoning me, telling me that anything was possible now. Any adventure I wanted to do, I could do it. It was all possible with time and perseverance. I thought I would be emotional today, but all I could do was smile. I couldn't stop smiling at my beloved animals that had brought me this far, and the wide expanse of blue ocean and the infinite possibilities for new adventures that lay beyond.

A wandering spirit

We left the beach, and for several tense, hair-raising hours navigated our way with the camels through the heavy traffic of Byron Bay to The Farm—a popular community farm and eatery that had agreed to hold my camels in one of their paddocks for a week.

I will never forget the sound of the gate being pushed shut and latched behind me and the camels. As soon as we were safely in the paddock, Keirin was honking the horn, Kathy was on the tray of the ute whooping and screaming, Uncle Steve, who had joined us for the final walk from the beach, was shaking like a bowl of jelly as he laughed, and Jimmy was yelling and hollering with the girls. It was mayhem, a chorus of noise and excitement. My support crew had officially clocked off—they had succeeded in keeping me and the camels safe and could no longer contain their joy. Everyone was yelling and screaming ecstatically. The camels plunged their heads into the thick green grass beyond the gate, taking vigorous mouthfuls.

And then, something broke within me. Like every ounce of energy that had kept me going for the past two years was zapped from my bones. My legs collapsed underneath me. I was unable to stand. I squatted in the long grass, the lead rope still clutched in my hand, with my head between my legs, and broke into silent uncontrollable tears. It was the moment I knew I had done it. I had led my camels safely across the country. I could finally release all the pent-up worry about their wellbeing that I had carried so heavily with me every step of the way. I no longer needed to be strong. The walk was over.

We celebrated that night around the camels' paddock with a barbecue and drinks with friends. It could not have been more perfect.

The next morning, I woke up next to Jimmy in the swag in the garlic-drying shed at The Farm—yet another unusual place we had camped together. It was a good thing we both liked garlic. I propped myself up on my elbow and looked at him. The trip had gifted me many things, but meeting someone along the way was not one I had ever expected. But now we were a team. We had worked well together from the start, and I knew that all the jobs we still had left to do—like packing up and trucking the camels back to the desert—would be shared with him.

Jimmy stirred, and we both looked out onto the green hills, bathed in sunlight.

'So, what are we going to do today, Soph?' Jimmy asked, his eyes brimming with excitement. I laughed. He was just like the camels. Every day was a new day and a new adventure for him. There was no nostalgia for the ending of the trip, only joyous anticipation of what the summer held for us.

'Let's go swimming,' I beamed back at him.

After a week in Byron at The Farm, we trucked the camels to Dad's property at Kilcoy. The camels would spend the summer there while Jimmy and I caught up with my friends and family and spent Christmas on the east coast.

It was January and the camels were happily at their temporary summer abode. Jimmy and I were now back in Byron, staying at Pete and Tori's place again, searching for a truck to transport the camels to the Flinders Ranges. I stood on their deck, looking out at the morning and picturing where the camels had grazed only a month and a half before. Once we sorted out the camel truck, we had a three-day trip ahead of us back to South Australia, where the camels would be agisted at Depot Springs Station. I was immensely happy with the arrangement. The owners were friends of Jimmy's, and the camels would be in a 3000-acre paddock, packed with their favourite feed, and only half an hour from Jimmy's place, where I would be living.

Before we had left Kilcoy the previous week, we'd said goodbye to the camels in their paddock. Jude particularly seemed to miss human company, so we lingered with him a long time, cuddling him and laughing at his goofy camel smile. I rubbed his big strong thighs affectionately, and kissed him on his cheek before we left.

As I stood on the deck, my phone rang. It was Dad. The moment I heard his voice, I knew something was wrong.

'It's the camels, Soph . . .' I felt my chest contract. 'One of the camels is dead.'

My entire world came crashing down around me. I felt like I had been walloped in the stomach with a sledgehammer and could barely breathe. Dad was fairly certain it was Jude. My biggest fear that I had carried with me for two years had come to pass. *How could this have happened? How could the trip have such a dark turn of events after such a happy ending?*

We rushed out of the house without saying goodbye to Pete and Tori. I sat curled in a foetal position in the passenger seat as Jimmy drove my ute back to Kilcoy. I gasped for air between shaking sobs, until eventually, after hours in the car, my sobs faded into quiet whimpers. I couldn't wait to get back to Kilcoy. I was so angry at myself for ever having left. Yet I was dreading our arrival.

Dad was standing by the shed in the paddock. I looked in horror, my big beautiful boy was sitting propped up between two pieces of machinery. At first, it looked like he had got himself stuck, but there was no sign of diarrhoea or anything to suggest he had struggled to get out of that spot. It seemed as if he hadn't felt well, and had sat himself down in that position to keep himself upright. He looked like he was resting, apart from his neck, which was flopped to one side, and the small pool of blood that had gathered under his head. His eyes were still, and I automatically touched his eyeball, as I had done with the wild bulls I had shot.

He was gone. I stroked his coat and lay my head against his side.

I never found out the cause of Jude's death. Dad had been away for two days, and when he saw the camels last, he'd reported that Jude didn't want to eat a carrot, and had a bit of foam on the side of his mouth. I should have known something was wrong then, but Dad checked on them again and reassured me that he was fine. A bit of froth around the mouth wasn't completely out of the ordinary for Jude. Consultations with a vet presented me with possible causes, but nothing conclusive. All I could think was that it must have been a poisonous plant or a snake, although neither were found in the paddock. Jude was at times a mystery of a camel, and his death will remain a mystery too.

Dad buried Jude that afternoon at Kilcoy. He felt terrible, but it wasn't his fault. We all experienced Jude's loss acutely, the other camels included.

I was swallowed by sadness, blame and regret that I hadn't been there to help Jude. I felt I'd failed him. I could barely look at the other camels, because all I would see was one missing. At night as I wallowed in my misery, I felt like I could almost hear Jude's deep breaths, the way he used to sigh as I rested my head upon his and wished him goodnight. I heard a quote at that time that I felt was applicable: 'Grief is a love that has nowhere to go.'

Jude had been everything to me. He was my soul camel, the one who would teach me the most. At times he had frustrated me beyond belief, but I loved him all the more for his acts of both insanity and deep trust and affection. Over the days that followed, the only comfort I could draw was knowing that he had made it the entire way. I thought of all the things that could have gone wrong on the trip. So many terrible scenarios could have happened, forcing me to leave him behind—or worse, to shoot him and walk away. All I could tell myself was that this was Jude's destiny, and now was his time to go. But still, it felt horribly unfair.

Eventually I clawed my way out of my sorrow. As my trip had taught me, we had to move forward. My main priority now was to get Mac, Charlie, Clayton and Delilah back to the desert country they were familiar with. Our truck was virtually unsafe to drive, but we had no other option than to patch it up and hope for the best. I wanted to get back to the Outback now more than ever.

We loaded the camels and I saw four heads sticking out of the stock crate, looking around in anticipation. It is an image that will haunt me forever. Jude deserved to be there. It had always been the five of them. He should have been going back to the desert country with his friends, where he belonged. But he was missing, and that image broke my heart.

A month had passed and Jimmy and I were living in the Flinders Ranges. We left home to check on the camels, as we did on a regular basis. We drove through the valley to visit them in their paddock with its ancient brown rolling hills on either side and open blue sky above. The track followed a wide dry creek bed, lined with the camels' favourite green prickly acacia, from which kangaroos, emus and occasionally goats darted out as we passed.

We hadn't spotted the camels so we climbed a small hill to see if we could catch sight of them. It was windy up here and we could see across the paddock, over the rolling ranges to the end of the Flinders and to the flatlands beyond. I felt that old expansiveness of spirit—the prickling feeling of being alive and free in this landscape. We both experienced it here. I looked out at the horizon and felt like I could reach out across the wide brown land and almost touch Lake Eyre and the Strzelecki Desert beyond, where I had walked. I could feel Jude up here too, wild and free, roaming the sand dunes where he pleased. Jimmy had had his bell inscribed, and it now hung in our house with Jude's halter. It read:

Jude

Circa 2013 – 23.01.22

Charismatic, affectionate, loopy, adorable, handsome and strong. The greatest camel ever.

We spotted the other camels and made our way down to meet them. They were all together, as they always were, contentedly grazing as the sun dipped low in the sky. I could feel

Jude here too, among his friends, in their peaceful presence. He was everywhere for me now. He was my constant reminder to trust in my own decisions, because he always trusted in mine. I'll never forget him, the camel I explored this wonderful country with.

I approached Mac, Charlie, Clayton and Delilah, greeting each of them, face to face, breathing out into their soft nostrils and allowing them to smell me in return. And then I whispered into their ears, telling them about the next adventure that we would all go on. Because camels are born to wander, and so am I.

Acknowledgements

I embarked on my camel trip to experience wild and remote places alone with my camels. What I never anticipated was how much richer the journey would be made by the people who made it possible.

It was not that many years ago that I knew nothing about camels. I now count myself incredibly fortunate that I stumbled into a diverse world of characters whose talent, knowledge and passion for working with camels would inspire me to dream of such a big adventure, facilitate its possibility, and make that dream come true. For this I would like to thank Chris Hill for sourcing my camels, giving me yards in which to train them, helping me to make my saddles and source my equipment and for many other generosities. I would like to thank Paul and

317

Karen Ellis for inspiring me by giving me my first taste of camel trekking and supporting me by trucking my camels to and from Coober Pedy as well as organising their agistment at Beltana Station during the summer in the middle of my trek. Also, to the other members of the camel community who have inspired my journey and taught me all I know about camels: Lauren Brisbane, Lionel Keegan, Andrew Harper, Doug Baum, Marlin Troyer, Don Anesbury, Bert Held, Saskia Wassermann, Steve Beetson and other international and Australian cameleers.

Camel training is often hard to do single-handed and in the year that I trained my camels at Uluru many of the staff rallied around me to help. For this I would like to say thank you to the 2019 Uluru Camel Tours crew—you were my camel family, my support and made the time training my camels there fun and often hilarious. Thank you to Greg Saunders for making the trip across to Western Australia with me and for being by my side in the early phases of the trip.

To all the pastoralists, managers, caretakers, rangers, Indigenous Elders, farmers and property owners whose country I walked across and whose homes I stayed in, thank you for your knowledge of the land and for the work you do in looking after the patch of Australia you call home. It was truly a profound experience seeing all the nooks and crannies of the bush that you are custodians of. I am constantly astounded by the hospitality I was given during my journey, and I consider many of my meetings the beginnings of a friendship that I hope will last for many years.

Mum and Dad—thank you for never questioning my crazy dreams (or at least not doing so directly). Your involvement in my trip has meant the world to me. Yours is a love and support I know I can always count on.

To my teammate in life, Jimmy, thank you for relentlessly pursuing me across the country. Your persistence paid off, and I'm very happy it did because now I can't imagine a life without you.

Keirin and Kathy—we've laughed together, cried together, got covered in camel shit and cud together, and despite all of this I know we will always be crazy camel chicks and have one another's backs.

The kind gestures I received while on the road were innumerable and there will always be more people than I am able to thank individually—from my friends who took time out to visit me while I was walking and those who supported me from afar, to all those who came to the beach at Byron to see me arrive; to the random truck drivers who slowed down and radioed one another about my camels on the road, to the people who leant out their car window and gave me a thumbs up. Humanity is truly amazing.

My camels' happiness and welfare has always been my greatest priority and I was adamant that I would find them a good place to live after my trek. I could not be happier with where they have ended up, at Depot Springs Station. Not only do they have an amazing paddock to roam freely but I have also become great friends with the Depot Springs family and will forever be grateful for their generosity in providing a safe and well-maintained patch of land for my travel companions.

Writing this book has been akin to the trek itself. In doing so I embarked on something that was completely new to me, and I was as untrained as my own camels were at the beginning of the walk. I jumped at the challenge of writing a book with the same naivety that I approached my own adventure. While I walked, people often asked me whether I would write a book, and my reply was that maybe I would produce a coffee-table book, as I never considered myself a writer. I now have a huge amount of respect for writers, editors and the publishing industry. I would like to thank Allen & Unwin for taking a chance on me, and especially my publisher, Tessa Feggans, who discovered my story and supported me through the entire process. I would also like to thank my editors, who have worked tirelessly on helping me with this book: Angela Handley, Katri Hilden and Dannielle Viera.

I have learnt as much from this experience as I did from my walk. It has had its ups and downs: days when the writing flowed and I made good progress, and days when I came to a grinding halt and, frustrated, had to pick myself up and keep going. I realised close to the end of my first draft that it is simply a case of putting one foot in front of the other. Focus on where you are at and enjoy the journey rather than stampeding towards the destination. Nothing can be achieved without time and persistence. Anything can be accomplished if you slowly and steadily keep on moving forward . . . but, for me, the best part was having my five best camel mates to share in the journey: Jude, Delilah, Charlie, Clayton and Mac.